RICK
STEIN
AT
HOME

KU-593-727

BBC
BOOKS

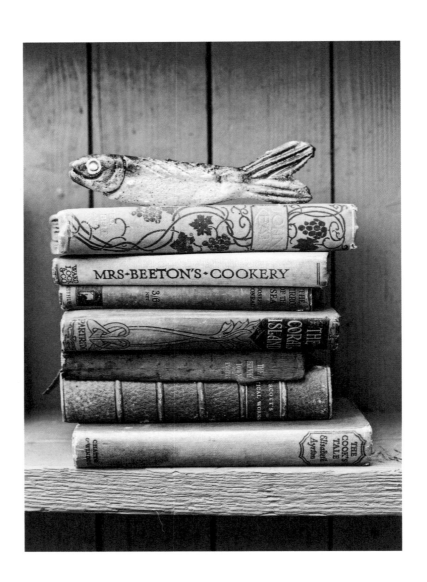

RICK
STEIN
AT
HOME

Yesterday afternoon, late November with London in lockdown, I went for a walk along the Thames with my wife, Sas. Normally I go swimming every day but all the pools, both indoor and outdoor, were closed. Like so many people now, I'm obsessed with steps and needed to get my total up to 10,000. It was a grey day, blowy and raining, the river in full-tide brown and flowing quite fast on the ebb down to Gravesend. The darkness of deep autumn makes it hard to keep the spirits up, particularly as normally we'd be at the Margaret River Gourmet Escape food festival in Western Australia at this time of year. There'd be a barbecue on the beach and I'd probably be cooking prawns on the grill and serving up plates of salmon marinated in passion fruit with chilli and coriander. But here we were in the gloom, with houseboats moored to the side and red, yellow and brown autumn leaves lying on the water between them and the bank. There had been a high tide and Chiswick Mall looked like a beach with driftwood and leaves and the odd black plastic bag.

I should have been full of the 'sere and yellow leaf', but I wasn't. I was thinking of dinner, just for me, Sas and my stepdaughter, Olivia. I'd had some hamburgers delivered from our butcher, Philip Warren in Launceston, Cornwall. I'd been to their shop in August and had seen what went into the burgers: just chuck and rib-cap steak to get the right balance of fat and some seasoning. That's it and they're perfect. I walked on through the drizzle, thinking about lighting the barbecue, even in this weather, and cooking the burgers on it; maybe toasting some brioche buns over the fire, too. Then I was turning over the accompaniments in my mind. I decided, since everyone is so particular about what they like in burgers, to get everything ready and laid out on a large rectangular serving plate. I'd bought some dill and cucumber pickles from the supermarket and had made my own chilli and red pepper ones – just sliced chillies and red peppers, ginger, salt, sugar and coriander seeds, all in distilled clear vinegar so that everything shows up brightly.

I was enjoying the thought of making mustard mayonnaise when I got home, using my own egg recipe with just English mustard, salt, vinegar and sunflower oil. I had an iceberg lettuce, some tiny tomatoes on the vine which, if you buy the expensive ones, do have a good flavour even at this time of year. I would thinly slice a red onion and an avocado. I also had a bottle of chipotle relish, a favourite of mine from the Cool Chile company, and a jar of mayonnaise for Olive. I'm a fan of Mexican beer with my burgers, but Sas is going through a fizzy water only phase and Olive favours cider flavoured with passion fruit, which is not my cup of tea at all.

We ate those burgers with great joy. I'd also melted some slices of Cheddar over them while they were on the barbecue. We tried some oven chips from the freezer, but they weren't very nice, and we succumbed to the strains of *Strictly Come Dancing* in the background. It was just a night at home but the stuff, I suspect, of sweet memories.

Like so many other people, I feel rather embarrassed to say that I've partly enjoyed lockdown because it's been a time to cook all the things I buy cookery books for and have been meaning to try some time. I've baked sourdough, made heaps of shepherd's pies, moussakas and pastitsios. I've taken the concept of not wasting anything to almost ludicrous lengths, started a serious compost heap and begun growing far more herbs and vegetables than I ever would have done normally.

I've revisited scores of recipes from my own books and sometimes complimented myself on their accuracy and at other times updated them. This was more often than not because they were just too complicated. In the 70s and 80s, I confess to being influenced by the book *Mastering the Art of French Cooking* by Julia Child, Louisette Bertholle and Simone Beck, a book from a time when you expected your readers not to know much about cooking and you felt the need to explain everything.

I also made a series of little videos for Instagram on what I was making at home. Spurred on by Sas, I decided to honestly record what I was cooking. For one, I made a nasi goreng, which I described as a great user-upper of leftovers. I included in it some pizza Margherita from the day before, some roast lamb and slices of avocado because there were just too many on the tree in the back garden at our house in Sydney, where

I spent five months of lockdown. I did videos for fish pie, Greek souvlaki, a roast egg curry from Thekkady in Kerala and beef tataki (Japanese sliced beef with soy and watercress), a recipe from Aya Nishimura, the stylist who cooked my recipes for the photos in this book.

Every Thursday, once it became possible, we used to invite Sas's stepmother, Janine, and her grandmother, Betty, round for dinner. There was me, Sas, Olive and a friend from down the road called Karen Balstrup who we always call KB. I never did any first courses but sometimes we'd have the odd nibble, like oysters or prawns with Marie Rose sauce. Once I made some pancakes with my sourdough starter, sprinkled them with pepper and salt, then served them with a taramasalata dip or a guacamole in an attempt to use up more avocados from the trees. Mostly, though, we'd go straight into the main course after the cocktails KB always made. The mains were just big dishes of pastitsio, fish pie, moussaka or lasagne, but occasionally I'd do roast beef or pork or slow-cooked lamb like kleftiko. On one occasion I cooked an Austrian tafelspitz – boiled silverside of beef with all the accompaniments, horseradish and apple, roast marrow bones, rösti potatoes, peas and lettuce.

Lockdown became, for me, a time to remember the joys of regular cooking at home in a world where the almost limitless possibilities of modern life had suddenly been shut down. The delightful importance of cooking regularly for family and friends was the new reality and what a pleasure it was. A few times in my life I've suddenly found myself waking up on a new morning to a world somehow changed for the better, like slipping through a crack in the wall.

Like maybe the first time I tasted squid cooked in its own black ink in Spain, or my first pint of beer with my Dad in the Cornish Arms aged 15 and stumbling into the hedge in the back garden on the way out. Or the first night of ravenous, unashamed sex with a Polish girl in Aynhoe Road in Hammersmith three years later, or just walking down Martin Place in Sydney on a sunny morning the next year with my flatmate Rob, wearing some white jeans and fancy brown suede loafers and thinking I'd finally cut loose from my family in this bright new country. Back in Sydney again it felt like I'd missed the point most of my life. We all need boundaries and boundaries were what we got during lockdown. Suddenly the importance of cooking at home became completely clear.

So that's the reason for this book, almost autobiographically to suggest great cooking experiences at my place. As if to immediately refute the idea of boundaries, I am lucky to have a few places to call home and there's no point in not admitting I'm a bit privileged. I've got a cottage in Padstow in Cornwall, a small house in London, a house in Sydney and, as if that wasn't enough, a beach house in Mollymook, next to Ulladulla in southern New South Wales. None of them are particularly grand; indeed all of them are falling apart somewhat because I have an unrequited love of DIY, and all of them regularly need my rather less than expert attention, so this is how I lead my life at home – between cooking and mending toilet seats.

But there's one person I've almost totally left out so far – my wife, Sas. This book would not have been written without her and, as you will see, her influence in everything that happens with dinner at home is overwhelming. I'm the cook but she is the entertainer. I don't doubt if she did the cooking it would be fabulous, but there is a very satisfactory division in our labour. I cook and she invites everyone, suggests what they might like to eat, decides on what the table is going to look like, rearranges the furniture, plans who is going to sit next to who, tells me that Bob Dylan and Leonard Cohen are not right for the evening, then gets everyone up and dancing at a particularly apposite point.

Big dinner parties are the best of times and the worst of times; the best being singing into spoons as if they were microphones at 1.30am to 'Don't Stop Believin' by Journey or 20 minutes later, when I'm beginning to flag and Sas puts on 'We Built This City', by Jefferson Starship. The worst of times is an hour before everybody is due to arrive, when I've left everything till the last minute. I was also going to say clearing up, but actually I rather enjoy it, along with slightly catty conversations about how badly some had behaved.

But cooking at home is not really about dinner parties, it's about nights in with the wife, weekends with the kids, Easter Sunday lunch, manic calorie counting, knocking a meal up from what's in the fridge, barbecues and picnics. It's about having friends over for a bite to eat and some nibbles, making your own snacks to scoff with a glass of champagne, trying to better Deliveroo by making spectacular takeaway food, and the joy of fruit cake with a cup of tea in the afternoon. It's deciding what to have with your eggs at breakfast and how to deal with the new reality of vegetarians and vegans.

I've also given in to the need to tell you about other occasional madnesses of mine, like the six-month quest to produce perfect sourdough and my obsession with stock. I've included recipes from my children, my wife and my friends and a piece on recipe testing using my chums as guinea pigs, with particular reference to the time I cooked 15 curries for 25 people, when writing my book on India. There are some thoughts about walks in the country and how they have to include coming back with a bunch of wild sorrel or some mushrooms, about chutney, jam and marmalade making, and the *Toy Story*-like goings-on in my garage, where sandwich- makers talk to dehydrators about how they ended up there. And finally, some serious stuff about the enormous role that food plays in our lives for cheering us all up.

The smell of that buttered toast simply spoke to Toad, and with no uncertain voice; talked of warm kitchens, of breakfasts on bright frosty mornings, of cosy parlour firesides on winter evenings, when one's ramble was over and slippered feet were propped on the fender; of the purring of contented cats, and the twitter of sleepy canaries.

From *Wind in the Willows* by Kenneth Grahame

Chapter One
BAR SNACKS

In the 1980s at the Seafood Restaurant we were all imbued with the glamour of 'nouvelle cuisine'. I bought every French cookery book I could afford on the subject: *The Nouvelle Cuisine of Jean & Pierre Troisgros*, Roger Vergé's *Cuisine of the Sun*, Georges Blanc's *Ma Cuisine des Saisons* in French, and my favourite, *La Cuisine Gourmande* by Michel Guérard. Then there was *Cuisine Naturelle* by Anton Mosimann, our own local – well, Swiss, actually – head chef at the Dorchester Hotel in London at the time. This book had the strapline 'elegant food for a healthy life'.

Once I was armed with these collections of mostly rather complicated recipes, things had to change at the restaurant. On the menu came lots of what I considered delicately sauced fish dishes, though mercifully for my British customers, the portion sizes didn't slim down much. Dishes included sea trout poached in hay, chilled crab consommé with chervil, sea bass fillets with lettuce leaves and my favourite – escalopes of salmon with a sorrel sauce. Looking back on all these now that the rubbishing of nouvelle cuisine that came later has passed, I find that they were just rather expert French dishes which we in the UK were not quite prepared for back then. Madly, with a small kitchen and not many chefs, I tried to excel with a few dishes like three fillets of fish: John Dory, monkfish and brill. These were sautéed in butter, chargrilled and steamed with three different sauces, the John Dory with salted cucumber, the monkfish with a roasted red pepper dressing and the brill with a cream and sorrel sauce.

As if dishes like this weren't too much already, I decided, like the Michelin-starred chefs, to have some little cups of soup, tiny skewers of fish dipped in rouille, bowls of peeled quails' eggs with mayonnaise, and plates of mussels stuffed with garlic butter to give away at the beginning of the meal. All these things the French call *amuse-gueule* or palette ticklers. The problem was that in our English-speaking kitchen, I wasn't about to start barking out '*fait marche les amuse-gueules s'il vous plaît*'. It had to be 'bar snacks for table 15, please'.

You might think that to call the opening chapter of my book 'bar snacks' is to purposefully take away any sense of exciting the appetite, but it is very nostalgic for me. If it seems a banal sort of phrase it is actually a no-nonsense way of describing types of dishes that are difficult to describe. Better still, when you consider the alternatives – nibbles, appetisers, hors d'oeuvres – bar snacks are just anything you don't need to sit down and eat with a knife and fork.

These days, formally sitting down to a first course as well as a main and pudding sometimes seems a little over the top. Even at Christmas we don't bother with a starter for lunch, simply because we're always late from having had two beers at the Cornish Arms, not just one. That's now the norm. And even when I've got something really rather special for dinner like grilled lobsters, we always start with some bar snacks to go with the champagne. The trick is not to appear to make too much of these dishes either, even though they might have been quite labour intensive to get together earlier. Some of my favourites are deep-fried coconut prawns with a sauce made from habanero chilli and ripe papaya to dip them into (page 22). Or a stalwart of mine – marinated salmon with passion fruit, lime and coriander (page 29).

Bar snacks have become such an integral part of our entertaining life that we quite often build the food of a whole night's eating around them by turning them into 'finger food'. For this, we either expand our little bar snacks or contract our main courses into things we can hand round for people to hold and eat while they chat. Some of the most popular of these are beef and pork meatballs with a spicy tomato sauce and olives (page 38), slow-cooked pork carnitas tacos (page 37), goujons of lemon sole with tartare sauce (page 23), feta and spinach filo 'cigars' (page 16), tempura oysters with sweet chilli dipping sauce (page 32) and, most important, strips of grilled rib-eye steak with béarnaise sauce (page 35).

For me too, there is an oft-forgotten imperative for a long and noisy party at about midnight, when the munchies attack and only Provençal fish soup or an Aussie meat pie will assuage the ravenousness.

Feta & spinach filo 'cigars'

This is a classic spanakopita filling, but I've used the filo pastry to make it into little cigar-shaped parcels that are easy to crunch.

MAKES 24

2 tbsp olive oil
1 medium onion,
   finely chopped
2 garlic cloves, grated
   or finely chopped
300g baby spinach,
   well washed
Big pinch chilli flakes
½ tsp dried mint or 2 fresh
   mint sprigs, chopped

200g feta cheese, crumbled
12 sheets filo pastry
   (about 1 x 220g pack
   depending on the brand)
110g butter, melted,
   or 110ml olive oil
Salt and black pepper

TIP
These can be made in advance and frozen before baking, then baked when needed. Just increase the cooking time to 15–20 minutes or cook until crisp and golden and the filling is hot right through.

In a wide pan, heat the oil over a low to medium heat. Add the onion and garlic and cook slowly for 5–10 minutes until softened but not browned. Add the spinach and increase the heat to allow the spinach to wilt and the liquid to evaporate. Stir in the chilli flakes, mint and feta and season to taste with salt and pepper. Remove from the heat and leave to cool.

Preheat the oven to 200°C/Fan 180°C. Place a sheet of filo on a board, brush with melted butter or oil and top with a second sheet – keep the rest of the filo under a slightly damp tea towel to prevent it from drying out. Cut the double sheet into strips measuring roughly 12 x 25cm.

Put a tablespoon of the mixture about 1cm from the end of the narrow side of a strip. Brush a little more butter or oil over the strip. Tuck in the sides and roll the pastry away from you into a fat cigar shape. Transfer to a baking tray lined with baking parchment.

Repeat with the remaining filling and pastry, then brush all the rolls with melted butter or oil.

Bake the 'cigars' for 10–15 minutes until golden and crisp, then serve them hot.

Debra's crab thingos

I am always keen to find things that taste hot, fresh and sharp to put in lettuce leaves. Not only do these look attractive but anything with lettuce also reassures the myriad of people on diets that this is not going to be bad for them. My favourite filling for lettuce leaves is the famous dish from Chiang Mai – larb. A chum of mine, David Thompson, has a chain of restaurants and serves a larb signature dish that's so hot that it's sort of a rite of passage, like a vindaloo. Our friend Debra's thingos are for polite cocktail parties.

MAKES ABOUT 15

200g white crab meat
1 red finger chilli, finely chopped
4 spring onions, finely sliced
2–3 tbsp coconut cream (enough to bind the mixture together)
Juice and finely grated zest of 1 lime

3 tsp Thai fish sauce
2 tsp brown sugar
Small handful coriander leaves, chopped, plus extra leaves to garnish
2 little gem lettuces, separated into leaves

TIP
The crab mixture is also lovely on toast.

Mix all the ingredients together except the lettuce and extra coriander, then refrigerate.

When it's time to serve, pile a teaspoonful of the crab mixture on to lettuce leaves and garnish with coriander.

Crispy chicken skin

I hate throwing food away. These are as good as pork scratchings.

Chicken skin from a whole chicken or chicken pieces, cut into strips

1 tsp soy sauce
Salt

Preheat the oven to 200°C/Fan 180°C. Spread the chicken skin pieces out on a baking tray, and sprinkle with the soy sauce and a little salt. Cook in the oven for about 20 minutes or until browned and crisp. Serve with cold beer.

Gouda quesadillas with caramelised apples & onion & salsa

I had a try at making quesadillas at the central market in Puebla, Mexico, using blue corn rather than flour dough. It was one of the low spots in my cookery programmes – a moment when the director says have a go and you know that your efforts alongside the lady who's been making them for 36 years will be frightful. So when I came to make some more, using flour tortillas, in my programme about Cornwall last year I felt almost like a pro. These are lovely and we made them to celebrate all things autumnal.

SERVES 8-10
as snack or 2-3
as a light lunch

15g butter
1 medium to large onion, sliced
2 Coxes or 1 large Braeburn
  apple, cored and sliced
1 tsp caster sugar
Sunflower oil
2 large flour tortillas
175g Gouda (Cornish,
  if available), grated
Black pepper

Salsa
2 large ripe tomatoes,
  finely diced
1/2 onion, finely chopped
1 green jalapeño chilli,
  finely chopped
Handful fresh
  coriander, chopped
1/4 tsp salt
Juice of 1/2-1 lime

TIP
These make a
great al fresco
camping meal,
cooked on a
frying pan over
an open fire or
a camping stove.

Mix the salsa ingredients together in a bowl and set aside.

Melt the butter in a frying pan. When it's foaming, add the onion and apple slices, sprinkle with the caster sugar and cook over a medium heat. Keep turning them until softened and golden brown, then season with black pepper.

Take a separate frying pan and wipe it sparingly with a little oil to prevent sticking. Warm a tortilla in the pan, then cover half of the circle with half the grated Gouda. When the cheese is starting to melt, top with half the onion and apple mixture and fold the empty side of the tortilla over to form a semi-circle. Turn it over, using a fish slice or a palette knife, and cook the other side for a couple of minutes or so until the cheese is melting and oozing. Transfer to a warm plate and repeat with the second tortilla.

Cut each quesadilla into wedges and serve immediately with the salsa and drinks.

Deep-fried coconut prawns

The sauce is a little on the hot side but so it should be, as habaneros are the chillies most often used in the Yucatán, where this dish comes from. It's proved to be one of the most popular recipes from my book The Road to Mexico. *I think it's to do with the exotic flavour of the coconut in the batter and the papaya and chilli in the dip.*

SERVES 8–12

24 raw king prawns,
    peeled but with tails on
    (about 600g frozen raw
    shell-on prawns)
1 litre sunflower oil,
    for frying
Salt

Batter
125g plain flour
1½ tsp baking powder
1 tsp salt
1 egg
150ml ice-cold water

Coating
50g plain flour
60g panko breadcrumbs
60g unsweetened
    desiccated coconut

Papaya dipping sauce
1 large papaya
½–1 habanero chilli, stem removed,
    deseeded and roughly chopped
1 banana shallot, roughly chopped
1 garlic clove, peeled and halved
3 tbsp cider vinegar
2 thin slices peeled root ginger
Juice of 1 lime
Juice of 1 orange
1 tbsp soft brown sugar
1 large pinch ground allspice
½ tsp salt

TIP
You can use mango
instead of papaya
for the sauce,
but the colour
is not so good.

For the sauce, peel the papaya, remove the seeds and chop the flesh. Put it in a blender with the other ingredients and process until smooth. Pour the sauce into a pan and bring to the boil, then turn the heat down to a simmer and cook gently for about 5 minutes. If it gets too thick, add a little boiling water.

For the batter, sift the flour, baking powder and salt into a bowl. Make a well in the centre and break in the egg, then bring in the flour from the sides. Whisk in the water to make a smooth batter.

Put the 50g of flour for the coating in one shallow bowl, the batter in a second, and the breadcrumbs mixed with the coconut in a third bowl.

Season the prawns with salt. Coat each one in flour, shaking off any excess, then holding it by the tail, dip it into the batter. Lift it out and let any excess batter drip back into the bowl. Roll the prawn in the coconut and crumbs mix, pressing it down so the mixture sticks, then put the prawn on a tray. Repeat until all the prawns are coated. Leave some space in between each one.

Pour the oil into a large pan and heat to 180°C. Deep-fry the prawns – a few at a time – for 1 or 2 minutes until golden and crisp. Drain them on kitchen paper. Serve at once with the sauce.

Goujons of lemon sole
with tartare sauce

Lemon sole is the best flatfish for goujons. Others, like plaice or dab, don't quite have the flavour, but in Australia I would concede that flathead is pretty good too.

SERVES 12

450g lemon sole fillets, skinned
1 litre sunflower oil, for deep-frying
50g plain flour
100g panko breadcrumbs
3 eggs
Salt
Lemon wedges, to serve

Tartare sauce
150ml Mustard mayonnaise (page 309)
1 tsp finely chopped green olives
1 tsp finely chopped gherkin
1 tsp finely chopped capers
1 tsp finely chopped parsley
1 tsp finely chopped chives

TIP
People tend to overcook goujons. They should be light brown, nothing more.

Mix all the tartare sauce ingredients together in a bowl and refrigerate until needed.

Cut each lemon sole fillet diagonally into strips about 2.5cm wide and lightly season them with salt.

Heat the oil in a large saucepan to 180°C or until a cube of day-old bread browns in about a minute. Line a baking tray with plenty of kitchen paper. Put the flour in a shallow bowl, the breadcrumbs in another bowl and beat the eggs in a third.

Coat the goujons, a few at a time, with the flour, then beaten egg and finally with the breadcrumb mixture. Make sure that they all take on an even coating and remain separate.

Drop a small handful of goujons into the oil and deep-fry for about 1 minute until crisp and golden. Lift out with a slotted spoon and place on the paper-lined tray to drain. Repeat until all the goujons are cooked, making sure the oil comes back to temperature each time.

Serve the goujons on a warmed plate with lemon wedges and tartare sauce.

Celebrations

If you have a lot of little jobs that need doing around the house, my advice is to find some cause for celebration and invite your friends round. There is nothing that galvanises me more strongly into mending the handle on the bathroom door, changing a light bulb in the hall, sorting out the recycling or fixing the sound system so it doesn't drop out in the middle of 'Fat-bottomed Girls', than knowing visitors are due. I've got a very good friend who half-painted the wooden fence around his house in a grey-blue colour – I think it was called something like 'cool marble' or 'clouded dawn'. It stayed like that for at least seven years and then he had a big party and it was finished. The reality is that none of us like to be shown up as being a bit slovenly but, more to the point, the euphoria of having people round also inspires us all, I would guess, with a desire that our house should look absolutely tippy top.

I think this is all part of the process of getting ready for Christmas and it's a classic example of the journey being as good as or better than the arrival. I just love the thought of the goose that's coming – should I be ordering one or two? Then there's the anticipation of the crisp fat on a goose, which is so much more rewarding than anything a turkey can offer, and the ham for Boxing Day. I love that combination of the smell of hot ham, cloves and cider and the sweet spiciness of the braising red cabbage. Plus there's the joy of butter melting when you split open the large baked potatoes, skins crisped in the oven, and the wonder of English mustard with it all. Or the beginning of mince pie season, which is surely at least a fortnight before Christmas; and Christmas Eve, the one time in the year when I get the fish kettles out, one for bass and the other a proper turbot kettle.

Actually I spend every other Christmas in Sydney and though I would love to describe prawns and salads on the beach or a Christmas beach barbecue, the reality is that Sas's family do pretty much the same food as we do back in England; apart from the absolute must of Aussie prawns and oysters to start.

However, my birthday in early January has turned into not just a celebration of that but also of midsummer in Australia. We managed to buy our house in Mollymook 12 years ago when property prices weren't too bad on the south coast of New South Wales, and it's a great place to spend summer. It's a beach house built in the 1950s to a design from California, so it's roofed in red cedar shingles and has a veranda all the way around. At the time, against all expectations that we would demolish it or split the property in half and sell one part, we restored it to its Beach Boys-style glamour. If you dressed in 60s fashion you could almost imagine Slim Aarons coming round to take some photos. You may have seen his marvellous pictures of groups of 60s girls with beehives and tight white miniskirts and men wearing light green jackets and white drainpipe jeans beside a pool in Palm Springs.

Sitting looking out over the Pacific at a long, narrow table seating 14 that came from a sheep-shearing shed, it's not a bad spot for a birthday barbecue. Actually not everything is cooked on the barbie. Sacha, my wife's cousin, takes care of that, cooking maybe a butterflied leg of lamb, a fillet of Scotch beef, some prawns, maybe a bit of snapper and a load of Aussie sausages, which I can't abide. But I'll have prepared oysters, prawns and my marinated salmon with passion fruit for nibbles. Then Sacha's partner Rose, who is from South Korea, will do her prawn fritters with soy, cider vinegar and chilli (page 30). I'll have made some big communal pie like a pastitsio (page 199) or fish pie (page 102), then we'll have salads, which everybody brings. To finish it's got to be pavlova, quite often with tropical fruits or strawberries, and a birthday cake. My favourite is Sas's family's version of Gretta Anna's hummingbird cake with bananas, pineapple and walnuts (page 275). I always mean to drink nothing but beer all night, but tend later to succumb to the charms of Aussie Shiraz or Cabernet Sauvignon, which is far too strong.

Similar happy anticipation happens for Easter. I like the fact that Easter is a movable feast, but for me it really has to be in April, with the feeling that daylight and daffodils are upon us. There's the annual indecision about spring lamb for Easter Sunday – there's not much flavour but it's more about the delicacy of the new season's meat, and the sheer specialness of serving it up versus the much greater flavour of the last year's lamb. But to me Easter is much more than that – it's the family gathering to celebrate the end of winter, surrounded by bluebells, daffodils and crocuses.

Running through the year, the next occasion that's special for my family is May Day in Padstow. This is a celebration of the coming of summer, which goes back as the locals say to 'time immemorial', whatever that means. Its roots are quite clearly a pagan fertility ritual. Two teams of 'Mayers', dressed in blue and white in one case and red and white in the other, dance through the streets of Padstow singing the 'Morning Song' which begins:

Unite and unite, O let us all Unite,
for summer is a-comin' today.

And whither we are going we will
all unite in the merry morning of May.

It's a festival that no one in Padstow would dream of missing and many return from all parts of the world to be there. I have only missed it three times since 1970, it's that important.

I don't cook much on May Day because everybody else does, but I do drink much. I have a few friends round at 9 o'clock in the morning for champagne and bacon sandwiches, and then everyone else invites us into their houses all through the day and night. Because my cottage is always filled with friends staying, I always leave a pot of fish soup on the stove with loads of baguettes, rouille and grated Parmesan cheese. I don't bother to tell anyone it's there; it just goes as people drift back late at night.

Moving on to June. Sadly, because we've now got so many staff, what we did for many years is no longer possible – a staff barbecue on a beach somewhere. We started at Tregirls beach on the Camel estuary, then as numbers increased we graduated to Treyarnon Bay for a few years and lastly to Harlyn Bay. By this time, the staff had got so big and the party had become so well-known, we found we were catering for everyone on the beach. The beer ran out and we repaired to the pub across the road and drank most of their beer too. Those glorious days have had to end, but whenever I think of beach barbecues I consider those the best days of my life.

These days I have a much more easy-to-control party with my chums in the garden of my cottage in Padstow and I enjoy the luxury of getting a couple of chefs and waiters from the restaurant to do all the work. As far as annual festivities are concerned, that's about it, but Sas and I can't go more than six weeks without some sort of reason to throw a party – birthdays obviously, anniversaries, weddings – and if there is nothing in the diary we'll make something up.

Not a celebration of meaning to anyone else but we always have a dinner party in August (in Sydney). It's winter there, of course, but it can be the most marvellous, clear, sunny weather and seems a good time to invite 20 or so people round for a midwinter jolly. Midwinter there, as I'm sure you are aware, is not much different to a UK summer, although it gets dark very early and Australian houses at an average temperature of about 12°C are very chilly. They just aren't built for colder weather.

'Sas and I can't go more than six weeks without some sort of reason to throw a party.'

Marinated salmon with passion fruit, lime & coriander

I came up with this recipe one New Year's Eve in Sydney about 15 years ago to serve at a party for Sas's closest friends, the Rosebuds. The idea of marinating raw tuna in passion fruit juice seemed very Aussie to me, but I quickly realised that there wasn't enough acidity to make this a ceviche, so I added lime juice as well as green chilli and coriander to give it a slightly Asian feel. It's been really quite successful and I still do it every Christmas down under. These days I tend to make it with salmon.

SERVES 8–12

3cm-thick piece of salmon fillet, weighing about 500g
2 passion fruit
1 tbsp lime juice
½ tsp Thai fish sauce
3 tbsp sunflower oil

1 medium-hot green chilli, finely chopped
1 tsp caster sugar
Small handful coriander, finely chopped
Salt and black pepper

TIP
You can make the marinade in advance, but leave adding the chopped coriander until the last minute.

Put the piece of salmon fillet on a board and slice it across into very thin slices. Lay the slices, side by side and butted close up together, on 4 dinner plates. Cover each one with cling film and set them aside in the fridge for at least an hour, or until you are ready to serve.

Shortly before serving, make the dressing. Cut the passion fruit in half and scoop the pulp and seeds into a bowl. Stir in the lime juice, Thai fish sauce, sunflower oil, green chilli, sugar and coriander, then season with half a teaspoon of salt and some black pepper.

To serve, uncover the plates, spoon over the dressing and spread it over the surface of the fish with the back of the spoon. Leave for 10 minutes before serving.

Rose's Korean prawn fritters with soy, cider vinegar & chilli

SERVES 4-6
as a bar snack
or more if served
alongside other
bar snacks.

Rose is Sas's cousin's partner and being Korean she has a fabulous repertoire of seafood recipes. What I love about this dish is its simplicity and the subtlety of soy and vinegar; also the fact that Rose finds parsley such an exotic herb. It's lovely to experience the flavour through somebody else's perception.

100g plain flour
20g cornflour
1 tsp salt
200g raw peeled
    prawns, chopped

Good handful flatleaf
    parsley, chopped
2 spring onions, trimmed
    and finely chopped
5 tbsp sunflower oil

Dipping sauce
5 tbsp soy sauce
1 tbsp apple cider vinegar
1 tsp chilli flakes
1 tbsp sesame oil

TIP
You can use
coriander
instead of
parsley, if
you prefer.

Whisk the plain flour, cornflour and salt with 200ml of water in a bowl to make a fairly runny batter. The consistency should be somewhere between single and double pouring cream. Leave the batter to rest in the fridge for an hour or so.

Make the dipping sauce by mixing all the ingredients together in a small bowl and set aside.

Preheat the oven to 180°C/Fan 160°C. Stir the chopped prawns, parsley and spring onions into the rested batter.

Add 2 tablespoons of the oil to a 28–30cm frying pan and place over a high heat. When the pan is hot, add half the batter, spreading it thinly to cover the base of the pan. Once the surface has lost its liquid texture and the underside is crisp and golden brown (2–3 minutes) slide the fritter on to a flat baking tray or plate. Add a little more oil to the pan, flip the fritter back into the pan and cook the other side for another 2–3 minutes until golden. Slide on to a baking tray and keep it warm in a low oven. Add another 2 tablespoons of oil to the pan and repeat with the rest of the batter.

Cut the fritters into roughly 3cm squares and serve immediately with the dipping sauce.

Tempura oysters with sweet chilli dipping sauce

A little snack that's absolutely intended for those who don't know if they like oysters or not. It's completely irresistible.

750ml sunflower oil,
   for deep-frying
50g plain flour
50g cornflour
Pinch salt
175ml ice-cold soda water
½ tbsp sesame seeds
12 oysters, shucked
   and shells reserved

Dipping sauce
2 tbsp fresh lime juice
2 tbsp Thai fish sauce
1 tbsp caster sugar
1 red bird's-eye chilli,
   very finely chopped
1 garlic clove, very
   finely chopped

TIP
You can make this with mussels instead of oysters, if you prefer.

Heat the oil in a wok or deep pan to 180°C or until a cube of day-old bread browns in about a minute. Line a baking tray with kitchen paper.

Mix the sauce ingredients together with 2 tablespoons of water and set aside in shallow dipping bowls.

Whisk the flours and salt with the soda water in a bowl and add the sesame seeds. Dip the oysters, a few at a time, into this batter, then gently lower them into the oil and fry until golden. Drain on the baking tray and keep them warm while you dip and cook the rest.

Serve the oysters on the half shell, with the dipping sauce alongside.

Grilled rib-eye steak with Rick's peppermix & béarnaise sauce

I know this looks like a recipe for a couple of nice steaks that you'd serve with salad and chips, because it is. But when the steak is sliced and served on cocktail sticks with the béarnaise as a dip it's the sort of thing that everybody — except vegetarians — absolutely loves. For me, it has the same effect as the first double gin and tonic of the evening of lifting my mood.

SERVES 8-10

2 rib-eye steaks (about 225g each), well marbled with fat (at room temperature)
2 tsp sunflower oil
Pinch salt
¼–½ tsp Rick's peppermix (page 308)

Béarnaise sauce
25ml white wine vinegar
2 tarragon sprigs, chopped
1 shallot, finely chopped
1 egg yolk
110g Clarified butter (page 312)
Salt and black pepper

TIP
If you have a digital thermometer on your oven, you can hold the cooked steak at 50°C for at least 20 minutes. This way you can get this cooked just before your guests arrive.

Preheat your barbecue. Brush the steaks with oil and season them on both sides with salt and the peppermix.

For the sauce, heat the vinegar, tarragon and shallot with a tablespoon of water in a pan. Season with plenty of black pepper and boil until the liquid has reduced to a tablespoon, then set aside.

Place a bowl over a pan of just-simmering water, making sure the bottom of the bowl is not touching the water. Add a teaspoon of water and the egg yolk and whisk with a balloon whisk until the mixture is creamy and increased in volume. Remove from the heat and gradually whisk in the clarified butter. Stir in the tarragon and shallot reduction, then keep the sauce warm in a bowl over a pan of warm water.

Cook the steaks for 1½–4 minutes per side depending on the thickness or how well done you like your steak (see the chart on page 319). If you prefer, cook the steaks on a preheated griddle pan.

Slice the steak and cut into bite-sized slices. Serve on cocktail sticks alongside the sauce.

Slow-cooked pork carnitas tacos

Carnitas is pork simmered very slowly in lard until it is very tender. It's very similar to French confit, but the recipe includes orange juice to cut the richness. Of all the taco fillings in my book The Road to Mexico, *carnitas is the one I use the most because it's so easy to make.*

SERVES 20

1kg boned pork shoulder, cut into 6cm chunks
½ medium onion, chopped
2 garlic cloves, chopped
2 tsp dried oregano
1½ tsp salt
250g lard
125ml whole milk
125ml fresh orange juice

Tortillas and garnishes
40 x 10cm corn tortillas
Guacamole and chipotle crema (page 311)
Pico de gallo salsa (page 311)
Handful coriander, roughly chopped
Handful radishes, sliced
1 banana shallot, sliced
2 limes, cut into wedges

TIP
Another way of enjoying carnitas is to pile it into burger buns and top with some kimchi and a teaspoon of Gochujang (Korean red chilli paste).

Put the pork in a pan with the onion, garlic, oregano, salt, lard, milk and orange juice. Cover the pan and simmer for about 45 minutes, then remove the lid and cook for a further 1¼ hours until the meat is tender.

Remove the pork with a slotted spoon and pull the meat apart with a couple of forks. Continue to simmer the juices until the liquid has all but evaporated. The fat will have separated and will be sitting on the top, so you can ladle it out to use again for cooking more carnitas, refried beans or delicious fried potatoes.

Scrape all the solids from the bottom of the pan and pour the reduced juices and solids over the shredded pork. Stir to combine. Spoon on to the warmed tacos and top with guacamole, chipotle crema and pico de gallo salsa.

Serve with chopped coriander, radishes, chopped shallot and lime wedges for squeezing.

Beef & pork meatballs with a spicy tomato sauce & olives

This recipe came from a stall in Prades market where they were cooking meatballs in a huge paella pan – and fabulous they were. They're flavoured with cinnamon and piment d'Espelette and cooked in an exquisite sauce. It was originally a pretty substantial dish with haricot beans, but just the meatballs and olives are a great accompaniment to champagne or cocktails.

SERVES 10-12

Meatballs
400g minced beef
400g minced pork
1 egg
3 garlic cloves, finely chopped or grated
Small handful flatleaf parsley, chopped
½ tsp ground cinnamon
1 tsp piment d'Espelette
   or sweet pimentón
Plain flour
3 tbsp olive oil
Salt and black pepper

Sauce
1 tbsp olive oil
1 onion, finely chopped
100g lardons or cubes of cooked ham
1 tsp piment d'Espelette or
   sweet pimentón
½ tsp ground cinnamon
6 tomatoes, tough cores
   removed, chopped
1 tbsp tomato paste
150g pitted green olives,
   drained and chopped

TIP
To turn this into a main course, bulk out the sauce with a 400g tin of haricot beans, drained, and serve with rice.

In a large bowl, mix the meat, egg, garlic, parsley, cinnamon, piment d'Espelette or pimentón and 2 tablespoons of flour. Season with salt and pepper and blend well. Using your hands, shape the mixture into walnut-sized balls, adding another tablespoon of flour if the mixture feels too wet to form into balls. Roll the balls in flour to lightly cover. Heat the oil in a large, preferably shallow, flameproof casserole dish and brown the meatballs all over. Set them aside.

For the sauce, heat the oil in the same casserole dish and fry the onion and the lardons or ham until the onions are softened. Add the spices and cook for a minute, then add the tomatoes, tomato paste and 250ml of water. Season with salt and pepper and bring to the boil. Turn the heat down, cover the pan and simmer for 15 minutes. Add the olives and meatballs to the pan, with any juices they have released.

Cover the pan and cook over a low heat for 30 minutes, then remove the lid and simmer for 10–15 minutes. Check a couple of times during cooking and add a little water if the sauce looks as if it is getting too thick. Serve with cocktail sticks.

Tarte flambée

I remember going on a bit too much in my book Secret France *about how the tarte flambée was France's answer to the pizza. Funnily enough, though, when we were filming in a village near Forcalquier in Provence, the pizzeria in the square not only had good pizza Margherita but also tarte flambée and very lovely it was.*

SERVES 12
as a snack

Dough
250g plain flour, sifted,
    plus extra for dusting
½ tsp salt
150ml tepid water
2 tbsp sunflower oil

Topping
250g full-fat crème fraiche
1 large onion, finely sliced
160g smoked bacon lardons,
    fried until golden brown
250g Emmental or Gruyère
    cheese or a mixture, grated
A few rasps freshly grated nutmeg
Salt and black pepper

TIP
If pushed for time, you can make this with 2 sheets of ready-rolled, all-butter puff pastry.

Mix the flour and salt in a bowl, then add the water and oil and bring everything together to make a rough dough. Transfer the dough to a floured board and knead well. Roll the dough into 2 rectangles, each measuring about 25 x 28cm.

Preheat the oven to 230°C/Fan 210°C or as hot as your oven will go. Spread the crème fraiche over the dough, leaving a little border around the edges, then dot with the onion, fried bacon lardons and grated cheese. Season with salt, pepper and grated nutmeg.

Bake for 10–12 minutes or until the base is crisp and the cheese is bubbling. Slide the tarts on to a wooden board and cut them into bite-sized squares. Serve immediately with drinks or as a light lunch with salad.

Chapter Two

FIRST COURSES

I'm fond of pontificating about the inadvisability of producing a first course at a dinner party – that is, if you're going to be doing everything on your own. It's what restaurants do and the contestants on *MasterChef*, but personally I get too involved with talking to everyone. Then I find I'm either not really listening to who I'm speaking to, or I'm having visions of the mackerel for the mackerel recheado burning on the barbecue, the beef in the tataki, which requires just seconds to cook, being well done, or the mussels cooked to graininess. All I'm thinking at this moment is please go away, but I'm filled with a sense of why could I not have planned this better? How did I not see that this was going to happen?

I now realise that it is always going to be the same. It reminds me of arriving at the Seafood Restaurant kitchen back in the 70s, an hour before service was due to start. I would be filled with excitement about changing the menu there and then, without a shred of caution, and there'd be panicky looks from the other chefs.

The problem at home is down to the curse of kitchens and dining rooms being all in one. The other night, in the first phase of coming out of lockdown, six of us had dinner in the garden at our house in Chiswick. All alone in the kitchen, with the others outside swaddled in coats, scarves and hats and warmed by a charcoal barbecue on one side and a fire pit on the other, I immediately felt in control.

I had been given a bit of a challenge to put Arbroath smokies on the menu at the Seafood Restaurant, so here was my opportunity to try out an idea for a dish which was simply scrambled egg made with far too much butter, the smokies (small haddock cooked over oak smoke), Cheddar cheese from Davidstow on Bodmin Moor, a little cream and parsley. Everything had to be done at the last minute, so it couldn't be worse, but having the freedom of the kitchen with everyone else outside was all I needed.

The dish was very well received and I've just managed to slip the recipe into this chapter, but then all went slightly pear-shaped. In my enthusiasm for keeping everyone warm and thinking the barbecue wasn't hot enough, I lifted the lid and aimed my leaf blower into the hot coals. Many of them took off, missed the guests but landed on the Astroturf lawn where they made a series of little melted black holes. Luckily, no one was burnt and it only seemed to contribute to the atmosphere of euphoria all of us felt at being together for a meal after so many months of isolation. The gardens either side were filled with laughter and the smell of barbecues – a special moment in a strange time.

Needless to say, all the recipes in this chapter are perfectly doable as first courses if you get a bit organised and try to keep your guests out of the kitchen. Some, like the minestrone (page 47) and the pea and lettuce soup (page 52) are easy to get ready in advance, so reducing stress. Others, such as the mackerel recheado (page 55) and the grilled scallops with toasted hazelnut and coriander butter (page 57) are quick to cook, but you do need a bit of peace so you can concentrate for those few moments.

Classic fish soup
with rouille & croutons

*I've always thought that a good fish soup is the best way to test
the quality of a fish restaurant. It's all to do with the depth of
flavour that comes from using lots of fish and shellfish with
saffron, tomatoes, red peppers, fennel, garlic and, always for me,
orange peel. I've made fish soup for 40 years and for the first ten
of those I used a mouli. I then upgraded to a giant stick blender,
but these days we use a centrifuge. Either way, the trick is to use
a sieve system that allows just enough, but not too much, of the
solids to pass through. You have to judge it, as you want a soup that
is not so thin that it tastes watery and not so thick that it borders
on porridge. At home, I use a conical strainer and then a finer sieve
if it's still too thick. It's never a good idea to include the bones though.*

SERVES 4

900g whole fish, such as
    gurnard or grey mullet or a
    mixture of fish on the bone,
    gutted, cleaned and skin on
85ml olive oil
75g each of onion, celery, leek
    and fennel, roughly chopped
3 garlic cloves, sliced
2 pared strips of orange zest,
    plus juice of ½ orange

200g tinned chopped
    tomatoes
1 red pepper, sliced
1 bay leaf and 1 thyme sprig
Pinch saffron strands
100g cooked North Atlantic
    prawns, shells on
Pinch cayenne pepper
½ tsp salt
Black pepper

To serve
Rouille (page 310)

Croutons
½ French baguette
Olive oil, for frying
1 garlic clove, cut in half
25g Parmesan cheese,
    finely grated, to serve

Fillet the fish and set it aside. Use the bones to make a fish
stock (page 306) – you'll need 1½ litres. Make the rouille.

Heat the olive oil in a large pan, add the onion, celery, leek,
fennel and garlic and cook gently for 20 minutes or until soft
but not coloured. Add the orange zest, tomatoes, red pepper,
bay leaf, thyme, saffron, prawns and fish fillets. Cook briskly
for 2–3 minutes, then add 1½ litres of stock and the orange
juice, bring to the boil and simmer for 40 minutes.

Meanwhile, for the croutons, thinly slice the baguette and fry
the slices in olive oil until crisp and golden. Drain on kitchen
paper and rub one side of each piece with the garlic clove.

Recipe continued overleaf

Liquidise the soup as finely as possible in a mouli or a blender. Then pass it through a conical sieve into a clean pan, pressing out as much liquid as possible with the back of a ladle. If the soup is very thick, pass half of it through a finer sieve. Return the soup to the heat and season to taste with the cayenne, salt and black pepper.

Pour the soup into a warmed tureen and put the croutons, Parmesan cheese and rouille into separate dishes.

To serve, ladle the soup into warmed bowls and leave each person to spread some rouille on to croutons, float them on their soup and sprinkle with Parmesan cheese.

Minestrone

This recipe is a basic guide – it's a fridge-drawer soup so you can use whatever you have, such as leeks, courgettes, peas, red pepper and other kinds of cabbage. The secret is to use plenty of Parmesan and to try to rid your head of the incessant 10CC song 'Life is a Minestrone' as you're making it.

SERVES ABOUT 10
as a starter or 6 as
a main course

4 tbsp olive oil, plus extra to serve
1 large onion, chopped
75g smoked streaky bacon
  or pancetta, chopped
3 celery sticks, chopped
3 carrots, chopped
2 garlic cloves, finely chopped
2 tbsp tomato paste
400g tin chopped tomatoes
1.7 litres Chicken stock (page 307)
Parmesan cheese rind (if available)
1 bay leaf

200g waxy new potatoes,
  scrubbed and cut into 1cm cubes
50g spaghetti, broken into
  2cm lengths
¼ small savoy or white cabbage,
  finely shredded
150g tinned cannellini beans, drained
1 rosemary sprig
Large handful flatleaf parsley,
  chopped
Grated Parmesan cheese, to serve
Salt and black pepper

TIP
Never throw away rinds of Parmesan, pecorino or Grana Padano cheese. Store them in a bag or box in the fridge, ready to toss into a pan of soup or a risotto.

Heat the olive oil in a large pan over a medium heat and add the onion, bacon or pancetta, celery, carrots and garlic. Cook for 3–4 minutes until the vegetables have softened a little. Stir in the tomato paste, then add the tomatoes, stock, Parmesan rind, if using, and bay leaf and cook for 30–40 minutes or so.

Add the potatoes, pasta, cabbage, beans and rosemary sprig. Season with salt and pepper and cook for a further 20 minutes. If the soup is too thick, add some water.

Add the parsley, then serve in warm bowls with an extra swirl of olive oil, plenty of freshly grated Parmesan and some good crusty bread. This is delicious on the day it's made but also great if cooked a day or two in advance.

Sourdough

Ingredients
500g strong white flour
300ml tepid water
150ml sourdough starter
15g salt

This is more a commentary on the making of sourdough than a precise recipe. Thanks to successive lockdowns: first, five months in Sydney, then a month in London in November and then shortly after Christmas in Padstow, I've been making sourdough bread, much of the time in half quantities due to Sas's love of eating it hot out of the oven. No amount of me saying, 'Please leave the bread for 45 minutes to cool down' makes any difference; it's that tantalising smell in the latter stages of baking. Like so many other people, I find making sourdough is almost like life itself – a sort of sine wave of elation and gloom. So, with the best part of a year's experience, here's what I now do.

Mix all the above ingredients together in a bowl. I used to use a spoon, but I now find fingers are better. Don't knead the dough, just mix until it's a rough ball, cover with a damp tea towel and leave for half an hour. Flatten the ball slightly into a rough rectangle in the bottom of the bowl, pick up the four corners and fold them into the centre. Do this two or three times more in the early stages of proving; this will develop the gluten sufficiently so you don't need to knead it in the usual manner of making bread. You can tell in the latter stages whether the gluten has developed sufficiently by pulling off a little of the dough and chewing it – having partly dissolved in your mouth there will be a residue like chewing gum.

Now here's the indecisive part. Proving can take up to 12 hours, depending on the temperature of the kitchen. My kitchen in Padstow is normally about 22 degrees and the dough will take 8–12 hours, depending on all kinds of things which I still don't understand: atmospheric pressure perhaps, humidity, definitely how perky the sourdough starter was when you began. You will know when the dough has reached the necessary expansion – it's much more than doubled in size and it has a sort of airiness and lightness you can't mistake. Plus, when you press it with your finger it should almost, but not quite, spring back.

Now's the time to shape the dough. I wet my fingers to make it easier to lift the puffy dough out of the bowl. I put it on a work surface, not floured, and again press the dough out to form a rough rectangle while trying not to push it down too much and thereby lose air. Then, as before, I lift up the four corners and fold them into the centre. I turn over the dough so it is seam-side down and gently shape the base of the dough with the edges of my hand, pushing slightly inwards at the bottom. This stretches the dough and gives a really good shape. I put it into the 'proving basket', seam-side up, in other words inverting it again. I cover it with a damp tea towel and leave it for the final prove, again until more than doubled in size. This could take up to two hours. In the latter stages of proving, I set my oven to 200°C Fan.

Proving basket: I find the most convenient shape for proving bread is a round banneton, which is a basket made from birchwood cane or rattan, but I also use a suitable bowl lined with a tea towel. In both cases I dust with copious amounts of flour using a dredger. This was a really important thing to learn because otherwise the proving bread sticks either to the cane or the cloth.

I have two ways of baking bread in a standard convection oven. One way is to use my red Le Creuset casserole dish, which I heat up in the oven. When the dough has proved I dredge the base of the dish with a little flour and drop the bread out of the banneton or bowl into it. I slowly slice it as deeply as possible using a razor blade with a wooden handle, called a 'lame', which you can buy very cheaply online. You can also use a very sharp small knife; the idea is to cut a slit across the dough to allow it to expand.

I put the lid on the casserole dish and slide it back into the oven. I bake the bread for 30 minutes with the lid on, then remove the lid and bake it for another 30 minutes with the lid off. Sometimes, if I'm feeling very energetic after the first 30 minutes, I take the bread, which is now sufficiently formed, out of the casserole dish and put it on the oven rack for the rest of the time; this gives it a slightly darker crust all round. Of course, I take the casserole dish, which the Americans call a Dutch oven, out. The point of the casserole dish is it keeps in enough moisture from the bread to delay the setting of the crust, making it relatively thin and crisp.

As long as Sas isn't around, I leave the bread to cool on a rack before slicing. I don't get it, but she actually prefers the inside of the bread to the crust.

The other option is to use a bread peel or, if I can't find it, a flat tray, I put a sheet of baking parchment on it and turn the turned and shaped dough out on to the parchment. I slide the parchment on to the base of the oven, heated as before, and I spray the surface of the dough with water for about 20 seconds. I close the oven door, then repeat after three minutes and six minutes. I bake the bread for about another 35 minutes; it cooks a bit quicker without the casserole dish.

'Like so many other people, I find making sourdough is almost like life itself – a sort of sine wave of elation and gloom.'

Sourdough starter

As far as I can tell, there's no real benefit in adopting somebody's time-honoured starter, since the dominant yeasts in a starter you make yourself will be in your kitchen, not somebody else's 10/50/100 years ago, but I could be wrong. The important thing is to take your time to get one going. It takes about five days. You start by mixing equal weights of grams of flour to millilitres of water, so start with say, 100g of flour and 100ml of water; this will give you a batter about the consistency of double cream. After a couple of days, the mix will start to bubble, first faintly and then much more vigorously. Every day pour away half of the mixture and replace it with about 50g of flour and 50ml of water. The object is to build up a strong yeast colony in the flour and increase the sourness of the starter. You may find that as it gets more and more vigorous you need to do this twice a day, but when you start using the sourdough starter the bubbling activity is particularly apparent.

Lots of sourdough starter recipes suggest you should draw a line, either with a felt tip or a piece of tape, to indicate the level of the sourdough when you add fresh flour and water and then use it when the activity has raised the level by about a centimetre, but now I can easily tell when the starter is vigorous enough to add to the dough. I find that if I'm not making bread for a while or I'm going away, putting the starter in the fridge will stop the activity, but it comes back when I take it out and add fresh flour and water.

I can't work out whether I'm going to give all this up when the pandemic is over. I think probably not. It's like making cheese or wine or anything that involves a living culture – there is an exciting commitment to getting it right but a depression when you get it wrong, normally because you're not really concentrating. This all might seem enormously complicated but actually it's almost instinctive in the end.

Pea & lettuce soup

This is a sort of soup version of cucumber sandwiches for afternoon tea — the ones with the crusts cut off for genteel purposes. It harks back to the times when orange or tomato juices were served as an appetiser, but when it's made with good chicken stock it's wonderful.

SERVES 6

50g butter
10–12 spring onions, trimmed and thinly sliced
4 little gem lettuce hearts, shredded
450g frozen peas
1.2 litres Chicken stock (page 307)
50ml single cream, plus extra to serve
Salt and freshly ground white pepper

TIP
You can use any sweet lettuce for this soup. Little gems work well and have a good colour, but butterhead lettuce or cos/romaine would also be fine. I sometimes add shredded sorrel at the last minute to give the soup a little acidity.

Melt the butter in a large pan, add the spring onions and cook gently for 3–4 minutes until soft without letting them colour. Add the lettuce and cook gently for 2 minutes, then add the peas and cook for a further 2 minutes.

Pour in the stock, season with 1½ teaspoons of salt and a little white pepper, then bring to the boil. Turn down to a simmer, cover the pan and cook for just 5 minutes.

Leave the soup to cool slightly. Blend until smooth and then pass through a strainer or coarse sieve into a clean pan. Bring back to a gentle simmer and adjust the seasoning if necessary. Stir in the cream and leave to cook for 1 minute but do not let the soup boil.

Serve in warm soup bowls and garnish with an extra swirl of single cream.

Jerusalem artichoke soup with crisp bacon

I love this soup. I've written the recipe to include a garnish of crisp bacon or pancetta, but what I really like — just to be a bit, shall we say, swanky or poncy — is salted pig's jowl or guanciale, which is a Roman cut of pork, essential for making proper spaghetti carbonara. The last time I was in Rome was just before the Covid outbreak and I couldn't get enough of the stuff. Its slightly-too-old flavour reminds me of the bacon we used to have hanging in the larder at the farm I was brought up on. That and the uncompromising sharpness of Pecorino Romano is what Italian food is all about; very local.

SERVES 4

600g Jerusalem artichokes
Lemon slices
30g unsalted butter
1 medium onion, chopped
2 celery sticks chopped
2 garlic cloves, chopped

1 litre Chicken stock (page 307)
200ml milk
60ml single cream
60g pancetta or bacon, chopped into
    small pieces and fried until crisp
Salt and black pepper

TIP
If you want a vegetarian soup, replace the bacon with 2 tablespoons of toasted, chopped hazelnuts and use vegetable stock.

Peel the Jerusalem artichokes, slice them fairly thinly and put them in a bowl of water with a couple of slices of lemon to prevent them from going brown.

Melt the butter in a large pan, add the onion, celery and garlic and sweat gently for 5–10 minutes until softened but not browned. Add the drained artichokes (minus the lemon slices) to the pan with the chicken stock and milk, then simmer for 25–30 minutes or until tender.

Blend the soup until very smooth and pass it through a sieve if necessary. Taste and season with salt and pepper. Serve in warmed bowls, add a swirl of cream and top with the crisp pancetta or bacon.

Mackerel recheado

I came across this recipe when I visited Goa for the first time in the 1980s. Then it was made with pomfret, a local fish, but I have since adapted it to a much simplified recipe for cooking freshly caught mackerel on the beach in my series Rick Stein's Cornwall. *I even went as far as buying a gadget online to drive my mini food processor from the cigarette lighter socket in a Land Rover, so I could make the fragrant masala paste.*

SERVES 2

6 small mackerel, filleted
(but preferably butterflied
so the fillets are still
joined by a piece of skin
and open like a book),
pin bones removed
Sunflower oil

Goan masala paste
1 tsp cumin seeds
1 tsp coriander seeds
2 tsp black peppercorns
1 tsp whole cloves
1 tsp ground turmeric
2 tsp crushed dried chillies
1 tsp salt
4 garlic cloves, roughly chopped
4cm root ginger, peeled and
roughly chopped
3 tbsp red wine vinegar

Kachumber salad
1 very large beef tomato
(or 2 large tomatoes),
very thinly sliced
1 shallot, very thinly sliced
2 tbsp chopped coriander
¼ tsp ground cumin
Pinch cayenne pepper
1 tbsp white wine vinegar
Salt

TIP
If your fillets
are separate,
not butterflied,
just spread the
paste on the flesh
side of a fillet and
sandwich it with
another. Tie as
in the method.

For the paste, grind the cumin and coriander seeds, peppercorns and cloves in a spice grinder. Put this mixture and the other paste ingredients in a food processor and whizz until you have a paste.

Spread about a teaspoon or less of the paste on the flesh side of one half of a butterflied mackerel fillet, then fold the other half of the fillet over. Take a couple of pieces of kitchen string and tie them around the fish to keep the fillets together. Repeat with the rest of the fish.

To make the salad, layer the ingredients in a large shallow dish in the order in which they are listed, finishing with the vinegar and salt. Don't mix the salad, just leave it to stand while you cook the fish.

When ready to eat, brush the fish with oil and grill on the barbecue for 2–3 minutes on each side. Serve with the salad.

Grilled scallops in the shell with toasted hazelnut & coriander butter

One of my oldest dishes. I can never quite put my finger on why the combined flavours of toasted hazelnuts and coriander go so well with scallops but they do.

SERVES 4

12 prepared scallops in the shell
Salt and black pepper

Toasted hazelnut and coriander butter
20g unblanched hazelnuts
100g salted butter, softened
Small handful coriander, roughly chopped
¼ banana shallot, roughly chopped
1 tsp fresh lemon juice

Spread the hazelnuts over a baking tray and toast under the grill for 4–5 minutes, shaking the tray now and then, until the nuts are golden brown. Tip them into a clean tea towel and rub off the skins. Leave to cool, then chop them roughly and tip into a food processor. Add the butter with the coriander, shallot and lemon juice. Season with a good pinch of salt and some pepper and process until well mixed.

Preheat the grill to high. Place the scallops on a large baking tray and season with salt and black pepper. Drop a tablespoon of the hazelnut and coriander butter on to each scallop, then grill for 4–5 minutes.

Stir-fried salt & pepper squid with red chilli & spring onion

This is one of the first Asian-style dishes I ever put on the restaurant menus and it's still there from time to time. The salad that accompanies it is entirely made up by me but does seem to encompass the flavours of Southeast Asian cooking.

SERVES 4

750g squid
½ tsp black peppercorns
½ tsp Sichuan peppercorns
1 tsp Maldon sea salt
1–2 tbsp sunflower oil
1 medium-hot red finger
   chilli, thinly sliced
3 spring onions, trimmed
   and sliced

Salad
¼ cucumber, peeled,
   halved and seeds removed
50g fresh bean sprouts
25g watercress sprigs,
   large stalks removed
2 tsp dark soy sauce
2 tsp roasted sesame oil
¼ tsp caster sugar
Pinch salt

TIP
Supermarket squid
is best avoided,
as it has the texture
of rubber bands,
so this is a recipe
to use when you've
visited a really
good fishmonger.

Cut the squid along one side of each pouch, open it out flat and pat dry. Score the inner side into a diamond pattern with the tip of a sharp knife, then cut it into 5cm squares. Cut the tentacles in half, if large, and set to one side with the pouches.

For the salad, cut the cucumber lengthways into short, thin strips. Put them in a bowl and toss with the bean sprouts and watercress. Whisk together the soy sauce, sesame oil, sugar and salt in a small jug and set aside.

Heat a frying pan over a high heat and add both peppercorns. Dry roast for a few seconds, shaking the pan until the peppercorns darken slightly and smell aromatic. Grind them coarsely in an electric spice grinder, then stir in the salt.

Heat half the oil and half the squid in the pan and stir-fry for 2 minutes until lightly coloured. Tip on to a plate and repeat with the rest of the oil and squid.

Put the first batch of squid back in the pan with the rest and add the salt and pepper mixture. Toss everything together for 10 seconds or so, then add the red chilli and spring onions. Toss again and serve with the dressed salad.

Barry Humphries's salmon,
caper & pink peppercorn fishcakes

For my television series Rick Stein's Cornwall, *I asked Barry to come to Cornwall to recount the story of how he nearly lost his life in his early twenties, when he slipped in an icy stream and went over the edge of a cliff only to be saved by a ledge lower down. He now refers to this as Barry's Leap. He insisted on bringing his own fishcakes for me to taste and I was looking forward to telling him to stick to the day job. Actually, though, they were astonishingly good, with the special ingredient of pink peppercorns.*

SERVES 6
as a first course

300g new potatoes
500g salmon fillet, skinned
Olive or sunflower oil
1 hard-boiled egg, chopped
1 egg, beaten
1 tbsp coarsely chopped parsley

1 tbsp capers (small or roughly chopped)
1 dessertspoon finely chopped gherkins
2 tsp pink peppercorns, crushed
About 50g fresh white or
    wholemeal breadcrumbs
Salt and black pepper

TIP
Also delicious
with the crisp
cabbage, walnut
and apple salad
(page 301).

Cook the new potatoes in their skins in salted water until tender. Crush them with a large fork and put them in a bowl.

Preheat the oven to 180°C/Fan 160°C. Brush the salmon with a little oil and season with salt and pepper. Cook in the oven for 3–4 minutes per 1cm of thickness – on average about 10–12 minutes.

Roughly flake the salmon and add it to the bowl with the potatoes, chopped hard-boiled egg, beaten egg, parsley, capers, gherkins, crushed peppercorns and ½–1 teaspoon of salt, then mix to combine.

Shape the mixture into 12 round patties, then flatten them slightly and coat with breadcrumbs. Heat about 1cm of oil in a pan and fry the fishcakes until golden.

Serve with tartare sauce (page 23) and a green salad.

Cornish mussels with cider

Here's another recipe from my Cornish TV series, something that I cooked on the turf above a beach just outside Mevagissey. I can't name the place because it's owned by a family. This is a version of moules marinière using Cornish ingredients — you can't go wrong really.

SERVES 4

1.75kg mussels
20g butter
1 garlic clove, finely chopped
4 or 5 spring onions, chopped
A few thyme sprigs and
 a couple of bay leaves
100ml dry cider

120ml double cream
Good handful wild sorrel
 leaves, coarsely chopped,
 or 200g baby spinach
 leaves, washed
Salt and black pepper
Crusty bread, to serve

TIP
I'm often asked if you should discard any mussels that don't open after cooking. In fact, there's nothing wrong with them, as they're cooked and should be fine. Once in a while, though, you will find that those that don't open are full of sand and mud, so probably best to throw them out.

Wash the mussels under plenty of cold, running water. Discard any open ones that won't close when lightly squeezed or tapped. Pull out any tough, fibrous beards protruding from the tightly closed shells and knock off any barnacles with a large knife. Give the mussels another quick rinse to remove any little pieces of shell.

Melt the butter in a large pan with a lid. Add the garlic, spring onions, thyme and bay leaves, then cook until softened. Add the mussels and cider, then turn up the heat, cover the pan and leave the mussels to steam in their own juices for 3–4 minutes. Give the pan a good shake every now and then.

Add the cream and the chopped sorrel or baby spinach and remove from the heat. Season with salt and black pepper. Spoon into large warmed bowls and serve with lots of crusty bread to soak up the tasty juices.

Arbroath smokies
with scrambled eggs

I remember getting very emotional when I visited the smokery at Arbroath run by Alex Spink & Sons, and I realised that smokies are a world-class delicacy. We do fabulous smoked fish in the UK and this is one of the best.

SERVES 4

1 Arbroath smokie, about 250-300g
10 eggs
60g mature Cheddar cheese, grated
50g butter
50ml double cream
Handful parsley, roughly chopped
Salt and black pepper
Sourdough bread, to serve

Remove the skin and bones from the smokie and flake the flesh. Whisk the eggs in a bowl and season with salt and pepper, then stir in the cheese.

Melt the butter in a frying pan until bubbling. Add the egg mixture and allow it to set a little, then scrape the bottom of the pan regularly with a spatula to create a lumpy finish. Add the fish halfway through, then just before the eggs are fully set, stir in the double cream and parsley.

Spoon on to 4 warm plates and serve with slices of toasted sourdough bread.

Gadgets

David Pritchard, the director I worked with for 25 years, and I used to have a long-running sad story about the gadgets in our garages. First in mine was the sandwich toaster, speedily followed by a fondue set (for beef, that is), but it wasn't until the electric carving knife arrived that the gadgets started to talk to each other. There was a lot of moaning about the length of time they'd all been out of the warmth of the kitchen and regular use, but as time moved on they were joined by others, notably a hot bag sealer and more recently a spiraliser and three generations of soda streams. After a while nobody bothered to even talk to the broken mini food processors – just the odd comment like, 'burnt out on an overload of swede puréeing, were you?'

There were a couple of very dusty things right in the cobwebs. They didn't speak and someone briefly remembered one of them made a cup of tea in the early morning and the other was a massive thing that apparently kept food warm. And then, very worryingly, the gadgets started to disappear. First to go, amazingly, was an old broken toaster with two little pouches for poaching eggs on the side, then a whole host of little plastic things, an omelette cooker for the microwave, a butter pat dispenser, a fat separator jug, an egg slicer and even a banana slicer. Then there was some upstart little green thing with a squeaky voice called a pepper prepper and some old goggles hanging from a hook: he claimed to stop the humans crying while cutting up onions.

These same humans would occasionally shower the dustbin with pickle pickers and egg graspers, silicon poaching sleeves, a myriad of little plastic extruding nozzles and grating plates waiting for the long dark trip to the landfill. Then there was a fruit spray, an electric tin opener, two broken steel tortilla presses, a quiver of wide Turkish kebab skewers, a pasta-maker without a handle, some rotisserie pieces, unidentifiable, and many layers of housing of a sophisticated food-drying system, all in light green plastic.

I wonder how much Amazon would admit that their enormous turnover comes not so much from book sales as from the combined addiction of gadget nerds like me and others. At least my purchases aren't going to bankrupt me. On order as I write are:

A canister of argon gas to spray on top of wine in a bottle to stop it oxidising – £15.87.

A set of digital scales going down to 0.1g – £7.99

A head torch, which I've decided would be helpful for staring into large pots – £5.99

A silver line spatula knife (15cm) for scraping sourdough off the work surface (and windows and tiles) – £1.00 – together with a bread cutter slashing and razor tool – £7.99.

A new handguard for my Benriner Japanese mandolin. At last, after 15 years, I've decided to cut my fingers no more on it when slicing garlic.

In spite of this carnage, though, there are some gadgets which have stayed in the kitchen. Not many, but they are probably there for the long run. The most important of these, despite a long history of frustration, is a wet and dry food processor. Back in the 1980s in Goa I fell in love with the Indian curry pastes called masalas. At the time there was nothing back in the UK that could grind whole spices and chop such things as fresh ginger, turmeric, lemongrass, chillies, onions and garlic into a paste, so I actually brought a small version of the spice grinders that were in every kitchen there back to England, courtesy of British Caledonian Airways. I described it at the time as being of the size and weight of a small petrol generator, it was the red Honda one I had in mind, which would have weighed about 10 kilos.

Back in Padstow I started making wet masala paste, notably for monkfish vindaloo, but after only six months, somewhat famously on my first television programme, *Taste of the Sea*, the machine disintegrated, wheels and bolts falling into the half-made paste. On subsequent trips to India, particularly when we filmed over the whole of India in 2012, I brought back various portable versions. I particularly remember a purple and white one, called Butterfly Desire, which until recently was used in our cookery school. In all the 15 years we've been using it I've never been totally confident, because in those days no kitchen devices from India had any sort of safety features whatsoever. If you're unlucky enough to have your hand in the flask when you switch it on, it would be, shall we say, Fargoed!

And then someone invented the Nutribullet, which as well as producing smoothies also made masalas. The secret is that not only does it have two horizontal blades, it also has two blades set at 45 degrees to the vertical, which makes all the difference. And then I discovered the Breville liquidiser, which unlike existing processors with two horizontal blades, had six: two pointing down, two horizontal and two pointing up. It changed my life.

Not quite so revolutionary but still massively important to me is the stick blender, first encountered in the restaurant as a version about the size of an old Seagull outboard motor, for making gallons of fish soup, whizzing up such things as fish bones and fillet, red peppers, chillies, orange peel, onions, garlic, Florence fennel and even sometimes lobster shells. Those would make the bearings and the seals go regularly. A mini-version of this is now in the drawer under the gas burners and is ideal for dealing with modest quantities of things like pea and lettuce soup, hummus from a tin of chickpeas, and blackcurrant fool.

Almost second only to the modern food processor is the microplane, used for grating anything from cheese to lemon zest; even the hardest, most dried-out Parmesan succumbs. It's made of toughened surgical steel and I'm much amused by the knowledge that it was developed by surgeons to rasp bones away during operations. Rather irritatingly, the microplane is so good that I threw out all the grating plates for my food processor, thinking I would never need them again. But, in addition to being a gadget nerd, I'm also very reluctant to throw any cheese out and sometimes leave it until it's so hard that even the microplane is a bit of a chore. Then I ask myself, 'Where did I put those graters?'

Don't worry, I could easily supply you with a list of soon-to-be obsolete gadgets, but realistically the only other one that really matters to me is the temperature probe. I used to feel guilty about using this because I thought that proper chefs could always tell whether a piece of meat or fish was cooked by pressing it. Well, I've been cooking for an awful long time and I still can't tell accurately enough. Of course, if a piece of meat is very rare it's squashy and when well done it's firm, but you need a bit more information and that's where the temperature probe comes in.

'First to go, amazingly, was an old broken toaster with two little pouches for poaching eggs on the side, then a whole host of little plastic things.'

Prawn molee

A molee is a spicy seafood and coconut dish. When I first tasted this in Kerala, southern India, I remember thinking it was so delicate it could quite easily be a recipe from a very smart French restaurant.

SERVES 8

2 tbsp coconut oil
¼ tsp ground black pepper
3 green cardamom pods, lightly
   crushed and left whole
6 cloves
2 medium onions, thinly sliced
3 garlic cloves, thinly sliced
5cm root ginger, peeled and finely grated
2 green chillies, seeds removed,
   finely sliced lengthways

1 tsp salt
Small handful fresh curry leaves
Small pinch of ground turmeric
400ml coconut milk
1½ tsp white wine vinegar
24 medium-sized tail-on raw prawns
   (defrosted, if frozen)
2 tomatoes, thinly sliced into rounds,
   to garnish

TIP
This dish will also serve 4 as a main course with plain boiled rice.

Heat the coconut oil in a heavy-based saucepan over a medium heat. Add the pepper, cardamom pods and cloves and fry for 1 minute until fragrant. Add the onions and fry for 5 minutes until translucent, then stir in the garlic, ginger, chillies, salt and curry leaves and fry for 1 minute.

Add the turmeric, coconut milk and vinegar. Bring to a simmer and simmer for 4–5 minutes until reduced slightly, then add the prawns and simmer for a further 4 minutes until the prawns are cooked. Scatter the tomatoes on top, turn off the heat, cover the pan and set aside for 3–4 minutes. Serve in small bowls.

Coarse pork & herb terrine with plum chutney

There's a restaurant in Paris that I visit quite regularly called La Régalade, which specialises in hearty French bourgeois cooking. A meal there always begins with the arrival of an oven-darkened terrine full of coarse meat and jelly, accompanied by cornichons and crusty bread. This is my attempt to recreate those wonderful textures and flavours.

SERVES 10

25g lard
175g onions, finely chopped
1kg rindless boned pork belly,
    cut into small pieces
175g rindless smoked streaky
    bacon, cut into small pieces
175g pig's or lamb's liver,
    cut into small pieces
4 garlic cloves, finely chopped
Large handful parsley leaves,
    finely chopped
1½ tbsp chopped rosemary
1½ tbsp chopped thyme
2 tsp salt
2 tsp Rick's peppermix
    (page 308) or black pepper

Plum chutney
Makes 4 or 5 x 450g jars
1kg dark-skinned plums,
    stoned and chopped
3 onions, finely chopped
150g sultanas
30g root ginger,
    peeled and grated
1 tsp chilli flakes
600g soft brown sugar
2 tsp fine salt
1 cinnamon stick
1 bay leaf
450ml red wine vinegar
½ tsp black pepper
⅛ tsp (large pinch) ground cloves

Heat the lard in a frying pan, add the onions and fry gently until soft but not browned. Transfer to a large mixing bowl and leave to cool.

Put the pork belly into a food processor and use the pulse button to chop it into a coarse, but not too coarse, mixture. Add this to the onions in the bowl. Put the bacon and liver in the food processor and coarsely chop, then tip into the bowl.

Add the garlic, chopped herbs, salt and peppermix or pepper and stir everything together really well – the best way of distributing the ingredients evenly is to use your hands.

Recipe continued overleaf

Preheat the oven to 170°C/Fan 150°C. Pack the mixture into a lightly oiled, 1-litre terrine dish or loaf tin and round off the top. Cover with a lid or some foil, then place the dish in a small roasting tin. Pour enough boiling water from a kettle into the roasting tin to come halfway up the sides of the dish. Bake for about 1½ hours or until the internal temperature registers at least 71°C with a temperature probe.

The terrine will have shrunk back from the edges of the tin and will be surrounded by meat juices. These will set to form a jelly that will keep the terrine moist.

Remove the dish from the roasting tin and leave to cool, then weigh down the terrine before placing it in the fridge to chill overnight. The easiest way to do this is to cover the terrine with a piece of foil, then cut out a piece of stiff cardboard that will fit snugly inside the rim of the dish. Place this on top of the foil and add a few weights or unopened cans on top.

To serve, slice or scoop out the terrine with the jelly and accompany with lots of crusty bread and plum chutney.

Plum chutney

Put all the ingredients in a large pan. Stir well, slowly bring to the boil and keep stirring frequently to make sure the sugar dissolves. Once the mixture is boiling, continue to bubble for 45–60 minutes until thick and syrupy and the plums have softened and are starting to break down. Remove the cinnamon stick and bay leaf.

Ladle into sterilised jars and ideally store for a week or two before eating. This chutney will keep for 6–12 months stored in a cool, dark place.

Vietnamese poached chicken salad with mint & coriander

SERVES 8–10
as a first course or
4 as a main course

What appeals to me about this salad is the combination of lightly poached chicken, bean sprouts, spring onions and herbs with roasted chopped nuts and sesame seeds, and the slightly gloopy fish sauce, lime juice and chilli dressing.

50g root ginger, peeled and sliced
4 small skinless, boneless, free-range
   chicken breasts
½ large cucumber
8 spring onions, trimmed, halved and shredded
150g fresh bean sprouts
Small handful mint, leaves torn into small pieces
Small handful fresh coriander sprigs
1 tbsp sesame seeds, lightly toasted
60g roasted, salted peanuts, finely chopped

Dressing
4 tbsp Thai fish sauce
2 tbsp red wine vinegar
2 tbsp lime juice
2 tbsp light soft brown sugar
½ tsp cornflour
1 medium-hot red chilli, finely chopped
1 garlic clove, finely chopped

TIP
When peeling ginger, use the bowl end of a teaspoon to scrape the skin off. It's much easier than using a peeler.

Put the ginger into a large, shallow pan with a litre of water and bring to the boil. Add the chicken breasts and leave them to simmer for 5–6 minutes. Turn off the heat and leave the chicken to cool in the liquid.

For the dressing, put the Thai fish sauce, vinegar, lime juice and sugar into a small pan and bring to the boil. Mix the cornflour with a teaspoon of water, stir this into the pan and simmer gently for 1 minute. Remove from the heat and leave to cool, then stir in the red chilli and garlic.

For the salad, peel the cucumber, cut it in half lengthways and scoop out the seeds with a teaspoon. Cut the flesh into 5cm-long matchsticks and add them to a large bowl with the spring onions, bean sprouts, mint and coriander, then toss together.

Lift the chicken breasts out of the poaching liquid and pull them into long chunky strips. Add these to the salad bowl and mix gently. Serve the salad with the dressing drizzled over the top and scattered with sesame seeds and chopped peanuts.

Aya's beef tataki

I'm always intrigued by the fact that the food stylist who cooks and presents the food for the photographs in my books is Japanese. I would have expected Aya Nishimura's plates to be precise and delicate, but she is a master of the fabulously rugged cooking that I love. Her versatility is apparent when you look through her book Japanese Cooking Made Easy, *which has all the delicacy and simplicity of Japanese art. This tataki is a case in point. The key is using the tail of a beef fillet, which is thinner (and much cheaper), so it will cook quickly.*

SERVES 4

400g beef fillet tail
2 tbsp mirin
2 tbsp sake
60ml soy sauce
2 tbsp rice vinegar
60ml orange juice
1 garlic clove, crushed with the
    back of a knife but left whole

1 onion, thinly sliced
    and kept in cold water
60g watercress, washed
200g daikon radish,
    finely grated (optional)
Salt and black pepper

AYA'S TIP
You can make a larger batch of the sauce and keep it in a clean, screw-top jar for up to 2 weeks in the fridge.

Take the beef out of the fridge and bring it up to room temperature. Season with salt and pepper.

To make the sauce, gently heat the mirin and sake in a small pan. Remove from the heat and add the soy sauce, vinegar, orange juice and crushed garlic, then set aside.

Heat a frying pan over a medium-high heat. Sear the beef for about 1–2 minutes on all sides. Remove it from the heat and leave to rest for at least 10 minutes.

Drain the onion and mix it with the watercress on a serving plate. Cut the beef into thin (5mm) slices and add them to the salad. Drain any excess liquid from the grated daikon, if using, and add the daikon to the salad just before serving with the sauce drizzled over the top.

I often get a little cast down when I suggest to Sas, my wife, that I should cook fish at home. There is a notable lack of enthusiasm. Lamb chops and peas – always; stir fry – yes; chicken and rice – oh, yes please; a roast, of course; even my mum's risotto, which isn't really a proper one, meets with approval, but not fish. In the end, I've had to ask her why. She says she doesn't like the smell of fish cooking in the house and she doesn't think it's going to be nice. She says she would never cook fish and nor do most of her friends because they all worry about getting it wrong, and it's expensive. It's weird, because whenever I do pluck up the courage and cook fish at home she loves it. Everyone does.

The other night, after I'd spent the day filming with a spider crab fisherman, I brought a large crab home. I boiled it in lots of salted water and served it up with mayonnaise, new potatoes, my own sourdough bread and a salad of lettuce, tomato and avocado. Sas went berserk, opened a bottle of champagne and declared it the finest crab she had ever eaten. She didn't even mind the fiddly business of picking the meat out of the shells, particularly difficult with spider crabs, as the insides of the shells are rough and the meat clings to them.

Most people do like crabs and lobsters, but indifference to fish is something I've had to face up to all my working life. Years ago, when we used to close the Seafood Restaurant right through the winter, I helped a local builder do improvements to the restaurant while we were closed. He once asked me if I ever cooked proper food, rather than just fish. I think it's as simple as that – many of us don't really like fish as much as meat and almost think it's not a substantial enough form of protein. Even when we eat a fish dish that's a delight, it doesn't change our attitude because, I think, it's not part of our childhood memories. Perhaps this explains why when we go to a restaurant or travel abroad we are much more amenable to eating fish; at home we want to eat things that are part of home.

I guess I'm lucky. Seafood was part of my childhood; the smell of cooking fish is part of my memories of summer holidays on Trevose Head in Cornwall. When I think of those days, I'm taken back to the scent of grilling mackerel and boiling runner beans, or the almost overpoweringly rich taste of lobster with my mother's olive oil mayonnaise.

There are a few fish dishes, though, that do hit the spot with all of us – fish and chips and fish pie, for instance. More than anything, their popularity is down to the fact that most of us have been eating them since we were kids. I haven't included a recipe for fish and chips in this book because I think it's not something you can do easily at home. You need a big fryer and lots of oil to fry three or four main-course portions of battered fish, and while I like the smell of grilling fish, I can't abide clouds of steam from cooking oil permeating the curtains. At our restaurants we fry in dripping – delicious but not something you want to bring into your house.

This chapter is filled with my favourite dishes and I'm very pleased to note that two of my three sons have elected to give me fish recipes – Ed's crispy mackerel with red cabbage and beetroot salad (page 109) and Jack's linguine con tonno (page 94). I'm thinking that my love of seafood has influenced the next generation, though Jack's recipe comes from his wife Lucie's Sicilian grandmother. But the last word for the recipes in this chapter must go to fish pie (page 102). That is indeed part of our collective memories.

Crab omelette

SERVES 2

I featured this in my television series Rick Stein's Cornwall. *I am always keen on recipes that don't overpower the flavour of crab meat and this is absolutely one of them. It's very difficult to explain this precisely, but sometimes brown crab meat is gorgeous and other times it can be thin and rather bitter. It's all down to the cycle of growing and shedding of new shells — most brown meat is simply very soft shell. If it doesn't taste nice, leave it out and add more white meat.*

15g unsalted butter
1 shallot, finely chopped
6 eggs
1 tbsp clotted cream
50g Parmesan cheese
   (or vintage Cornish Gouda
   if you have it), finely grated

100g white crab meat
50g brown crab meat
2 tbsp chopped herbs
   (mix of parsley, chives,
   chervil and tarragon)
Salt and black pepper

Heat the butter in a 20–23cm non-stick omelette pan or frying pan. Add the shallot and fry for a couple of minutes until softened. Lightly beat the eggs with the clotted cream in a bowl, then stir in the cheese, crab meat and herbs and season with salt and pepper.

Pour in the egg and crab mixture. Turn the heat down to low and, using a spatula, occasionally draw in the sides of the omelette as they start to set. While the egg is still wobbly and soft, flip one side of the omelette over the other to form a semi-circle. Slide it on to a plate, cut it in half and serve with a side salad and bread.

Crab linguine with parsley & chilli

This is the original introduction to this recipe from my book Coast to Coast *and it's as valid now as it was then, so here goes: Though the recipe for this is very short, there are a number of nuances that need to be explained. First, it's very important that the pasta is cooked perfectly al dente. I've suggested a cooking time of 7–8 minutes, but I always test pasta by biting it. Second, when I say warm the sauce ingredients over a gentle heat, I really mean it – the temperature should never get much above 60°C. Last, try not to break up the crab meat if it's fresh and has been hand-picked, because lumps of crab meat folded through the pasta look very appetising.*

SERVES 4

450g dried linguine or spaghetti
3 vine-ripened tomatoes, skinned, deseeded and chopped
300g fresh white crab meat
1 tbsp chopped parsley

1½ tbsp lemon juice
50ml extra virgin olive oil
Pinch dried chilli flakes
1 garlic clove, finely chopped
Salt and black pepper

TIP
These days I'm not so doctrinaire about skinning and deseeding tomatoes, but for some recipes like this one, it is a good idea. The main reason, by the way, for deseeding tomatoes is to remove liquid.

Cook the pasta in a large pan of boiling, well-salted water for 7–8 minutes or until al dente.

Meanwhile, put the tomatoes, crab meat, parsley, lemon juice, olive oil, chilli flakes and garlic into another pan and warm through over a gentle heat.

Drain the pasta, tip it back into the pan, add the sauce and gently fold together. Season to taste and serve immediately on warm plates.

Ensenada fish tacos
with chilli & avocado

If you ask me about cooking fish and chips at home, I'd say don't. The quantities of hot oil required to properly cook fish in batter plus copious thick chips is too much, especially if your fryer is indoors. Fish tacos are a different matter, because you're only cooking small pieces of fish in hot oil. This a great party dish, as you can prepare everything beforehand, then fry the fish at the last minute.

SERVES 6

12 x 15cm corn tortillas
600g white fish fillets,
   such as cod
100g plain flour
1 litre sunflower oil
Salt

Batter
200g plain flour
¼ tsp salt
½ tsp baking powder
275ml ice-cold beer

Toppings
¼ small white cabbage,
   finely shredded
1 avocado, stoned,
   peeled and diced
Pico de gallo salsa
   (page 311)
Hot chilli sauce, such
   as Cholula or Huichol

Chipotle crema
2 Chipotles en adobo
   (page 311 or bought)
3 tbsp mayonnaise
3 tbsp soured cream
Juice of ½ lime

TIP
Because corn tortillas are naturally gluten-free you can make this for gluten-intolerant guests. Use gluten-free flour as well as gluten-free beer for the batter, which incidentally produces a lovely crisp result.

Warm the tortillas in a dry frying pan, a microwave or the oven. Get your toppings – shredded cabbage, diced avocado, pico de gallo salsa and hot chilli sauce – ready. Mix the ingredients for the chipotle crema together and set aside.

To make the batter, sift the flour, salt and baking powder into a roomy bowl. Using a balloon whisk, incorporate the beer until you have a smooth batter. Set aside.

Cut the fish into fingers about 1cm thick and season with salt. Heat the oil in a large pan to 190°C. Dip a few pieces of fish into the flour, shake off the excess, then dip them into the batter. Fry for 2–2½ minutes until crisp and golden. Repeat until you've cooked all the fish, draining each batch briefly on kitchen paper to remove the excess oil. Serve the fish immediately in warm tortillas, with the toppings on the table for guests to help themselves.

The art of stock making

I used to say that what separates Western from Eastern cooking was stock. French cuisine, which is really my main influence, is based on what they call *le fond* – the foundation. Latterly, I discovered that Asian cookery also features some wonderful stocks. There's a great film that any food lover should watch called 'Ramen Heads' – it's about a group of mostly ageing Japanese cooks who, every day, try to produce the perfect bowl of ramen noodles. Perhaps more important than the noodles themselves is the stock, and it's the same with Vietnamese pho. The name 'pho' dates back to the early 1900s when the French occupied Vietnam, and some think the word pho is possibly derived from the French word *feu*, as in the dish, pot au feu.

As a chef who taught me at college used to say: you can cook an awful lot better with a sharp knife. The same goes for a good stock, if you see what I mean.

So it's understandable in a way that I am obsessed with stock. There is no aspect of cooking that gives me greater pleasure or more secret satisfaction than realising when someone really likes a dish I've cooked that it's due to the stock.

The other great pleasure of making stock is that it satisfies my innate parsimoniousness. I *hate* wasting food. I really don't know where this came from – my parents, perhaps, who went through both world wars, or maybe 50 years of working in restaurants and worrying endlessly about kitchen profits. Either way, the pleasure of not throwing anything away that could conceivably be added to a stock is enormous.

It's rare that I go and buy the ingredients for making any stock because mostly I buy meat, poultry or fish on the bone. This is partly because I can make stock from the bones, but it's also more economical, plus anything on the bone is likely to be of better quality than meat or fish that's been processed. As far as fish is concerned, as soon as it is filleted the flesh will deteriorate more quickly through exposure to the air.

It's similar with poultry and actually with any cut of meat – buying a bigger piece on the bone enables you to tell much more accurately the quality of what you're buying. Obviously I'm not suggesting you buy large parts of a sheep or cow, but consider the enormous pleasure of buying a three- or four-rib joint of beef for a Sunday roast as opposed to the sirloin – and you've got the ribs to use for a delicious beef stock.

I guess I'm being a bit controversial when I say that I'm not averse to making chicken stock using what's left of the roast chicken, plus the bones from my family's plates. I have this completely illogical reservation about doing the same with the leftover bones on my guests' plates, considering everything goes into the stockpot or pressure cooker and is boiled. Any bones or, indeed, lobster, langoustine or prawn shells, are perfectly acceptable from the family's plates.

I'm never short of vegetables to go into a meat or veg stock. I've always got onions, carrots and celery in the fridge and more often than not some leeks or garlic that are beginning to dry out or those bulbs of garlic with the tiniest fiddly cloves that drive you mad trying to peel them. Almost all veg is suitable for stock, apart from things like potatoes, red peppers and aubergines, or too much cabbage. I even add the odd wrinkly chilli. There is no need to peel the vegetables, just give them a good scrub clean.

Seeing a couple of bendy carrots or limp spring onions that are too old to go into a stir-fry in the veg drawer is not a reason to throw them out. If I've got raw bones or meat that's too full of cartilage I will often freeze it for the next time I make stock. If there is too much fat on meat, I'll trim it off and render it – that is, heat it in the oven to use for frying meat for a stew – but I'm also quite happy to add a fair amount of fat to a stock because I can skim it off the top or let the stock cool and remove it anyway. The golden rule here is not to let stock boil furiously, as it will make an emulsion and give you a fatty, cloudy stock.

I've become inordinately fond of induction cooking for making stock because it's so controllable. You can turn the setting down so low that you hardly notice that it's heating at all and after a few hours there's a perfectly clear liquid ready to pass through a sieve and perhaps reduce a bit more. There's no point in freezing bulk stock. Much better to reduce it once the solids and fat have been removed, so it takes up far less room in the freezer.

My problem is that I now have two freezers full of beautiful stock, but what can I do with it? Well, fortunately for me, my deli is down the road so every now and then I'll knock up five litres of pea and ham soup and send it round to them. But that's the only problem with my excessive enthusiasm. The reality is I've got the best material for making soups, gravies, sauces, stews, risottos, pilafs and boulangère potatoes. I might use a little lick of reduced beef stock to swirl into the pan after frying steaks, or a dash of hot chicken stock in a salad dressing to make the perfect salade tiède. Stocks really are the foundation of good cooking.

'There is no aspect of cooking that gives me greater pleasure or more secret satisfaction than realising when someone really likes a dish I've cooked that it's due to the stock.'

Crisp fried fish with a hot,
sour & sweet sauce

*My family isn't terribly keen on eating whole fish because
of the bones, but the Thai sauce with this is too good to miss,
so I've adapted it to make with fillets.*

SERVES 4

8 bass fillets, each 75–80g
75ml Thai fish sauce
Sunflower oil
50g shallots, thinly sliced
5 garlic cloves, thinly sliced

3 red bird's-eye chillies,
   thinly sliced
50g soft brown sugar
10g tamarind paste

TIP
You'll probably
like this dish so
much, you'll want
to make it again,
so don't throw
away the oil –
cool and sieve
it, then reuse.

Put the fish in a bowl and sprinkle about 25ml of the fish
sauce over the flesh side. Set aside for 5 minutes, then remove
and pat dry.

Pour oil to about 1cm deep in a large frying pan and place
over a medium-high heat. Add the shallots and fry, stirring
now and then, until they are crisp and golden, then drain on
kitchen paper. Repeat with the garlic and chillies, cooking
each briefly until lightly golden, then set them aside.

Put the sugar, tamarind paste and 4 tablespoons of water in
a small pan with the remaining 50ml of fish sauce. Bring to
the boil and simmer for about 1 minute until thickened.

Add a film of oil to the frying pan. Add 4 of the fillets,
skin-side down, to the pan and cook for 5 minutes to give a
nice crisp skin. Turn them over and cook for another minute,
then remove and keep warm while you cook the rest.

While the fish is frying, bring the sauce back to a gentle
simmer and stir in half the fried shallots, garlic and chilli.
Serve the fish on warmed plates and spoon over some of
the sauce. Scatter over the remaining fried shallots, garlic
and chilli, and serve with boiled rice and steamed pak choi.

Hot smoked salmon kedgeree

This is the perfect dish for hot smoked salmon, which I now think makes the best kedgeree. I wonder whether my mother, sadly long departed, would have agreed because it was she who introduced me to kedgeree as a child in the first place. I often think how important the British Raj dishes were for instilling a love of Indian food into my baby boomer generation. They may be dismissed now as poor copies of the real thing, but we grew up familiar with the flavours of cumin, coriander, cardamom, turmeric and even a little chilli, albeit in the form of curry powder.

SERVES 6

½ tsp fennel seeds
1½ tsp cumin seeds
½ tsp ground turmeric
¼ tsp Kashmiri chilli powder
350g basmati rice
1 tsp salt

4 eggs
50g butter
350g hot smoked salmon,
    skinned and roughly flaked
Large handful parsley, chopped
1 tbsp lemon juice

TIP
You can now buy undyed smoked haddock with quite a heavy smoke which also works really well with the spice in this recipe. You'll need to poach it first, though.

Place half the fennel seeds and half the cumin seeds into a dry frying pan over a medium heat and fry for about 1 minute until fragrant. Stir in the turmeric and Kashmiri chilli, then tip everything into a spice grinder and reduce to a powder.

Put the rice into a saucepan with 600ml of water and the salt and bring to the boil over a high heat. Reduce the heat to low, cover and simmer for 8–10 minutes until all the water has been absorbed and the rice is just tender. After 8 minutes, check it by squeezing a grain between your fingers. You want rice that is soft on the outside, but still firm within. When done, stir gently with a fork to separate the grains.

Put the eggs in a small pan of simmering water and simmer for 8 minutes. Drain and cover with cold water until cool enough to handle. Peel the eggs and cut them into quarters.

Melt the butter in a heavy-based saucepan over a medium heat, add the remaining fennel and cumin seeds and fry for 30 seconds. Add the ground spices and hot rice and fry for 5 minutes until steaming hot. Gently fold in the salmon, parsley, lemon juice and eggs, then serve at once.

Mussels with black beans,
garlic & ginger

I originally found this dish in the late 80s in a book called
Yan-Kit's Classic Chinese Cookbook. It was an early encounter
with Chinese seafood cooking which was as much a revelation
to me as the fish curries of Goa. Soon after I put this dish on the
restaurant menu Yan-Kit came to the restaurant and I was in
awe. Sadly, she's no longer with us but I still refer to her book
regularly. The ingredients that make this dish are the fermented
and salted beans that are still sold in little cardboard drums in
Asian supermarkets. You can use black bean sauce instead, but it's
not quite the same. And here's a thing – the dish is still on our menu.

SERVES 4

1.75kg mussels
1 tsp Chinese salted
   black beans
¼ tsp sugar
3 spring onions
2 tbsp groundnut oil
4 garlic cloves, finely chopped

15g root ginger,
   peeled and finely chopped
1 tbsp dark soy sauce
2 tbsp Chinese rice wine
   or dry sherry
3 tbsp Chicken stock (page 307)
1 tbsp chopped fresh coriander

TIP
If you prefer
a thicker sauce,
transfer the mussels
to a serving dish
and mix a teaspoon
of arrowroot with
a little cold water.
Add this to the
sauce and bring
to the boil, stirring.
Pour over the
mussels and serve.

Wash the mussels under plenty of cold, running water.
Discard any open ones that won't close when lightly squeezed
or tapped. Pull out any tough, fibrous beards protruding from
the tightly closed shells and then knock off any barnacles with
a large knife. Give the mussels another quick rinse to remove
any little pieces of shell.

Rinse the black beans and mash them together with the sugar.
Trim and thinly slice the spring onions, separating the white
parts from the green.

Put the oil in a wok or large, deep frying pan and heat until
very hot. Add the garlic, ginger and the black bean mixture
and stir-fry until the smell of hot ginger and garlic rises. Add
the whites of the spring onions and stir-fry for a few seconds.
Add the mussels, soy sauce, rice wine or sherry and stock.
Cover and steam the mussels open for about 3–4 minutes.

Add the coriander and the green parts of the spring onions,
toss together and serve.

Linguine con tonno

This recipe is by my son Jack and here's what he has to say: This is a store-cupboard staple in my home. The dish itself comes from my wife Lucie's nonna, who was Sicilian. The Italians revere tinned and preserved food because they can catch or pick things at the right time and then enjoy them for the rest of the year. The key here is the Parmesan rind in the sauce which gives it a wonderful savoury taste. Pay particular attention to your salad – it needs to have a good kick of acidity to counter the tuna pasta sauce.

SERVES 4-5

60ml extra virgin olive oil,
    plus extra for serving
1 onion, diced
3 garlic cloves, chopped
1 Parmesan rind
1 tsp dried oregano
1 tbsp tomato paste
2 x 400g tins chopped tomatoes
300g tinned tuna, well drained
500g dried linguine
Salt and black pepper
Grated parmesan, to serve

Salad
120g mixed salad leaves
½ small red onion, chopped
100ml extra virgin olive oil
30ml white wine vinegar

Put the 60ml of olive oil in a large pan over a medium-high heat. Add the onion and a little salt, soften the onion for 5 minutes without allowing it to colour, then add the garlic, Parmesan rind and oregano. Cook for a further 2–3 minutes, then add the tomato paste and cook for another minute. Add the tinned tomatoes, season with more salt to taste and when the sauce begins to bubble, turn the heat down as low as it will go. Keep stirring every 20 minutes for a couple of hours, adding a splash of water if it starts to stick.

Add the tuna to the sauce once it is ready. Cook the linguine for 2 minutes less than the packet instructions, then drain. Scoop the sauce into the pasta and mix it through. Serve on warm plates, drizzled with a little more olive oil and sprinkled with grated Parmesan. Season with black pepper.

Dress the salad leaves and onion with oil and vinegar, season with salt and serve with the pasta.

Madras fish curry of snapper, tomato & tamarind

When I ate this dish in the seaside town of Mamallapuram in Tamil Nadu, it was made with snapper, but in the UK I recommend using any of the following: monkfish fillet, because you get firm slices of white, meaty fish; filleted bass, preferably a large fish because although you'll get softer flesh it has plenty of flavour; or gurnard. I think more than anything else that this dish underlines my belief that really fresh fish is not ruined by a spicy curry. I can still remember the slightly oily flavour of the exquisite snapper in that dish I ate in Tamil Nadu, because fish oil, when it's perfectly fresh, is very nice to eat. I always think oily fish goes well with curry anyway, particularly with the flavours of tomatoes, tamarind and curry leaves.

SERVES 4-6

60ml sunflower oil
1 tbsp yellow mustard seeds
1 large onion, finely chopped
3 garlic cloves, finely crushed
30 fresh curry leaves
2 tsp Kashmiri chilli powder
2 tsp ground coriander
2 tsp ground turmeric
400g tin chopped tomatoes

20g tamarind paste mixed
 with 80ml water
2 green chillies, each sliced
 lengthways into 6 pieces,
 with seeds
1 tsp salt
700g monkfish, sea bass or
 gurnard fillets, cut into
 5cm chunks

Heat the oil in a heavy-based saucepan over a medium heat. When it's hot, add the mustard seeds and fry for 30 seconds, then stir in the onion and garlic and fry gently for about 10 minutes until softened and lightly golden.

Add the curry leaves, chilli powder, coriander and turmeric and fry for 2 minutes, then stir in the tomatoes, tamarind, green chillies and salt. Simmer for about 10 minutes until rich and reduced.

Add the fish, cook for a further 5 minutes or until just cooked through, and serve with rice (page 305).

Baked sea bream Rota-style

This dish originally comes from Rota in the Bay of Cadiz. It has particularly nostalgic memories for me because I asked my three sons, Ed, Jack and Charlie, to go with me to Cadiz to get a feel for the city prior to filming there for my Long Weekends *series. Bream is a farmed fish, but none the worse for it. If you are lucky enough to get hold of a 1.4kg or 1.5kg bream, double the quantities of the other ingredients and you can serve four. Precooking the vegetables in the oven allows for a briefer cooking time for the fish.*

SERVES 2

5 tbsp olive oil
1 large onion, sliced
1 garlic clove, chopped
1 large green pepper, sliced
400g tomatoes, chopped,
    or a 400g tin of tomatoes
1 bay leaf
3 large waxy potatoes, peeled

2 x 400g whole sea bream,
    scaled and gutted
Juice of ½ lemon
6 black peppercorns
60ml dry sherry
Small handful flatleaf
    parsley, leaves chopped
Salt and black pepper

Picada
Small handful flatleaf
    parsley, chopped
2 large garlic cloves,
    roughly chopped
½ tsp sea salt

TIP
Other fish you could cook in this way are sea bass, John Dory, snapper or red mullet.

Heat 2 tablespoons of the oil in a frying pan over a medium-low heat. Fry the onion, garlic and green pepper for 10–15 minutes until soft. Add the tomatoes, bay leaf and a splash of water, cover and continue cooking for about 20 minutes.

Meanwhile, heat the oven to 180°C/Fan 160°C. Cut the potatoes into thick slices and arrange them in an ovenproof dish that's large enough to accommodate the sea bream later. Season with salt and pepper and drizzle with 2 tablespoons of the olive oil, then bake in the oven for about 20 minutes.

To make the picada, grind the parsley, garlic and salt together with a pestle and mortar, then set aside.

Season the fish with salt and pepper and place on top of the cooked potato slices. Spread the picada over the fish. Add the lemon juice and a couple of tablespoons of water to the dish, then pour the tomato mixture over everything. Drizzle over the remaining oil, add the peppercorns and sherry, then bake for 20–25 minutes. Scatter with chopped parsley and serve.

Nasi goreng with mackerel & prawns

Like so many rice or noodle street dishes from Southeast Asia, nasi goreng is a bit of a 'put whatever you like into it' sort of dish and I have written about this in my essay 'Waste not, want not' on pages 174–76. However, it should always include a good spice paste, some thinly sliced omelette and plenty of crisp fried shallots. I always put prawns in my nasi goreng and I love some broken-up, well-flavoured fish like mackerel in it too.

SERVES 4

225g long-grain rice
400ml just-boiled water
2 mackerel fillets
2 large eggs
Sunflower oil, for frying
6 large shallots, thinly sliced
175g peeled, cooked
   North Atlantic prawns
1 tbsp soy sauce
5cm piece of cucumber, quartered
   lengthways and sliced
4 spring onions, chopped
Salt and black pepper

Nasi goreng paste
3 tbsp groundnut oil
4 large garlic cloves,
   roughly chopped
20g root ginger, grated
2 large shallots, roughly chopped
15g roasted salted peanuts
6 medium-hot red chillies,
   roughly chopped
1 tbsp tomato paste
½ tsp blachan
   (dried shrimp paste)
1 tbsp soy sauce

TIP
You can use
the tubs of fried
onions available in
the supermarket.

First make the nasi goreng paste: simply put all the ingredients into a food processor and blend until smooth.

Put the rice in a pan with the just-boiled water and bring back to the boil. Put a lid on the pan, turn the heat down to a simmer and cook for 10 minutes. Turn off the heat and leave to cool.

Preheat the grill to high. Season the mackerel fillets on both sides with salt and pepper. Lay them on a lightly oiled baking tray, skin-side up, and grill for 3–4 minutes. Leave to cool and then flake the flesh into large pieces. Discard any bones.

Next, beat the eggs in a bowl and season with salt and pepper. Heat a little oil in a large, non-stick frying pan and pour in the eggs to make a very thin omelette. Cook until the eggs have lightly set on top, then flip over and cook for a few seconds on the other side. Roll the omelette up and thinly slice into strips.

Recipe continued overleaf

Pour oil into the frying pan to a depth of 1cm. Add the shallots and fry over a medium heat until crisp and golden brown. Lift them out with a slotted spoon and drain on kitchen paper.

Spoon 2 tablespoons of the oil from frying the shallots into a large wok and get it smoking hot. Add 2 tablespoons of the nasi goreng paste and stir-fry for 2 minutes. Add the cooked rice and stir-fry over a high heat for another 2 minutes, until it has heated through.

Add the prawns, strips of omelette, fried shallots and flaked mackerel and stir-fry for another minute. Add the soy sauce, cucumber and most of the spring onions, toss together well and then spoon on to a large, warmed serving dish. Sprinkle with the remaining spring onions and serve straight away.

Whole poached bass with hollandaise

The great thing about poaching larger fish is that this method of cooking is very forgiving. When you bake or barbecue a big fish it's quite difficult to keep it from being charred and overcooked or partly raw. Agreed, for poaching you do need to have a fish kettle which allows you to keep the whole fish bathed in water at the right temperature until it's ready to serve. You also need a cooking probe thermometer, but you'll never go wrong and everyone will be amazed at the sheer succulence of the fish.

SERVES 6-8

1.5kg whole sea bass, gutted and cleaned
Salt

Hollandaise sauce
3 egg yolks
335g Clarified butter (page 312), warmed
Juice of ½ lemon
10–12 turns freshly ground white pepper
A good pinch of cayenne pepper
¾–1 tsp salt

TIP
Hollandaise sauce is best used as soon as it is made, but will hold for up to 2 hours if kept covered in a warm place, such as over a pan of warm water.

Put the fish in a fish kettle and barely cover with water salted at a ratio of 1 teaspoon of salt per 600ml of water. Bring the water temperature up to 90°C, checking with the probe, then turn off the heat and let the water cool until the internal temperature of the fish at its thickest part is 60°C. You may need to give the odd burst of heat to achieve that. Keep the water at 60°C and the fish will stay perfectly cooked while you make the sauce.

Put the egg yolks and 3 tablespoons of water into a stainless steel or glass bowl set over a pan of simmering water. Make sure the base of the bowl is not touching the water. Whisk until voluminous, thick and creamy. Remove the bowl from the pan and gradually whisk in the clarified butter until thick. Whisk in the lemon juice, white pepper, cayenne pepper and salt.

Once the sauce is made, remove the bass from the fish kettle and put it on a board. Peel back and discard the skin, then, using a palette knife, carefully lift the fillets from the bones. Serve with the hollandaise spooned over, some new potatoes dressed with chopped parsley and vegetables of your choice.

Fish pie

This is as simple a recipe for fish pie as you can imagine, but if the fish is good (and that includes the smoked fish which must be of the best quality), there are few better fish dishes in the world than British fish pie with hard-boiled eggs and parsley, of course.

SERVES 6

1 small onion, sliced
2 cloves
1 bay leaf
600ml whole milk
300ml double cream
225g undyed smoked
   haddock fillet

450g unskinned cod fillet
150g large, peeled, cooked
   king prawns
4 hard-boiled eggs
100g butter
45g plain flour
5 tbsp chopped flatleaf parsley

Freshly grated nutmeg
1.25kg floury potatoes,
   such as Maris Pipers
   or King Edwards, peeled
1 egg yolk
Salt and freshly ground
   white pepper

TIP
Try making this
with haddock or
hake instead of
cod. I just think
smoked haddock
is essential.

Put the onion and cloves in a large pan with the bay leaf, 450ml of the milk and the cream. Bring just to the boil and simmer for 10 minutes. Add the fish and cook for about 3 minutes until just set. Lift the fish out and strain the liquor into a jug. Flake the fish, discarding the skin and any bones, then put it in a shallow 1.75-litre ovenproof dish with the cooked onion. Add the prawns, then peel the eggs, cut them into chunky slices and arrange on top of the fish.

Melt 50g of the butter in a pan, add the flour and cook for 1 minute. Take the pan off the heat and gradually stir in the reserved cooking liquor. Put the pan back over the heat and bring the sauce slowly to the boil, stirring all the time. Leave it to simmer gently for 10 minutes. Remove from the heat again, stir in the parsley and season with nutmeg, salt and white pepper. Pour the sauce over the fish and leave to cool. Once cool, chill in the fridge for 1 hour.

Boil the potatoes for 15–20 minutes. Drain, mash and add the rest of the butter and the egg yolk. Season with salt and white pepper. Beat in enough of the remaining milk to form a soft, spreadable mash.

Preheat the oven to 200°C/Fan 180°C. Spoon the mash over the filling and mark the surface with a fork. Bake for 35–40 minutes, until piping hot and golden brown.

Pan-fried fillet of monkfish
with new season's garlic & fennel

*I wrote this recipe ages ago and it's almost the cook's version
of hearing the first cuckoo in spring for me. It was inspired by
seeing the first purple green heads of garlic and early fennel bulbs,
all from the Mediterranean. These days I stir in a few leaves of
local ramsons – wild garlic – and some wild fennel herb. This is
really a seasonal dish but I think it's nice made any time of the year.*

SERVES 4

16 large garlic cloves,
   ideally new season's
100g semolina
A couple of fennel herb sprigs
100g unsalted butter
500g fennel bulb, thinly sliced
600ml Fish stock (page 306)

4 x 200g pieces of
   prepared monkfish fillet
4 tbsp sunflower oil
2 tsp lemon juice
Splash of Pernod
   or Ricard
Salt and black pepper

TIP
You can also make
this with fillets of
John Dory. They
are thinner, so
simple pan-frying
will be enough;
no need to heat
up the oven.

Put 2 of the garlic cloves, the semolina and all but 1 sprig
of the fennel into a food processor. Blend to an aromatic
pale green powder and set aside.

Cut the rest of the garlic cloves lengthways into long thin
slices. Melt half the butter in a pan, add the garlic and sliced
fennel and fry over a medium heat until lightly browned. Add
the fish stock, season with salt and pepper, then simmer for
15 minutes until the fennel is tender.

Preheat the oven to 200°C/Fan 180°C. Coat the pieces
of monkfish in the semolina mixture. Heat the oil in an
ovenproof, non-stick frying pan, add a small knob of butter
and the monkfish. Fry over a moderate heat, turning the
fish now and then, until golden brown all over. Transfer
the pan to the oven and cook for a further 10 minutes.

Remove the monkfish from the oven and slice diagonally into
thick pieces; keep it warm. Add the sautéed fennel mixture,
lemon juice, Pernod or Ricard and the remaining fennel sprig,
finely chopped, to the pan in which the monkfish was cooked.
Simmer rapidly until slightly reduced, then add the remaining
butter and simmer until it has blended in to make a rich sauce.
Serve the fish with the sauce spooned around it.

Indonesian seafood curry

Added to the fact that I often cook this at home, it's also possibly the most popular dish on the menu in any of our restaurants, both here and in Australia. I think it's really down to the Indonesian spice paste, which has a mixture of fragrance and heat – that and the coconut milk. I don't know if I am alone in recognising that coconut milk in Asia has the same effect in recipes as cream does in milk-producing countries. It's important to realise that although the nurturing effect of delicious fat is a worry for those wanting to lose weight, it is also a glorious enhancer of flavour and texture and a valuable part of a normal diet.

SERVES 4

400g fish fillets, such as monkfish, John Dory, barramundi, gurnard or sea bass, skin on
250g squid pouches
12 large raw peeled prawns
1 tsp salt

Freshly ground white pepper
1 tbsp lime juice
200g (8 heaped tbsp) Indonesian spice paste (page 308)
2 tbsp sunflower oil

4 Kaffir lime leaves, torn into small pieces
2 fat lemongrass stalks, halved and bruised
120ml Chicken stock (page 307)
250ml coconut milk

TIP
If you want to give your regular chicken stock some Asian flavour, infuse it with fresh root ginger and lemongrass.

Cut the fish into 3–4cm chunks. Slit the squid pouches open, lay them flat and use the tip of a sharp knife to score the inside surface with a diamond pattern. Cut the squid into strips and then into squares about the same size as the fish.

Put the fish, squid and prawns into a shallow bowl. Sprinkle with the salt, some pepper and the lime juice and mix together well.

Heat the oil in a large pan over a medium heat. Add the spice paste and fry gently for 2–3 minutes until it starts to smell fragrant. Add the lime leaves, lemongrass and stock and simmer for 1 minute.

Add the fish, squid and prawns to the pan, then pour in the coconut milk and simmer for 4 minutes. Season to taste with a little more salt and lime juice and serve.

Cornish bouillabaisse with mash

I suppose this is a bit of a plug for my autobiography, Under a Mackerel Sky, *in which I recall first tasting a bouillabaisse made by some French friends of my parents in Church Cove on the Lizard Peninsula in Cornwall. Matt Bennett, the director of my* Rick Stein's Cornwall *series, read it and said we had to include a recipe for a Cornish bouillabaisse in the programme. Actually, I've been making dishes like this forever but now it's got a name.*

SERVES 4

Fish
2 whole gurnard, about
   600g total weight, filleted
   (ask for the head and bones)
6 cooked langoustines,
   cut in half lengthways or
   6 large prawns, shell on
12 mussels in the shell

Bouillabaisse
5 tbsp olive oil
2 shallots or 1 onion
   chopped, skin and all
3 garlic cloves, roughly
   chopped, skin and all
1 small fennel bulb, chopped
100ml dry white wine
600ml Fish stock (page 306)
   or water
2 large tomatoes,
   roughly chopped
1 tbsp tomato paste
2 strips of orange peel
Pinch saffron
Pinch cayenne pepper
Salt and black pepper

Mash
1kg potatoes, peeled
   and cut into quarters
150ml whole milk
   or cream
Pinch saffron
50g butter

TIP
Whisking the potatoes with an electric handheld whisk, such as you'd use to make cakes, gives mash a wonderfully light, whipped texture - and no lumps.

Start with the bouillabaisse. Heat the olive oil in a fairly deep, wide pan and fry the shallots or onion, garlic, fennel and gurnard heads and bones until soft. Add the wine, the stock or water, tomatoes, tomato paste, orange peel and saffron. Bring to the boil, then turn the heat down to a simmer and cook for 30–40 minutes.

Meanwhile, make the mash. Boil the potatoes in well-salted water for 20–25 minutes until tender when prodded with a knife. While the potatoes are cooking, warm the milk or cream in a small pan with the saffron and butter. When hot, turn off the heat and leave the saffron to infuse the milk.

Drain the potatoes well. Push them through a potato ricer, whisk with an electric whisk or use a masher. Beat the saffron liquid into the mash until light and smooth. Taste and add salt as required. To keep the mash warm, cover it with buttered foil and put it in a low oven.

Recipe continued overleaf

Working quickly, push the bouillabaisse mixture through a sieve with a wooden spoon or the back of a ladle, or pass it through a mouli to extract as much flavour as possible from the fish bones and vegetables. Discard the solids.

Rinse the pan, pour the soup back into the pan and heat it through, seasoning to taste with salt, pepper and cayenne. Add the gurnard fillets and the langoustines or prawns and cook for 2 minutes, then add the mussels and cook for a further 2–3 minutes until the mussels have opened.

Spoon some mashed potato on to each warmed plate and top with some fish, prawns or langoustines and mussels. Spoon over a little more of the sauce and serve immediately.

Crispy mackerel with red cabbage & beetroot salad

A recipe and note from Ed Stein: Years ago, an Indian chef named Rui was at our family house in Cornwall and he showed us a way of dusting fish fillets with flour and turmeric before frying. It's a simple way of achieving a wonderful golden spicy coating. The salad recipe works well, I think, with the crisp mackerel.

SERVES 4

¼–½ tsp salt
Juice of 1 lime
8 mackerel fillets
1 tsp ground turmeric
3 tbsp plain flour
4 tbsp vegetable oil
Mango chutney,
    to serve

Salad
½ red cabbage,
    finely shredded
2 beetroots, peeled and
    finely sliced or grated
1 red or green finger chilli,
    finely sliced

Dressing
Olive oil
Balsamic vinegar
Salt

Mix the salt with the lime juice and rub the mixture well into the mackerel fillets. Mix together the turmeric and plain flour and dust over the fillets on both sides.

In a large bowl, combine the red cabbage, beetroots and chilli. To make the dressing, mix 3 parts olive oil and 1 part balsamic vinegar and season with a pinch of salt. Add the dressing to the salad and toss to coat.

Heat the oil in a large, non-stick frying pan over a medium-high heat. Add the mackerel fillets and fry for 2–3 minutes on each side until crisp. Serve the crispy fried fish with the salad and some mango chutney on the side.

Lobster & clotted cream quiche with tarragon & parsley

I write this at the risk of offending some people, but the point of this quiche is to use up all the meat left over from a feast of lobster. Most people don't really know about or bother with all the lobster meat in the head section or indeed in some parts of the claws and the legs, so if I've got a pile of lobster shells, there's the makings of a great quiche there. And if I'm not up to doing that, I'll bash the shells a bit and make shellfish stock (page 307).

SERVES 6-8

1 quantity Rich shortcrust
  pastry (page 312)
Flour, for dusting
1 egg white
750g cooked lobster
  in the shell

175ml whole milk
100g clotted cream
3 large eggs
2 tsp finely chopped tarragon
2 tsp finely chopped parsley
Salt and black pepper

TIP
This is equally
good made with
langoustines.

Preheat the oven to 200°C/Fan 180°C. Roll out the pastry on a lightly floured work surface and use it to line a 23cm loose-bottomed flan tin with a depth of 4cm. Prick the base here and there with a fork and chill for 20 minutes.

Line the pastry case with a sheet of crumpled greaseproof paper, add baking beans, then bake for 15 minutes. Remove the paper and beans and return the pastry to the oven for 5 minutes. Remove once more and brush the base of the case with the unbeaten egg white. Put it back in the oven for 1 minute. Remove and lower the oven temperature to 190°C/Fan 170°C.

While the pastry is baking, take the lobster meat out of the shell. In a bowl, gradually mix the milk into the clotted cream until smooth. Beat in the eggs and stir in the herbs, three-quarters of a teaspoon of salt and some black pepper.

Scatter the lobster meat over the base of the pastry case and pour over the egg mixture. Bake the quiche for 25–30 minutes until just set and lightly browned. Remove and leave it to cool slightly before serving with a soft lettuce salad with an olive oil and garlic dressing.

Smoked haddock with dugléré sauce

SERVES 2

*This sauce is one of the first classic French sauces I used
in the Seafood Restaurant and it is still a favourite.*

2 x 150–170g fillets
of undyed smoked
haddock, skin on

Dugléré sauce
1 tomato (about 85g),
skinned
30g butter
1 small shallot or ½ banana
shallot, finely chopped
50ml dry white wine

2 tsp plain flour
200ml Chicken stock
(page 307)
50g cold butter, cubed
Small handful flatleaf
parsley, chopped
Salt and black pepper

TIP
This makes a
good starter
too, in which
case 2 x 100g
fillets will
be enough.

Put the smoked haddock fillets, skin-side down, in a pan
and cover with cold water. Bring to the boil, allow the
water to bubble momentarily, then turn off the heat and
leave the fish in the water to cook for about 6–8 minutes
or until the flesh is almost opaque.

Chop the tomato finely, put it in a sieve and shake off
the watery juices. Set aside.

To make the sauce, melt the butter in a saucepan, add the
chopped shallot and sweat over a low heat until softened
but not browned. Turn up the heat, add the wine and bring
to the boil. Reduce the wine by half, then stir in the flour
and cook for a minute before adding the stock. Continue
to bubble until reduced by about a third. Taste the sauce
and if the flavour needs concentrating, reduce a little more.
Using a small balloon whisk, whisk in the butter, a cube
at a time, until you have smooth, silky sauce. Stir in the
tomato and parsley.

Carefully remove the fish from the water and drain it
well. Serve on warm plates and spoon over the sauce.
Nice with some boiled new potatoes.

Salmon Wellington with a white wine & cream sauce

I am quite a sucker for salmon in puff pastry, as is indeed virtually everyone I know. In the 80s at the Seafood Restaurant, I used to do individual parcels of wild salmon in puff pastry with tarragon and butter and served it with the same sauce as below. The problem that I almost didn't want to admit was that the internal butter and juice from the salmon made the pastry a bit soggy. The point of a beef wellington, and this fish version, is to surround the flesh with something that will encase the moisture, so now the pastry is really nice and crisp and vies for star status on our Christmas Eve dinner menu.

SERVES 6
as a main course

1kg side of salmon, skinned
500g block of all-butter
    puff pastry
Flour, for dusting
1 egg, beaten with
    1 tsp water

Mushroom filling
20g unsalted butter
1 tsp sunflower oil
2 shallots, finely chopped
300g mushrooms, finely
    chopped (shiitake, oyster,
    portobello or whatever
    you like)
120g mascarpone cheese
Zest of ½ lemon
3 or 4 tarragon sprigs,
    leaves stripped from
    the stalks and chopped
Small handful flatleaf
    parsley, chopped
Small handful chives, chopped
Salt and black pepper

White wine sauce
20g butter
1 shallot, finely chopped
100ml white wine
300ml Fish stock (page 306)
    or Chicken stock (page 307)
150ml double cream
40g unsalted butter,
    cold and cubed
1 tbsp chopped chives
1 tbsp chopped parsley

TIP
This dish can be made 24 hours ahead of time. Prepare it to the stage where you cover it with cling film and put in the fridge to chill, then cook as required. It is also delicious served cold the next day with mayonnaise.

Start by making the mushroom filling. Heat the butter and oil in a frying pan and when the butter has melted, add the shallots. Let them soften for a minute or so, then add the mushrooms and cook over a medium heat until they have released their liquid and it has evaporated. Allow to cool completely. Stir in the mascarpone, lemon zest and herbs and season with salt and pepper.

Cut the salmon fillet in half and trim, then set it aside in the fridge. Preheat the oven to 220°C/Fan 200°C.

Recipe continued overleaf

Cut about a third off the pastry block, then wrap the rest and put it in the fridge. On a floured board, roll out the pastry third to a rectangle a little larger than one of the pieces of salmon – they will be stacked one on top of the other. Put the rolled-out pastry in a shallow baking tray lined with baking paper and prick it all over with a fork to prevent it from rising too much. Bake in the oven for about 15 minutes until crisp and golden, then remove and leave to cool.

Take the remaining piece of pastry and roll it out into a rectangle a couple of inches larger than the first piece. Smooth half of the mushroom mixture on to the cooled, cooked pastry base and top with both pieces of salmon, one on top of the other. Spread the remaining mushroom mixture over the top piece of salmon and around the sides. Now drape the remaining pastry over the fish and tuck it under the pastry base as if you were making a bed and tucking the sheet in. Using the rounded end of a teaspoon, mark the pastry all over to replicate fish scales. Brush all over with beaten egg, then cover with cling film and chill in the fridge for 30 minutes.

When you're ready to cook, preheat the oven to 220°C/ Fan 200°C. Remove the wellington from the fridge and glaze again with the remaining beaten egg. Bake for 30 minutes, then reduce the oven temperature to 200°C/Fan 180°C and cook for a further 15 minutes until the pastry is crisp, risen and golden. Using a temperature probe, check that the thickest part is 55°C. Remove from the oven and leave to rest for 10 minutes before cutting and serving.

While the fish is in the oven, make the sauce. Melt the butter in a pan and soften the shallot. Add the white wine, bring to the boil and reduce by a third. Add the stock and cream and bring back up to the boil, then reduce the heat and whisk in the butter, a cube at a time, Season with salt and pepper and stir in the chopped chives and parsley. Keep the sauce warm and serve alongside the salmon, with a crisp watercress salad or green beans and buttered new potatoes.

Sautéed red mullet with parsley, garlic & spaghettini

This makes four large servings, but I always think that a good pile of pasta is what everybody really likes. The great thing about it is that the well-flavoured skin of the red mullet goes slightly grainy when it's fried and seems to coat the spaghetti with the sweet taste of seafood. I also make this with monkfish, John Dory, bass or bream; it's just a lovely way of cooking fish.

SERVES 4

4 x 150g red mullet, filleted
450g dried spaghettini
4 tbsp olive oil
2 garlic cloves, finely chopped
1 medium-hot red chilli, finely chopped
4 plum tomatoes, chopped
Handful flatleaf parsley, finely chopped
Salt and black pepper
Extra virgin olive oil, to serve

TIP
This is lovely with the very fine spaghettini but it's great with spaghetti or linguine too.

Cut the red mullet fillets across into strips 2cm wide. Bring a large pan of water to the boil and season with salt. Add the spaghettini, bring back to the boil and cook for 5 minutes or until al dente. Drain the pasta well and tip it into a large warmed serving bowl.

Meanwhile, heat the oil in a large frying pan. Fry the strips of mullet, skin-side down, for 3–4 minutes, then season with salt and pepper. Add the garlic and chilli to the pan and fry for 30 seconds, then add the tomatoes and fry for 30 seconds more.

Tip the contents of the pan into the bowl with the pasta, scraping up all the little bits that may have stuck to the bottom of the pan. Add most of the parsley and gently toss everything together so that the fish just begins to break up. Serve immediately, drizzled with extra virgin olive oil and sprinkled with the remaining parsley.

Seafood pancakes

MAKES ABOUT
8 PANCAKES
Serves 8 as a starter
or 4 as a main course

In the 70s, seafood pancakes became the staple of every frozen food company and I had to drop them from the restaurant menu. Fortunately, the craze has passed so it's nice to be able to feature them again. They make a fabulous first course too.

Batter
120g plain flour
½ tsp salt
1 egg, beaten
300ml whole milk
1 tbsp sunflower oil,
 plus extra, for frying

Filling
120g sole, plaice or hake
 fillets, skinned
1 tbsp butter
1 small onion, finely chopped
60ml dry white wine
300ml Fish velouté (page 309)
Juice of ¼ lemon

90ml double cream
1 tsp chopped parsley
1 egg yolk
Pinch cayenne pepper
120g shelled cooked prawns
60g white crab meat
60g Gruyère cheese, grated
Salt and ground white pepper

TIP
These are pretty deluxe, but you can just use white fish and they are still really good. Maybe up the cheese quantity a little if not using prawns and crab.

For the batter, sift the flour and salt into a bowl, make a well in the centre and add the egg. Slowly whisk in the milk and the tablespoon of oil until you have a smooth batter.

Heat a 20–23cm frying pan and swirl in a little oil, then tip out any excess. The pan should be just coated. Pour in enough batter to coat the bottom of the pan evenly and place over a medium heat. After a minute or so, loosen the edges and flip over to cook the other side. Repeat to make 8 pancakes.

Cut the fish into 2.5cm-wide strips. Grease a shallow pan with butter, add the onion and lay the sole on top. Pour over the wine and season with salt and pepper. Cover the pan with baking paper and poach the fish very gently until it has just firmed up. Heat the velouté in a pan and add the cooking juices from the fish and the lemon juice, cream, parsley and egg yolk. Season with cayenne. Turn on the grill to heat up.

Add prawns and crab meat to the pan of fish and pour in enough of the sauce to bind everything together. Reserve the rest of the sauce to pour over the pancakes.

Spoon the mixture into the centre of each pancake, then roll them up and place in a buttered, shallow, ovenproof dish. Pour over the remaining sauce and sprinkle with the cheese. Place under a hot grill until golden and bubbling, then serve.

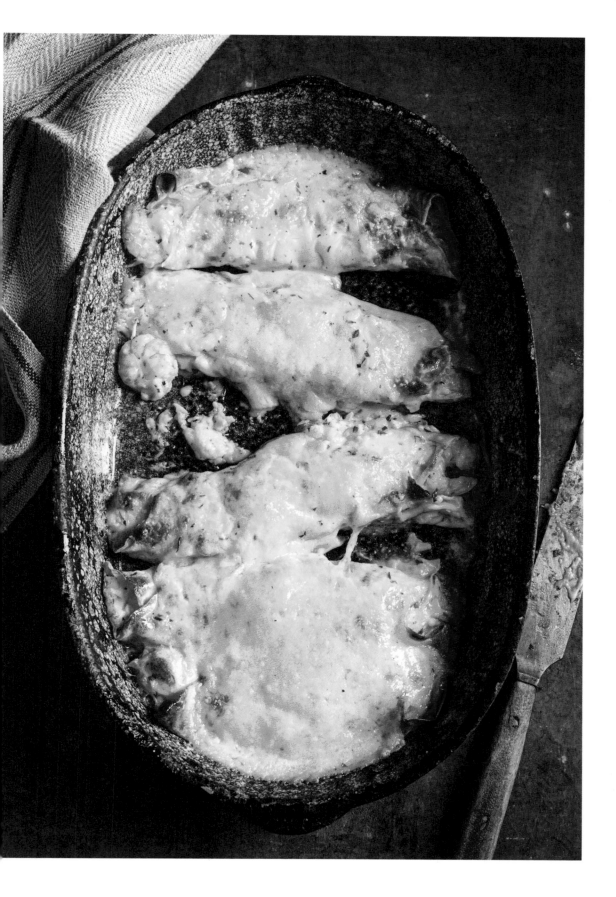

Barbecued whole sea bass with fennel mayonnaise

This is my favourite way of cooking whole fish on a barbecue, but it can be quite tricky and you might want to try cooking it under a grill the first time round. What really works in this is the mayonnaise that's flavoured with fennel herb as well as a splash of pastis and some chopped chives. They give the sauce a bit of onion flavour which seems to work so well.

SERVES 2

2 x 450–500g sea bass, cleaned and trimmed of fins
2 tbsp olive oil
1 bunch fennel herb
2 tsp Pernod
Salt and black pepper

Fennel mayonnaise
1 egg yolk (at room temperature)
1 tsp white wine vinegar
150ml olive oil (not extra virgin)
½ tsp Pernod

½ tbsp finely chopped fennel herb
A few chives, finely chopped

TIP
You can also make this with sea bream, red mullet, snapper or John Dory.

Preheat a barbecue or an indoor grill.

Slash each fish 3 or 4 times down each side and rub them with olive oil. Season well, inside and out, with salt and pepper, then push some of the fennel herb into the gut cavity.

For the mayonnaise, put the egg yolk, vinegar and a pinch of salt into a bowl or food processor and whisk together. Start adding the oil very slowly, literally a drop at a time at first. If you go too quickly, your mayonnaise will split. Then keep adding the oil in a very slow, fine stream until the mixture is really thick. Stir in the Pernod, the chopped fennel and chives. Check the seasoning, adding more salt if required, then set aside.

Barbecue the fish for 5–7 minutes. Sprinkle each with a teaspoon of Pernod, then carefully turn them over and cook for a further 5–7 minutes until they are cooked right through to the backbone. If you're using an indoor grill you probably won't need to turn them over, but they may take a few more minutes. Use the browned side as the presentation side.

Carefully remove the fish from the barbecue or grill and serve with the mayonnaise, boiled new potatoes and a green salad.

Chapter Four
POULTRY

Cusgarne Farm is just 100 acres of organic land quite near Truro in Cornwall. Nothing from the hedges, fields, orchards or ditches has been sprayed with chemicals since 1988. Greg and Teresa Pascoe and their daughters Zennor, Lamorna and Veryan have turned their family farm into a vision of what farming could be like without the pressure to produce cheap food. Nowhere is this more apparent than when watching the chickens in their enclosure – a large paddock dominated by a chicken hut built on the chassis of an old muck spreader.

The birds on the Pascoe's farm behave like chickens do if they're left alone to live naturally. It's thoroughly engrossing to watch and you can quickly see that chickens know where they stand with each other. You notice the dominant individuals reminding less important ones of their status with a peck – the pecking order. It's not necessarily a polite or just way of living but it's harmonious and you instantly realise that space is key to happy hens. Given that our requirements from chickens are no less altruistic than their behaviour to each other, it would seem only right that we should at least let the birds lead the life they would normally lead, rather than treat them as a cash crop.

It is easy to be considered elitist in pointing out the incredible difference in taste between a proper free-range chicken and one reared in a little box, but is there anything more depressing about the way we eat now than much of the poultry section of a supermarket? Rows of opaque plastic boxes filled with legs, breasts and thighs, increasingly with no skin. What is this strange substance that looks like it could have been grown hydroponically? Is this to be the basis of what we're proud to call home cooking? I'm not going to lie. I've bought these things, but even when I've turned the chicken meat into perhaps a chicken pie, butter chicken or a poached chicken dish I've felt ashamed.

Instead, let us celebrate these fascinating birds and go out and spend some money on a proper chicken from a farm shop, then cook something special. I find chicken with morels as irresistible on a menu as turbot with hollandaise sauce. These days, I suppose people frown on a savoury dish with lots of cream in it, but the French invented this way of cooking and there is something so luscious and comforting about a beautiful free-range chicken cooked with a cream and wine sauce with the smoky flavour of dried morels (page 149).

Or try my spatchcocked chicken with tarragon recipe on page 135 for a quicker than usual way of roasting a bird. Split the chicken open along the backbone, mix some softened butter with chopped tarragon, garlic, salt and black pepper and spread it under the skin. Roast it in a hot oven and serve with sautéed potatoes and a salad.

I suspect the real reason for roasting chicken for a long time traditionally would have been to ensure that the inside cavity reaches a high enough temperature to kill any pathogens. Splitting the chicken open and flattening it like this means that the inside is cooked quickly and therefore the rest of the meat is much juicier, particularly if some flavoured butter has been tucked under the skin.

My mum's risotto

I still love this. I'm sure any family with a parent or grandparent who is a good cook will have a not-exactly-PC dish that everyone adores. Even my children love this and my mother was still making it when it was perfectly easy to get arborio rice. I use long-grain as she did, so it's actually more of a pilaf in the cooking than a risotto, but it'll always be my mum's risotto to me and it still tastes wonderful.

SERVES 4

75g butter
60g shallots, finely chopped
3 garlic cloves, finely chopped
100g button mushrooms,
    quartered
120g courgettes, chopped
350g long-grain rice
150ml white wine
620ml Chicken stock
    (page 307), heated
120g frozen peas

25g raisins
250g leftover roast chicken,
    chopped into 1cm pieces
75g cooked ham or unsmoked
    bacon, cut into 1cm pieces
40g Parmesan, freshly grated
    (plus extra at the table)
Handful flatleaf parsley, chopped
Salt and black pepper

TIP
Add a Parmesan rind, if you have one, when you add the stock. It'll impart a delicious salty, tangy flavour to the risotto.

Melt 50g of the butter in a wide pan over a medium heat. Add the shallots, garlic, mushrooms and courgettes and sweat until soft, but not coloured. Add the rice and stir well to coat the rice in the butter. Cook for a minute or so, then add the white wine. Let it bubble and reduce a little before adding the chicken stock, peas and raisins.

Bring to the boil, stirring constantly, then turn the heat down low, put a lid on the pan and cook for 10 minutes. Stir in the chicken and ham, then remove the pan from the heat, replace the lid and leave to rest for about 3 minutes.

Stir in the Parmesan, the rest of the butter and the chopped parsley. Season with salt and pepper to taste. Serve in warmed bowls with extra Parmesan for guests to add at the table.

The best chicken pie in Greece

I hate to say it, but I sort of think the Greek chicken pie is even better than our own. This recipe came from a filming trip to Epirus in northern Greece and is made from a whole chicken. The chicken and onions are first poached, and the liquid then reduced to a gelatinous sauce. It is the sweetness of the onions that really counts here and the almost complete reduction of the cooking juices.

SERVES 6-8

1kg onions, chopped
30g butter
2 tbsp olive oil, plus extra
    for greasing and brushing

1 free-range chicken (about 1.5kg)
3 eggs, beaten
6 sheets filo pastry
Salt and black pepper

TIP
Filo pastry has no fat so dries out really quickly. Always cover it with a faintly damp tea towel to prevent it from becoming brittle and difficult to work with.

Put the onions, butter and olive oil into a large pan or stockpot with a lid. Add the whole chicken and pour in enough water to almost submerge the bird. Cover, bring the water to the boil, then turn the heat down to barely a simmer and poach the chicken for about 1½ hours.

When the chicken is cooked, remove it from the pan and strain the liquid into another pan. Set the onions aside for later. Now boil the liquid hard to reduce to a tasty gelatinous stock – about 150–180ml. When the chicken is cool enough to handle, strip all the meat off the carcass, discarding the bones and skin. Put the meat and the reserved onions into a large bowl and mix well. Add the eggs and reduced stock and season with 1½ teaspoons of salt and some black pepper.

Heat the oven to 230°C/Fan 210°C. Grease a 30cm round pie dish with oil. Line the dish with 3 sheets of filo, alternating the direction each time and brushing each layer with a little oil. Add the chicken mixture and fold the overhanging edges in. Top with a further 3 layers of filo, again placed at different angles to one another. Fold in the overhanging edges to seal the pie and brush all over with more olive oil.

Bake for 15 minutes. Remove the pie from the oven and cut it into 6 or 8 wedges while still in the dish. Reduce the heat to 200°C/Fan 180°C and bake for a further 45 minutes. Allow to rest for 10–20 minutes, then serve, still warm.

A quiet night in

Thanks to the pandemic, virtually every night is a quiet night at the time I'm writing this, but it used to be that Sas and I would look forward to an evening at home with extreme longing, simply because whether it was in London, Padstow or Sydney, we were always going somewhere.

The main criteria of the quiet night in was that we would drink fizzy water and eat something that would give us a sense that we were at last starting to redress the calorie imbalance. I know lots of our friends swear by those diets where you just eat two bananas twice a week and then go bonkers for the rest of the time. I'm much too in love with cooking and eating to do something so mundane, so I've evolved a number of dishes which are lovely but very low in calories.

The first one came from an early trip to Singapore many years ago when I tried Chinese white-cooked chicken (page 150) for the first time. If you haven't ever tried it you absolutely must. It's a whole chicken simmered for a brief time and left to go cold in the poaching liquor, which has lots of sliced ginger added to it. The chicken is then cut up on the bone and served with rice, a lettuce and coriander salad and, most importantly, three accompaniments: bird's-eye chillies thinly sliced and immersed in rice wine or white wine vinegar with a little sugar, dark soy sauce with finely chopped spring onions and ginger, and a dry peppermix of coarse salt, Sichuan and black peppercorns lightly crushed. There is not a hint of fat anywhere in the dish, apart from in the chicken itself, which is very lean anyway.

In Shanghai I later observed that you can buy special chickens for this dish, which are quite small and presumably 100 per cent free of anything like salmonella, because the poaching time is very short indeed. The essence of the dish is to achieve extreme softness and succulence of the chicken; it is one of those dishes that astounds me with its simple sophistication.

Next on my list of reasons to love being at home of an evening would be a two-egg omelette with a lettuce, tomato and avocado salad and a miserly number of sweet and delightful new potatoes. I evolved this very simple combination after reading Elizabeth David's wonderful compilation of essays: *An Omelette and a Glass of Wine*. Every time I make this supper there is always a glaring element missing – the glass of wine – and the compensation for me is that I add freshly grated Parmesan to the omelette. It's so lovely and makes up a little for the lack of a glass of, say white Côtes du Rhône, scented with a little Viognier.

The other great contribution to sensible quiet nights in is soup. There is a theory among dietitians, to which I very much subscribe, that soups are great appetite suppressors because the body registers them as food, not drink, even though they contain lots of liquid. As far as I'm concerned, as an obsessive maker of all kinds of stocks, soups are a must, otherwise the freezer just gets completely rammed.

I find to make soups interesting you need to have some sort of hook. In other words, you don't just make pea soup, you make pea and lettuce soup (page 52), or you add a little bit extra, like some crisp fried pancetta or toasted hazelnuts on a Jerusalem artichoke soup (page 53).

'The main criteria of the quiet night was that we would drink fizzy water and eat something that would give us a sense that we were at last starting to redress the calorie imbalance.'

Hainanese chicken & rice
Khao man gai

This recipe is similar to the white-cooked chicken on page 150, but my family insisted on both being included, as they are so loved. Interestingly, you can tell that both came from the same place as the cooking is very similar, but the subtle details are so different. One is fresh tasting, with clean flavours of chilli and coriander, while this dish is all about the beautiful softness of the rice and the unique flavour of the ginger, chilli and yellow bean sauce.

SERVES 4-6

1 x 1.5kg free-range chicken
(at room temperature)
25g peeled root ginger,
thickly sliced
3 garlic cloves
6 spring onions, trimmed
½ cucumber, peeled, halved
lengthways and sliced
Salt and freshly ground
white pepper

Rice
1 tbsp sunflower oil
350g Thai jasmine
rice, rinsed
1 tsp sesame oil
1 pandan leaf, tied
into a knot (optional)

Thai ginger and chilli
dipping sauce
5 garlic cloves
25g peeled root ginger,
thinly sliced
1 medium-hot red chilli,
thinly sliced
2 tbsp soft brown sugar
2 tbsp white wine vinegar
2 tbsp yellow bean sauce
2 tbsp dark soy sauce
1 tbsp white peppercorns,
coarsely ground

Remove the fat from the cavity of the chicken and set it aside for later. Season the chicken inside and out with salt and white pepper.

Take a large, deep pan in which the chicken will fit snugly – if the pan is too large, the amount of water needed to cover the bird will result in a watery stock. Add 4 litres of water (enough to cover the chicken), bring to the boil and add the ginger, garlic, 4 of the spring onions and a little salt. Immerse the chicken in the water, bring almost back to the boil and then leave it to simmer very gently for 12 minutes.

Turn off the heat, cover and leave for 30 minutes. Remove the chicken from the pan, cover and set it aside. Skim the fat from the stock and boil until it's reduced to 1.2 litres, then set aside.

For the rice, heat the oil in a pan over a medium heat. Add the reserved chicken fat and leave for 2–3 minutes until melted. Remove from the heat, lift out any solid bits and discard them. Put the pan back over a medium heat, add the rice and stir-fry for a couple of minutes to coat the grains.

Add 600ml of the hot chicken stock and bring it back to the boil, then add the sesame oil. Stir once, add the pandan leaf, if using, then cover the pan, lower the heat and leave to cook for 10 minutes. Then turn off the heat and leave to sit, still covered, for 10 more minutes.

Meanwhile, separate the chicken meat from the bones and slice it. Cut the remaining spring onions in half and thinly shred them lengthways.

To make the dipping sauce, blend all the ingredients in a small food processor.

Spoon some of the cooked rice on to each plate, top with the cooked chicken and garnish with the cucumber. Reheat the remaining chicken stock and season to taste. Ladle this into small soup bowls and sprinkle with the shredded spring onion. Serve each person with a plate of chicken and rice, dipping sauce and a bowl of soup, then tuck in.

Spatchcocked chicken with tarragon

I'm much more likely to roast a chicken that I've spatchcocked than a normal one. The reason is not only that it reduces the cooking time significantly but also allows for the even cooking of every part. It's also the only way to cook it properly on a barbecue if you don't have a rotisserie.

SERVES 4–6

1 free-range chicken (about 1.75kg)
90g butter, softened
3 or 4 tarragon sprigs, leaves stripped
   from stalks and roughly chopped
2 large garlic cloves, grated or very
   finely chopped
Salt and black pepper

Gravy
75ml white wine
300ml Chicken stock (page 307)
30g cold butter, cubed
2 tarragon sprigs, leaves stripped
   from stalks and chopped

TIP
Always keep the bones to make chicken stock. Freeze them if you don't have time to use them immediately.

Preheat the oven to 200°C/Fan 180°C. To spatchcock the chicken, place it on a board, breast-side down. Using poultry shears or heavy scissors, cut down either side of the backbone and remove it. Turn the bird over and press down to flatten.

Mix 75g of the butter with the tarragon and garlic. Loosen the skin on the chicken breasts and thighs, then gently use your fingers to create a pocket between the meat and skin. Using your fingers or a butter knife, spread the mixture over the meat taking care not to break the skin. When the breasts and thighs are well covered, smooth the skin down. Anoint the outside with the remaining butter and season all over.

Place the chicken in a roasting tin that's just large enough to hold it. Roast for 40–50 minutes or until the internal temperature is 70°C. When the chicken is ready, remove it from the oven, place it on a warmed plate and cover with foil. Leave to rest for 5–10 minutes while you make the gravy.

Place the roasting tin on the hob and add the wine. Allow it to bubble up and boil, then add the stock. Stir to lift any tasty bits that have stuck to the tin and turn down the heat to a simmer. Season to taste and whisk in the butter a cube at a time and add the tarragon. Serve the chicken with the gravy, sautéed potatoes (page 304), and green beans or a salad.

Chicken & prawn stir-fry with black bean sauce & coriander

I can't claim this is an authentic Chinese recipe. It's just something I make because the flavours of the black bean sauce, Chinese 5-spice and plenty of chilli appeal to me. I often cook this dish with strips of pork tenderloin, but most popular with my family is this chicken and prawn version. The cooking of the vegetables is a bit arbitrary; all you need to ensure is that they retain plenty of crunch. My stir-fries vary – sometimes I use baby corn, sometimes courgettes. It's really down to what you have in the fridge.

SERVES 6

1 x 1.3kg free-range chicken, boned and skinned, or 2 chicken breasts, 2 thighs and 2 drumsticks, boned and skinned
45ml sunflower oil
4 garlic cloves, chopped
10cm root ginger, peeled and sliced or grated
2 tbsp black bean sauce
½ tsp Chinese 5-spice
60ml Shaoxing wine or dry sherry

30ml soy sauce
½ tsp salt
1 tsp sugar
1 red pepper, sliced
2 red chillies, sliced
100g green beans, topped and tailed and cut in half
100g mangetout
100g button mushrooms, sliced
100g raw peeled prawns
100g bean sprouts

1 tbsp cornflour, mixed with a little water
30g coriander, roughly chopped
1 bunch spring onions, trimmed and sliced diagonally

To serve
Steamed jasmine rice (page 305)
Chilli oil or soy sauce

TIP
When making this, keep the chicken bones for stock and the skin for delicious crispy chicken skin snacks (page 18).

Cut the chicken into finger-sized pieces. Heat 3 tablespoons of the oil in a wok over a high heat. Add the garlic and ginger and stir-fry until fragrant and golden. Add the black bean sauce, Chinese 5-spice, Shaoxing wine or sherry, soy sauce, salt, sugar and chicken, then fry until the chicken is browned but not fully cooked through. Remove the chicken pieces with a slotted spoon and keep them warm.

Add a little more oil if needed, then the red pepper, chillies, green beans, mangetout and mushrooms. Cook for a minute or so, then put the chicken back in the wok and add the prawns, bean sprouts and 100ml of water. Let the mixture bubble, add the cornflour paste and cook until the chicken is cooked through and the sauce has thickened to a silky, clear honey-like consistency that clings to the chicken. Stir in the coriander and spring onions and remove from the heat.

Serve with steamed jasmine rice and chilli oil or soy sauce.

Chicken in the fridge

My wife explains the curious disappearance of food from the fridge and cupboard by saying the mice have been around again. Long ago, I realised that it wasn't mice that were eating the remains of the roast chicken in the fridge and decided on a simple call up the stairs, 'There's chicken in the fridge'. Here are a couple of ideas for using up leftover roast or poached chicken.

Coronation chicken

SERVES 4
as a light lunch salad
or a sandwich filling

300g cold roast or poached
    free-range chicken
1 tbsp sunflower oil
1 small onion, finely chopped
1 tbsp medium curry powder
60ml Chicken stock (page 307)
1 bay leaf
½ tsp tomato paste
25g sultanas

2 tbsp mango chutney
    or apricot jam
125g Mayonnaise (page 309)
50ml double cream, lightly
    whipped, or Greek yoghurt
½ tsp lemon juice
1 tbsp chopped
    coriander leaves
1 tbsp toasted flaked almonds

TIP
Although designed
for chicken, this
curried mayo also
makes a delicious
dressing for
shredded cabbage
and carrots as a
curried coleslaw,
or to dress cold,
boiled new potatoes.

Remove all the bones and skin from the chicken and shred the meat. Heat the oil in a small pan over a medium heat and add the onion. Cook for about 3 minutes until soft but not coloured. Add the curry powder and fry for a minute then add the chicken stock, bay leaf, tomato paste and sultanas. Cook for 5 minutes until the stock has greatly reduced, then stir in the mango chutney or jam. Stir well, remove the bay leaf and leave to cool.

When cool, add the mayonnaise, double cream or yoghurt and the lemon juice. Stir in the shredded chicken and coriander and fold together.

Serve as a sandwich filling with sourdough bread or on a bed of salad, garnished with additional coriander leaves and/or a tablespoon of toasted flaked almonds.

Georgina's chicken sandwich filling

ENOUGH FOR
4 GENEROUS
SANDWICHES

225g cold roasted or poached
   free-range chicken
75g Mayonnaise (page 309)
30g walnuts, chopped
2 celery sticks, finely chopped
1 small dessert apple, such as a Cox,
   peeled and chopped (optional)
4 slices white bread
4 slices granary bread
Salt and black pepper

Remove all the bones and skin from the chicken and shred the meat. In a bowl, mix the chicken with all the other ingredients and season with salt and pepper. Make each sandwich with one slice of white bread and one slice of granary bread.

For a bar snack or buffet, remove the crusts and cut each sandwich into 3 fingers. The filling is also delicious with chopped tarragon or parsley or a pear in place of the apple.

Butter chicken

In Australia, butter chicken is as ubiquitous as chicken tikka masala is in the UK. I make the comparison with reason because they're virtually the same dish. This does lead me to wonder whether all the stories about how chicken tikka masala was invented in the UK are true. The most common one of these is that it was a way Indian restaurants had of refreshing chicken which had been cooked in the tandoor but not sold – by putting it in a spicy tomato sauce and reheating it. In fact, the practice of marinating chicken in spiced yoghurt and cooking it in the intense dry heat of a tandoor, then adding a delicious sauce of slow-cooked garlic and ginger with chilli, coriander, cinnamon, tomato, cream and a paste of cashew and pumpkin seeds, is an Amritsar classic.

SERVES 4-6

4 large free-range chicken
    breasts, skinned, each cut
    into 2 or 3 pieces at an angle

First marinade
Juice of 2 limes
1 tsp Kashmiri chilli powder
1 tsp salt

Second marinade
50g natural yoghurt
50g double cream
4 garlic cloves,
    roughly chopped
5cm root ginger,
    roughly chopped
1 tsp Garam masala
    (page 308 or bought)

1 tsp ground turmeric
¾ tsp ground cumin
½ tsp beetroot powder
    (for colour – optional)

Sauce
50g ghee
5 garlic cloves, finely crushed
5cm root ginger, finely grated
400g tomato passata
½ tsp Kashmiri chilli powder
½ tsp ground coriander
½ tsp ground cumin
½ tsp ground cinnamon
½ tsp Garam masala
    (page 308 or bought)
1 tsp desiccated coconut
1½ tsp salt

25g cashew nuts
25g pumpkin seeds
2 tbsp boiling water
1 tbsp dried fenugreek leaves
½ tsp caster sugar
45ml double cream

To finish
Pinch chat masala
Handful coriander leaves,
    roughly chopped
3cm root ginger,
    finely shredded

TIP
Kashmiri chilli powder is used for its deep brick-red colour. The real thing is quite mild and if you can't get it, you can substitute it with 3 parts sweet paprika and 1 part cayenne pepper.

For the first marinade, mix the lime juice, chilli powder and salt in a large bowl. Add the chicken pieces, then cover and transfer to the fridge to marinate for 1 hour.

For the second marinade, put all the ingredients into a mini food processor. Blend until smooth, then add this to the marinated chicken and stir well to coat. Cover and transfer to the fridge for 4 hours.

Recipe continued overleaf

Preheat your grill to its hottest setting. Thread the chicken on to lightly oiled metal skewers and grill until lightly charred in places but not completely cooked through, as you'll finish cooking them in the sauce.

For the sauce, heat the ghee in a pan over a medium heat. Add the garlic and ginger and fry for a minute, then stir in the passata and bring to a simmer for 5 minutes. Add all the spices, the coconut, salt and 100ml of water and simmer for a further 10 minutes.

In a mini food processor, blend the cashew nuts, pumpkin seeds and boiling water to a paste. Stir this into the sauce, followed by the chicken pieces and another 100ml of water.

Simmer for 10 minutes, or until the chicken is completely cooked through, then stir in the fenugreek, sugar and cream and cook for a further 2 minutes. Sprinkle with chat masala and garnish with fresh coriander and ginger, then serve.

Chettinad chicken

The dish is very peppery, but you know you're experiencing real country cooking. It also has one of those ingredients that is transformational but quite hard to get hold of. It's the lichen off a tree, known as dagarful, kalpasi or stone flower, with a flavour like cinnamon. You can find it online, but if it proves elusive, just add more cinnamon. While I'm writing this, I'm tasting some dagarful out of the jar and noting how faint the taste is, but the reality is if it's not in the dish, you will notice a slight change of fragrance.

SERVES 4

Spice blend
1 tbsp fennel seeds
1 tbsp cumin seeds
1 tbsp coriander seeds
1 tbsp black peppercorns
1 tbsp Kashmiri chilli powder

Chicken
50ml sunflower oil
1 tsp fennel seeds
5cm cinnamon stick
1 tbsp very roughly chopped dagarful or an extra 3cm cinnamon stick
150g shallots, diced
Handful fresh curry leaves

700g skinless, boneless, free-range chicken thighs, cut into 5cm pieces
4 garlic cloves, finely crushed
4cm root ginger, finely grated
1 tsp sugar
1 tsp salt
Steamed basmati rice (page 305), to serve

TIP
If you do have some dagarful, sort through it and remove any pieces of bark before using.

For the spice blend, put the spices in a spice grinder and process to a powder.

For the chicken, heat the oil in a sturdy frying pan over a medium heat. Add the fennel seeds, cinnamon and dagarful, if using, and fry for 1 minute. Add the shallots and curry leaves and fry for 10 minutes until the shallots are softened and golden.

Add the chicken and stir it around in the pan for a minute or so, then add the garlic, ginger, sugar, salt and all of the spice blend and fry for 2 minutes. Add 100ml of water, and cook for about 10–15 minutes, until the chicken is cooked through and the sauce thick, reduced and clinging to the chicken. Keep stirring often and add more splashes of water if needed to stop the chicken sticking to the pan. Serve with rice.

Roast goose with sage & onion stuffing & apple sauce

I can understand why turkey overtook goose as the preferred bird for Christmas in the 19th century – turkeys are much meatier – but I wonder if we're not missing a treat. The flavour of goose, particularly of the fat, is so much more interesting. I've tried lots of different types of stuffing, but in the end I think a simple sage and onion is best. Anything with more punch, like apricots, prunes, chestnuts or sausage meat, merely competes for attention with the sublime flavour of goose.

SERVES 8

1 x 4.5–5kg oven-ready goose
Salt and black pepper

Sage and onion stuffing
3 large onions,
   finely chopped
75g goose fat
400g fresh white breadcrumbs
Finely grated zest of 1 lemon
4 tbsp chopped fresh sage
3 tbsp chopped parsley
1 large egg, beaten
Salt and black pepper

Gravy
4 rashers streaky
   bacon, chopped
Goose giblets
1 small onion, chopped
1 carrot, chopped
2 celery sticks, chopped
2 bay leaves
6 black peppercorns
1 tbsp flour

Apple sauce
4 Cox's apples, peeled,
   cored and sliced

Preheat the oven to 220°C/Fan 200°C. Remove all the clumps of excess fat from the inside of the goose cavity, put it into a pan and leave over a very low heat until melted. Pass it through a fine sieve into a bowl.

Season the goose inside and out with salt and place it on a rack set over a large roasting tin. Roast for 30 minutes. Remove it from the oven and lower the temperature to 180°C/Fan 160°C. Lift the goose on to a board with 2 wooden spoons (you don't want to pierce the skin), pour off the excess fat from the roasting tin and then replace the goose on the rack. Keep the fat for future roast potatoes. Put the goose back in the oven and roast for a further 1½–2 hours, or until the juices run clear when the thickest part of the thigh is pierced with a skewer. Halfway through the cooking time, pour off any excess fat if necessary.

Meanwhile, for the stuffing, fry the onions in about 75g of the goose fat until soft and very lightly browned. Put the breadcrumbs, lemon zest, sage and parsley in a bowl, add the onions and season with salt and pepper to taste. Stir in the beaten egg to bind the mixture together. Spoon the stuffing into a well-greased terrine dish or loaf tin, cover with a lid or foil and set aside to cook later.

To make the giblet stock for the gravy, fry the bacon, giblets and vegetables in a little goose fat until golden brown. Pour off the excess fat, add 1.2 litres of water, the bay leaves and peppercorns and simmer for 1 hour. Strain through a sieve and set aside.

For the apple sauce, put the prepared apples and 100ml of water into the pan and simmer for 12–15 minutes, stirring now and then, until soft and smooth. Season with a pinch of salt and keep it warm.

When the goose is cooked, lift it on to a board, cover it with foil and leave it to rest for at least 20 minutes. Put the stuffing in the oven and cook for 25–30 minutes.

Set the roasting tin on the hob and stir in a tablespoon of flour. Add the giblet stock and deglaze the tin by rubbing the base with a wooden spoon. Season to taste, then pass through a sieve into a warm gravy boat.

Not being a very neat carver, I like to carve in the kitchen and take the slices of goose to the table on a large, warm plate. I cut off the legs and cut each one in half, then carve the breast meat away from each side into long, thin slices. I serve the stuffing, apple sauce and gravy separately, with some roast potatoes (pages 204–5) and vegetables.

Chicken fricassée with morels

For me, this dish seems to be the very heart of French cuisine.
It also happens to be a wonderful partner for a nice white Burgundy.
Traditionally, this was made with poulet de Bresse and Savagnin,
the Jura wine that has a slight sherry-like flavour. My preference
is for Noilly Prat but sherry would be a good substitute.

SERVES 4

20g dried morels
200ml tepid water
40g unsalted butter
4 boneless, free-range
    chicken breasts, skin on
1 banana shallot,
    finely chopped

90g chestnut mushrooms,
    cleaned and quartered
100ml Noilly Prat or dry sherry
130ml Chicken stock (page 307)
150g full-fat crème fraiche
150ml double cream
Salt and black pepper

TIP
I have purposely
written this for
dried morels,
as fresh ones are
hard to get hold
of. They used to
grow in my sandy
garden at Trevose
Head, but it was
so long ago that I
didn't realise what
they were. Using
fresh morels
changes the dish,
as you lose the
smoky flavour of
the dried ones,
but in its place is a
succulent subtlety.

Soak the morels in the tepid water for about 15 minutes,
then drain them in a fine sieve over a bowl. Strain the liquid
and reserve 75ml for the sauce. Rinse the morels under cold
running water to remove any debris and dry them on kitchen
paper. Cut them in half lengthways.

Melt half the butter in a large sauté pan or frying pan.
Fry the chicken breasts, skin-side down, for 2–3 minutes
until light golden brown, then turn them over and repeat on
the other side. Take the chicken out of the pan and set aside.

Add the remaining butter to the pan. Fry the shallot over a
medium heat until softened, then add the morels and chestnut
mushrooms and fry for a few minutes. Add the Noilly Prat or
sherry, the morel soaking liquid and the stock and bring to the
boil, then turn the heat down and simmer for 2–3 minutes.

Stir in the crème fraiche and cream. Put the chicken back in
the pan, along with any juices. Cover the pan and cook the
chicken over a medium heat for about 8 minutes or until
it is cooked through. Season with salt and plenty of black
pepper and serve immediately with rice or potatoes.

Chinese white-cooked chicken
with ginger, spring onions & coriander

This recipe really brings out the best in a free-range chicken. I first had it in a restaurant in Singapore where my then very young sons sat entranced by the number of lizards running across the walls. I love hot and cold food – here, the cold chicken and the hot rice. The three dips and the crisp lettuce with coriander go towards making a fascinatingly complex combination of flavours – the best food ever, especially if you're on a diet!

SERVES 4

5cm root ginger, sliced
1 x 1.5kg free-range chicken
(at room temperature)

Seasonings
1 tsp Sichuan peppercorns
1 tsp black peppercorns

1 tsp Maldon sea salt flakes
4 spring onions, trimmed
1 slice root ginger, peeled
and finely chopped
3 tbsp dark soy sauce
1 medium-hot red bird's-eye
chilli, thinly sliced

1 tsp caster sugar
2 tbsp rice wine vinegar
or white wine vinegar

Salad
½ iceberg lettuce, torn into pieces
Handful fresh coriander leaves

TIP
The secret of the success of this dish is in the cutting of the chicken. The pieces need to be on the bone and you can only cut it up cleanly when the chicken is cold and firm.

Pour 3 litres of water into a pan that's just large enough for the chicken. Add the ginger and bring to the boil. Add the chicken and bring back to the boil, then turn the heat down and simmer for 12 minutes. Take off the heat and let the chicken go cold in the liquid.

Remove the chicken from the pan and cut it into 5cm pieces. You will need a large kitchen knife that's sharp enough to cut through chicken bones; some poultry shears are also useful. Cut off the legs and cut them in 2 at the joint, then cut each thigh section in half. Remove the breasts, still on the bone, from the carcass: to do this, cut horizontally just under the breasts from the cavity end of the chicken, working through all the rib bones and down towards the wings. Separate the 2 breasts by cutting through the breastbone and then cut each breast into 3 pieces. Finally, cut off the wing bones. Arrange all the pieces attractively on a cold serving platter.

Coarsely grind the peppercorns in an electric spice grinder. Stir in the salt and tip the mixture into a dish. Thinly slice the spring onions and mix with the ginger and soy sauce in a second dish. Mix the chilli, sugar and vinegar in a third dish.

Mix the lettuce and coriander in a salad bowl. Serve the chicken and salad with the seasonings and some steamed rice (page 305).

Chicken tinga tacos

This great dish, found all over Mexico, has a deep smoky flavour and is most popular as a filling for tacos but also often appears in tostadas, burritos and tamales. Make a batch using a whole chicken and you can feed a crowd or freeze half for later use.

SERVES 4-6

1 free-range chicken
    (about 1.3kg)
1 onion, peeled and halved
1 carrot, scrubbed and
    cut into 3
1 celery stick, cut in half
1 garlic clove, bashed
1 thyme sprig or bay leaf

Sauce
3-4 tbsp Chipotles en adobo,
    to taste (page 311 or bought)
4 ripe tomatoes, quartered
1 tsp oregano
150ml chicken stock
    (from poaching the chicken)
2 tbsp olive or sunflower oil
2 medium onions, sliced
2 garlic cloves, chopped
Salt and black pepper

To serve
Corn tortillas
Shredded lettuce
Soured cream
Crumbled Lancashire
    or feta cheese
Chopped onion
Chopped coriander
Sliced radishes
Lime wedges

TIP
The sauce is delicious with leftover shredded roast turkey after Christmas. Also consider using chicken tinga as the filling for a cottage pie.

Put the chicken in a large saucepan with the vegetables, garlic and thyme or bay leaf and add cold water to cover. Place the pan over a medium-high heat, bring the water to the boil, then skim off any foam that rises to the top. Turn the heat down, so the surface just blips from time to time, and poach the chicken for 30–40 minutes. Turn off the heat, remove the chicken from the pan and leave it until cool enough to handle.

Strip off the meat and discard the bones – use the skin to make crispy chicken skin (page 18). Strain the stock and reserve 150ml for the sauce – use the rest for soup or freeze it.

For the sauce, put the chipotles en adobo, tomatoes and oregano in a blender with the 150ml of stock and a teaspoon of salt. Whizz to a smooth sauce and set aside.

Heat the oil in a saucepan and fry the sliced onions and garlic over a medium heat until soft and golden. Turn the heat up to high for a minute, then tip in the tomato and chilli mixture. Cook for 5–10 minutes to reduce and thicken the sauce, then add the chicken meat. Taste for seasoning, add black pepper and a little more salt if required. Serve with corn tortillas and the other accompaniments.

Duck confit parmentier

This recipe, one of the highlights of my book Secret France, *came from the village of Auxey-Duresses in Burgundy and is for feeding hungry grape pickers at lunchtime. Lucky them. I think the reason it's so popular is that it's reminiscent of cottage pie but has a sort of Gallic luxuriousness from the use of duck, rather than beef, and plenty of grated Comté cheese on top.*

SERVES 6

4 confit duck legs (page 312 or bought)
4 shallots, chopped
A few fresh thyme sprigs,
    leaves stripped and chopped
175ml red wine
200ml Chicken stock (page 307)

Handful flatleaf parsley, chopped
150–200g Comté cheese, grated
800g potatoes, cut into 5cm chunks
100–125ml warm milk
Salt and Rick's peppermix
    (page 308) or black pepper

Warm the confit duck legs over a gentle heat to release the fat, then pour the fat into clean jam jars. You will need some for this dish, but save the rest for roasting potatoes another day.

Remove the skin from the duck legs and discard it or slice and roast it as a nibble. Pull away the duck meat with a couple of forks and shred it, discarding any bones and gristle.

Heat a couple of tablespoons of the duck fat in a pan, add the shallots and thyme, then season with salt and peppermix or black pepper. Once the shallots are golden, add the wine and stock, bring to the boil and cook for a few minutes. Add the shredded duck meat and chopped parsley and stir well.

Preheat the oven to 210°C/Fan 190°C. Boil the potatoes in a pan of well-salted water for 20–25 minutes until tender. Drain well, then add the warm milk and mash until smooth. Season to taste.

Grease a baking dish with a little duck fat and spoon in the meat mixture, then cover with mashed potatoes. Sprinkle the grated cheese on top and bake for about 25 minutes, until heated through and browned on top. Nice served with stir-fried Brussels sprouts with shallots and chestnuts (page 303).

Christmas

Being somewhat self-obsessed, I was watching a Christmas Special I made called *Rick Stein's Cornish Christmas* last weekend, it being December. The excitement that comes between December 24th and January 1st is beginning to appear, maybe with the turning on of the Christmas lights around Padstow harbour. Until recent years, they were in it, too. They used to have what looked like a glittering Loch Ness monster rising out of the inner harbour, but when the health and safety boys started to look at the meeting of 240-volt electricity with sea water it was gone forever. Shame really, because it's what made our Christmas lights unique.

In that Christmas programme there were two wonderful sequences: first, a wassailing at Cotehele on the Tamar in real snow with a pantomime horse, twice the height of anyone there, and a Green Man pouring cider on the roots of the trees to bring on the fertility of next year's crop. The other sequence was a remarkable Saturnalia in Penzance, where everyone was dressed up as if for the carnival in Venice, but if anything, more sinister, with big black beak masks and ominous-looking capes. It struck me then and now how incredibly ancient and important to us all Christmas is. I guess the real reason for it, as I said in the programme, is that setting aside the Christian traditions, we'd all go quietly mad in the depths of winter without something to celebrate – and celebrate we do. Perhaps one of the reasons Australia is so joyous at this time of year is that not only do they have beautiful weather but all the fun of Christmas too.

It's a time of great joy and happiness – and, for most of us, mind-bending stress. This is partly to do with the annual presence of our dearly beloved relatives, some of whom we don't really get on with, and also the pleasure and frightening reality of cooking so much food for so many people. I must confess that every year I mess up the cooking in one way or another. With me, generally it's to do with the one pint at lunchtime at The Cornish Arms, which always ends in two by which time the realities of cooking goose for 12–14 people have become a mere bagatelle and everybody knows that we won't be eating until about 3.30pm. Before I get locked in to the inevitability of it happening all over again this year, let me suggest some simple rules for a stress-free Christmas lunch, which in no way will I actually follow myself.

First, if there's any way of cooking anything hours or even days beforehand, do it. The only vegetables that you need to cook on the day are plainly boiled brassicas like Brussels sprouts or green cabbage. Any other veg – in my case, braised red cabbage, a purée of carrot and swede, even roasted artichokes or parsnips – you can get ahead with.

Also, make any sauces like bread sauce, cranberry sauce, apple sauce and custard, if you like to serve it with your Christmas pudding. The point is that any time you spend cooking on Christmas Eve or indeed the 22nd or 23rd, is far more time efficient than on Christmas Day itself, when everyone wants to talk and open presents.

I like to cook something quite meaningful on Christmas Eve too, so the need to pre-prepare is even more important. Cooking on Christmas Day is a bit like restaurant cooking. I always think of it as a balance between expediency and perfection, and over Christmas, expediency is king. By the time anyone starts Christmas lunch or dinner there's probably an average of two glasses of something alcoholic in their system, so the little dimming of the flavours caused by earlier cooking will not be noticed. You thrashing around in the kitchen swearing and telling people to get out, in colourful terms, definitely will be. But what is so extraordinary is that it doesn't matter how big the disaster in the kitchen, it's very rare that it spoils things because everybody is so ultimately under the spell of the magic.

Here are some more ideas for things you can make in advance. You certainly wouldn't want to make your Christmas pudding any later than Stir-up Sunday, which is the last Sunday before Advent (late November) and named after the beginning of the collect for the day in the Book of Common Prayer: 'Stir up, we beseech thee, O Lord, the wills of thy faithful people'.

Similarly, Christmas cake needs to be made around the same date to allow plenty of time to moisten the freshly baked cake with brandy, sherry or whatever.

Mince pies can be made a week ahead or longer if you freeze them in the patty tins. They keep perfectly well for a few weeks. Obviously your own mincemeat is going to be the best and it's got to be my mum's shortcrust (page 285), but you can buy really good mincemeat and actually even not so good versions can be enlivened with a bit of grated apple, orange zest and chopped dried fruit.

Every September or thereabouts, since I became at all well-known, I'm asked for a new spin on Christmas, but it really doesn't require any spin whatsoever. Christmas needs to be the same as it ever was. It's the same sort of question we always ask ourselves in restaurants: should the menu consist of those dishes that the customers really love or should it be full of new and exciting ideas? Well, at Christmas there's no contest. It's not a time to be telling anybody how exciting the cooking is; it's a time to be saying how absolutely lovely it is, without question the ultimate comfort food.

People often joke about the interminable nature of leftovers after Christmas Day, especially if turkey was the main event; there's just so much meat on it. And this is when what's left of a whole cooked ham comes into its own. For me, the prospect of at least three days of cold meats with baked potatoes and a winter salad accompanied by as many chutneys, pickles and cold sauces as you can muster on the table is a joy. It's food I could eat forever. I also have an utter passion, since my trip to Mexico, for turkey cooked down with smoky chipotles en adobo and tomato, until it's falling apart and becomes the centre of a Mexican taco – turkey tinga.

Just consider these, hopefully helpful, suggestions:

If you have a frozen turkey it will take a long time to defrost, so take it out of the freezer the day before.

You probably never cook anything else as big as a turkey or goose, so make sure the bird fits in your oven.

Write a timetable for the 24th and 25th and stick it on the fridge. Invest in a timer or use the one on your phone! Don't order too much and don't cook too much.

Don't forget that in the UK at least – sorry to all you Aussies and Kiwis – the outside is your fridge. You'll have far too much food and booze to cram into your normal domestic fridge. It was my wife who observed how easy it is to keep beer and champagne cold outside.

Inveigle others to bring part of the meal. Especially Christmas pudding. It's common practice in Australia and I like it because it gives everyone a sense of being involved.

Don't leave any last-minute vegetables until the last minute. Cook, refresh them and then reheat them in the microwave. Don't tell me you haven't got a microwave.

Make plenty of gravy because it's the one thing you can serve boiling hot, even if plates, veg and turkey are getting a bit on the cool side by the time everyone's been served. Serve the gravy last and plenty of it.

When someone asks, 'Can I do anything?', don't be proud like me and say, 'No, I'm fine.' Have a few suggestions ready, such as 'Will you empty the bin?' or 'Would you be a sweetie and do the washing up?'

On this note, last Christmas at my son Jack's insistence, we plated everything in the kitchen. I wasn't keen because I like a big display of veg in pretty dishes on the table, but it instantly cut down on washing up and waste, and everyone said it was the best Christmas lunch ever. I suspect that's because when you're having a fabulous conversation, having to stop to help yourself is a pain. Also, it's a nice gesture to decide for people how much they need of everything. Otherwise, some are taking too little and others too much.

Remember this little homily from Benjamin Franklin: 'By failing to prepare, you are preparing to fail.'

Duck breast with sea buckthorn berries, chilli & ginger

We were filming my series Rick Stein's Cornwall *at Nancarrow Farm, near Truro, and had been to an orchard where Seth Pascoe grows nothing but sea buckthorn, a coastal berry that's deep orange in colour, sour but with a beautiful aftertaste reminiscent of passion fruit. I realised that their orange acidity would be great with duck because of its high fat content. I remembered a dish I'd done for my book* Far Eastern Odyssey *– Vietnamese braised duck with orange – and came up with a sautéed duck breast with lots of Southeast Asian flavours. It's really rather good. Serve with wok-fried greens.*

SERVES 2

2 duck breasts
(about 150g each)
Sunflower oil
100g sea buckthorn berries
500ml freshly squeezed
orange juice
5cm root ginger, peeled
and finely chopped
1 large garlic clove, finely chopped
1 lemongrass stalk, finely sliced

2 spring onions, white parts
finely sliced on the diagonal,
green parts set aside
1 bird's-eye chilli, finely chopped
2 star anise, broken
1 tbsp Thai fish sauce
1–2 tbsp caster sugar
(depending on tartness
of berries)
Salt and black pepper

Wok-fried greens
1 tbsp sunflower oil
1 large garlic clove, chopped
4cm root ginger, peeled
and chopped
1 small head spring greens,
finely sliced
3 or 4 stalks curly kale, finely
sliced (woody stems removed)
2 tsp soy sauce (or more, to taste)

TIP
If you don't have
sea buckthorn
berries, use
600ml of orange
juice and add half
a teaspoon of
cornflour mixed
with a little of the
measured orange
juice to thicken
the sauce. Orange
juice hasn't got
the viscosity of
sea buckthorn.

Season the breasts and place them in a pan brushed with oil. Cook for 4–5 minutes until the skin is brown and some fat has been rendered, then turn them over and cook for 2 or 3 minutes more. Remove and set aside, covered, to rest for 5–10 minutes.

In a separate pan, simmer the berries and juice for 5 minutes until softened. Pass through a sieve and discard the seeds.

Pour off the excess fat from the duck pan and add the ginger, garlic, lemongrass, white parts of the spring onions, chilli and star anise and fry until softened. Add the orange and buckthorn juice and simmer to reduce. Add fish sauce and sugar to taste.

Slice the rested duck breasts on the diagonal and add them to the pan to cook through in the sauce. Throw in the green spring onion tops and let them wilt.

Heat the oil in a wok, add the garlic and ginger, then stir-fry for a minute. Add the greens and kale and stir for a minute or so, then season with soy sauce. Serve with the duck.

Duck noodle soup

This was a star turn when we were filming at Or Tor Kor market in Bangkok. David, the director, and I had two bowlfuls each, so excited were we by it, but that led me to think it would be better to serve it as a main course than a soup. I often make this at home and I confess to doing the unpardonable thing common in Southeast Asia of sprinkling it with Aromat, which is basically MSG. I'm sure I shouldn't be saying this but the reality is that MSG is very much part of the taste of the cooking in countries like Vietnam, Cambodia and Thailand, and I recently read an article in the NY Times pointing out that it is no more bad for you than salt.

SERVES 6

1 x 2.25kg oven-ready duck
2 tbsp hoisin sauce
Salt and black pepper

Soup
2 tbsp sunflower oil
8 garlic cloves, thinly sliced
300g dried fine egg
noodles or 400g fine
ready-to-use noodles
2 litres Duck broth (page 307)

3 tbsp Thai fish sauce
1 tbsp dark soy sauce
4 tsp rice vinegar
1 tbsp soft brown sugar
1 red bird's-eye chilli,
thinly sliced
3cm root ginger,
finely shredded
400g fresh bean sprouts
1 bunch coriander,
roughly chopped

6 fat spring onions, halved
lengthways and thinly
sliced on the diagonal

To serve
2 red bird's-eye chillies,
thinly sliced
3 tbsp Thai fish sauce
3 tbsp rice vinegar
Dried chilli flakes
Soft brown sugar

Preheat the oven to 230°C/Fan 210°C. Pull out any excess fat from the cavity of the duck and season inside with a little salt and pepper. Place the duck on a rack in a roasting tin and brush all over with the hoisin sauce and season with salt.

Roast for 20 minutes, then lower the temperature to 180°C/Fan 160°C and continue to roast for 1 hour and 10 minutes. Pour off the fat from the roasting tin into a bowl.

Leave the duck until cool enough to handle, then cut off the legs and cut away the breasts in one piece and slice thinly. Pull the meat off the duck legs and cut into bite-sized pieces and set aside with the breast meat. Use the leg bones and carcass, to make the broth (page 307).

Recipe continued overleaf

Heat the oil in a small frying pan over a medium heat, add the garlic and fry until crisp and golden. Lift the garlic out with a slotted spoon and place on kitchen paper. Put the noodles in a large bowl and pour over boiling water from a kettle to cover and leave them for 3–4 minutes until tender. Drain, mix them with a little oil and set aside. (No need for this soaking stage if you're using 'ready-to-use' noodles.)

For the flavourings to serve alongside the duck, mix 1 sliced bird's-eye chilli with the fish sauce and the other with the rice vinegar. Put these and the chilli flakes and sugar into 4 small serving dishes.

Put the duck broth into a pan and bring to the boil. Reduce to a simmer and add the fish sauce, soy sauce, rice vinegar, sugar, chilli and ginger. Turn the heat down to low and leave for 5 minutes.

Drop the noodles and bean sprouts into the stock and heat through for 3 minutes. Ladle the soup into 6 warmed soup bowls, distributing the noodles and bean sprouts as evenly as possible. Top with the duck breast and leg meat, fried garlic, coriander and spring onions and serve with the flavourings.

NB. If you don't have time to make the duck stock, just use 2 litres of chicken stock and add the fish sauce, soy sauce, rice vinegar, sugar, chilli and ginger as above. Bring to a simmer for about 5 minutes, then turn the heat off and leave to infuse for 20–30 minutes. Then continue with the recipe as above.

Chapter Five
MEAT

Eating at our pub, The Cornish Arms, between the lockdowns was for the most part spent sitting in a gale, wearing a vest, a thick shirt and a jersey, my blue quilted Barbour jacket, a scarf and a woolly hat. Being Australian, Sas wore even more layers, including a variety of different coloured beanies – a couple of them with little sparkling rabbit's ears. Rugs and heaters were supplied and at one point, I thought about providing hot-water bottles too.

All of it was worth it to be eating with other people and also because of my favourite starter there – devilled kidneys with mushrooms. To me, it's a bit like when you see sticky toffee pudding on a menu– it's what you really want but you feel a bit shamefaced about ordering it because you have it every time. The kidney dish came from cooking at home on Sundays, the one day in the week when I do cook something a bit special for breakfast. The devil in the detail is just cayenne pepper but was there ever a better vehicle for lamb's kidneys? You'll find the recipe on page 211.

Inevitably, when tucking in with others of a similar age, talk will come round to lamenting that younger generations don't eat offal like we do. In fact, they don't eat meat like we do either and many of them don't eat it at all. Time will come, I'm told, when most of the meat we eat will have been cultivated in a factory. I don't think I'd find it hard to get used to that if it put a stop to the intensive rearing of animals and provided there was still the opportunity to buy meat from well-reared, free-range animals for my Sunday roast, my Christmas ham glazed with mustard, cloves and brown sugar (page 183), or for braised beef short ribs with red wine and caramelised shallots and carrots (page 189).

And times and tastes change. When I first wrote the recipe for belly pork on page 185 some 20 years ago, belly pork was as cheap a cut of meat as you could get. I think it's a bit like the discovery of gurnard 30 years ago – then it was a fish only used for baiting lobster and crab pots, but now, like belly pork, it's expensive. I feel partly to blame for the gurnard, but with belly pork I think it is more because people have realised just how delicious it is.

Putting the recipes together for this chapter has been a mixture of elation at what I've chosen and regret at having to leave out some much-loved dishes. It contains 23 recipes and is a bit like a greatest hits compilation. As with all the chapters in this book, the intention is to try to cover what my family and I cook at home, not just for big dinners but for whatever we are doing. I've also included my son Charlie's minced pork chilli and garlic dish with Thai basil – pad kra pao (page 195) – which is a great favourite.

Not all the dishes are new. Some have appeared in my other books but I've recooked all of them and made some, mostly slight, changes. These are often because I've realised that a lot of the processes I would have described in detail have become easily understood, as nearly everyone cooks much more knowledgeably these days.

Fennel & sausage ragù with tagliatelle

This is the sort of pasta dish I always seek out in Italian restaurants because I love fennel-flavoured sausages. At home, I find it's easiest to reproduce the flavour by using good-quality sausage meat and adding fennel seeds, chilli, garlic, rosemary, salt and black pepper. What I love about this dish is that it is nurtured with plenty of cream and served with home-made egg tagliatelle.

SERVES 4

400g coarse pork sausage
    meat or 400g sausages,
    skins removed
1 tbsp olive oil
1 small onion, finely chopped
1 large garlic clove, grated
2 celery sticks, chopped
¾ tsp fennel seeds,
    roughly ground
¼ tsp chilli flakes
1 fresh rosemary sprig,
    leaves finely chopped

150ml dry white wine
150ml double cream
150ml Chicken stock
    (page 307)
50g Parmesan cheese,
    freshly grated, to serve
Salt and black pepper

Pasta dough
400g 00 pasta flour
4 eggs, lightly beaten
2 tsp salt

TIP
This is also very good with bought dried pasta, cooked according to the packet instructions.

For the pasta, combine the flour, eggs and salt in a food processor. Tip the mixture out on to a work surface and bring it together in a ball of dough. Cover with cling film and leave to rest for 20–30 minutes. Roll out the pasta into a couple of sheets about 2mm thick. Run them through a pasta machine, or use a knife to cut them into 5mm-wide ribbons. Hang them over the back of a chair or a broom handle to dry.

Break up the sausage meat into a large ovenproof pan and add half the oil to start with. If the sausage meat is fatty, it might render quite a bit of fat and you won't need the rest of the oil; if it's quite dry, you will. Cook over a medium heat for about 10 minutes, stirring from time to time. Add the onion, garlic, celery, fennel seeds, chilli flakes and rosemary, season, then cook for a further 15 minutes. Pour in the wine, cook for few minutes until reduced by half, then add the cream and stock. Put a lid on the pan and simmer gently for half an hour – take the lid off near the end if the sauce needs thickening up.

Cook the tagliatelle in plenty of boiling salted water for about 4 minutes until al dente. Drain, add to the ragù pan and mix. Serve in warmed bowls with freshly grated Parmesan.

Macaroni cheese with bacon & breadcrumbs

This is a recipe from California which is just so delicious, mainly I think because it flows a little bit when you spoon it out – it's sort of silky rather than stodgy. To begin with I was a bit put off – too much sauce, too much cream, too much cheese, not a bit like Italy. But then, while into my second glass of Sonoma-Cutrer Russian River Chardonnay, I began to think to myself, this isn't Italy, it's California and if they want to reinterpret classic dishes why shouldn't they? Someone I met in Palermo once told me that the secret of a good Italian dish, as taught to her by her grandmother, is esagerare, *meaning put more of everything in, and so it is with this recipe – there's masses of cheese and plenty of bacon.*

SERVES 6-8

90g butter, plus extra
  for greasing
90g plain flour
1 heaped tsp Dijon mustard
1.5 litres whole milk
100ml double cream
1 bay leaf

400g mature Cheddar, grated
5-6 rasps of nutmeg
500g macaroni
100g lardons or pancetta, diced
50g white breadcrumbs
50g Parmesan cheese, grated
Salt and black pepper

TIP
To make a vegetarian version, substitute the bacon with sliced sundried tomatoes.

Melt the butter in a large pan and stir in the flour to make a roux. Cook for a minute, add the mustard, then take the pan off the heat and whisk in the milk and cream. Add the bay leaf, put the pan back over the heat and cook the sauce, stirring constantly, until it boils and is thick and bubbling. Take off the heat, remove the bay leaf and stir in the Cheddar and nutmeg. Keep stirring until the cheese has melted; the sauce will thicken considerably. Season with pepper.

Preheat the oven to 200°C/Fan 180°C. Cook the macaroni in lots of salted boiling water for about 10 minutes or until al dente, then drain well. Fry the lardons or pancetta until crisp and add them to the cheese sauce.

Stir the cooked macaroni into the sauce, then pour into a buttered ovenproof dish measuring about 35 x 20cm. Mix the breadcrumbs with the Parmesan and scatter over the top. Bake for 15–20 minutes until golden and bubbling. If you've prepared this in advance and let it cool before baking, increase the cooking time to 25–30 minutes. Serve with a green salad.

Salad of Parma ham with rocket, tomatoes, figs, Gorgonzola & basil

I'd love to know who first invented this – for me, it's the perfect main course salad. I'm surprised it doesn't have a proper name, like Caesar salad does, because the basic structure of it appears in so many restaurant menus and recipe books: Parma ham, some interesting salad leaves like rocket or endive, tomatoes, a rich creamy cheese, such as Gorgonzola, Taleggio or burrata, and a sweet fruit element, such as figs or peaches. I think pears work better than apples; the exotic fragrance of a ripe pear is what you are aiming for.

SERVES 6

200g mixed bitter leaves
   (cime di rapa, puntarelle,
   radicchio, chicory or curly endive)
100g rocket leaves
6 ripe figs, quartered, or 2 ripe
   white peaches, stoned and
   sliced, or 2 pears, peeled,
   cored and sliced
10 slices Parma ham, torn
50g Parmesan cheese shavings

90g Gorgonzola dolce,
   cut into chunks
500g ripe tomatoes, core
   removed, cut into wedges
1 tbsp capers, drained
Handful basil leaves
40g toasted pine nuts
60ml olive oil
30ml sweet aged balsamic vinegar
Salt and black pepper

TIP
I know that this is blindingly obvious but everything needs to be at room temperature.

Mix the bitter leaves and rocket in a large serving bowl. Top with the figs, peaches or pears, the ham, Parmesan, Gorgonzola, tomatoes, capers, basil leaves and pine nuts. Season to taste and drizzle with olive oil and balsamic vinegar, then toss well and serve.

Braised belly pork
with soy & black vinegar

I got this recipe when on a filming trip to Shanghai where I visited a restaurant run by chef Anthony Zhao. Apparently Shanghainese cooking isn't particularly well regarded in China, but I certainly didn't notice anything second rate, although I don't have a massive knowledge of Chinese cuisine. Everything was great, particularly some dumplings filled with pork, prawns and some stock so that your mouth was filled with a glorious squirt of flavour as you bit into them. But the star turn for me was this dish which is also known as red braised pork and was Mao Zedong's favourite. The belly pork needs to be well layered with fat – in Shanghai they call it five-layer belly pork.

SERVES 4

2 tbsp sunflower oil
6 spring onions, cut on the diagonal into 3cm lengths
10g root ginger, peeled and finely sliced
5cm cinnamon stick
1 star anise
1 bay leaf

600g belly pork with rind off, cut into 3cm pieces
4 tbsp dark soy sauce
3 tbsp Shaoxing rice wine or dry sherry
½ tsp salt
40g soft light brown sugar
¾ tbsp black vinegar

TIP
If you can't get black vinegar, use rice vinegar or at a pinch, balsamic, which is sweeter so cut back on the sugar by 5g.

Heat the oil in a wide pan. Add the spring onions, ginger, cinnamon, star anise and bay leaf and slowly sauté until the spring onions are golden brown and fragrant. Add the pork and lightly colour the outside of the meat.

Add the soy sauce, rice wine, salt, sugar, black vinegar and enough water to barely cover the meat, then stir. Simmer for 30 minutes with a lid on the pan. Remove the lid and simmer for a further 15–20 minutes or until the liquid has reduced down to a sticky glaze that generously coats the pork. Serve immediately with rice.

Waste not, want not

Tonight I'm making bolognese sauce for four of us. I'm not entirely sure what's going to go into it because I haven't looked in the fridge yet. I've got a recipe for ragù bolognese (page 186), but I don't always follow it exactly. It's got pork and beef mince, chopped carrots, celery, onion and garlic, smoked bacon, tinned tomatoes and tomato paste, salt and pepper and red wine and that's about it. The recipe first appeared in my book *From Venice to Istanbul,* and came from the grandmother of a chef at a very ordinary commercial hotel in Ravenna.

I may be completely out of order here, but I know a lot of my friends would agree, in thinking that a ragù is where things get used up, basically anything that can go into a rich, red wine sauce. So, in confessional mode, here's what might go into mine: chopped mushrooms, obviously, in many different varieties and certainly ones that have partially dried out. Then there are livers – chicken or duck liver, but even lamb's or pig's. The secret here is to keep this element restrained – my mother always put chicken liver, very finely chopped, into pasta sauce and provided it's a small amount it gives it a nice bite. Then there are Parmesan rinds; you never need to throw these away, just drop them into the simmering sauce for half an hour or so and they give the sauce a salty umami flavour. When the rind has gone really soft you can retrieve it and it's rather nice to eat. I'm always keen to add a small amount of cream or yoghurt, too, if it's hanging around in the fridge.

I'm not at all particular about what sort of red wine I use, and sometimes I add white wine anyway. I also have two bottles of what the Italians call vincotto, one red and one white. For this, I take all the almost finished bottles of wine hanging around the house and cook the remnants down very slowly with a cup of sugar until the mixture becomes a deep red syrup or, in the case of white wine, a honey-coloured syrup. You'll find a recipe on page 312 and it makes all the difference in boosting the vinosity of a stew or even a white wine sauce for fish or chicken fricassee.

Ragù also allows me to make use of all those little dried ends of salami or chorizo which, once chopped up, will rehydrate in the sauce. The recipe doesn't mention stock, but I tend to use up any leftover chicken or beef stock in my ragù. For herbs, I favour thyme or rosemary and as a great fan of a very similar Greek version of ragù bolognese called kokkinisto, I will quite often vary the pasta sauce with copious amounts of Greek wild thyme.

I do the same thing with pimentón to give the sauce a Spanish flavour. This is also a good opportunity to empty some of the tins that my wife buys regularly – in fact, every time she finds yet another pretty red and yellow tin with some Spanish beauty pictured on the front. Other enthusiastic additions are soy sauce, especially if the colour looks a bit wan, and even HP sauce but very sparingly. The basic principle is to get a deep-flavoured, deep-coloured sauce to accompany the pasta. Personally, I think ragù bolognese is all about the pasta rather than the sauce – that and plenty of freshly grated Parmesan or sometimes pecorino.

For me, there's something completely satisfying about cooking at home in a way that allows me to waste very, very little. This involves recycling or using up food to the point where nothing goes into the dustbin and only inedible food goes into the compost bin.

The problem these days is that food has become, for many people, relatively cheap and therefore the emphasis on not wasting it has become less important. But I guess because of my upbringing with my parents, who lived through the second world war, it doesn't matter how little money I save by not throwing food out, it just seems wrong to do it and absolutely right to use everything I can.

This can cause problems with my wife who, being a tad younger than me, finds it very difficult to deal with wrinkly, shrivelled mushrooms, yoghurt that's so out of date it's nearly catching itself up next year, little blocks of rock-hard cheese, garlic cloves and ginger almost dried out, excessively bendy carrots, squishy tomatoes and red peppers, perfect for a sofrito next week, no rush! I'm constantly having to justify all the, to coin an Australian phrase, 'dagginess' in the fridge, but the reality is that all this horror often leads to spectacularly wonderful dishes. The only problem is that I never write down what I've put into them and could not possibly repeat what I've made.

It's not just ragù that works with this mindset, of course. It's also stir-fried rice dishes like nasi goreng (page 99), classic fish soup (page 45), risottos, and any amount of soups and stews; minestrone (page 47) is a great one.

The other great avoider of waste, though, is the deep freeze, so mine is filled with tiny packets of such things as a single chicken liver, prawn shells, the outer frills that lie around a scallop, chicken carcasses and ends of bread for breadcrumbs. There are pieces of sponge for trifles, ends of puff pastry (for cheese straws, perhaps), little plastic boxes of tomato, chilli and red pepper labelled with notes, such as 'for tacos', 'breakfast sauce' or 'fish soup veg'. I'm rummaging in my freezer as I write this and there's a big box of veg stew dated 2018, but that won't be a dish in it's own right, and a packet saying ham stock 2018 – not sure that it is even from 2018 because my writing isn't great. I have a bag of lovely lobster stock and some salt cod from the same year and a slice of duck parfait that I have to say that even I won't be using.

In a way I'm slightly dreading Christmas because I'm roasting three geese this year and, knowing my parsimonious nature, everything we don't eat will be turned into stock and I'm not sure I've got enough room in the freezer. I might even have to buy another one!

'It doesn't matter how little money I save by not throwing food out, it just seems wrong to do it and absolutely right to use everything I can.'

Pork in milk

This is one of the dishes I really want people to try, even if, on first impression, you might think the combination of milk and pork doesn't sound appetising. What happens is that as you slow-cook the pork, which is two-thirds immersed, the milk curdles and gradually the liquid reduces until you are left with a ricotta-like cooked milk flavoured with fennel, garlic and sage. The pork is almost falling apart and you serve it in thick slices with the grainy sauce all around. It is totally wonderful, particularly if eaten with something bitter like the radicchio and anchovy salad on page 302. Serve with plain boiled or mashed potatoes or polenta.

SERVES 8

2kg pork loin, skin and half the
thickness of fat removed,
then rolled and tied
30g butter
1 tbsp olive oil
6 garlic cloves, crushed
or finely chopped

6 sage leaves, torn
1 tbsp fennel seeds
Zest of 1 lemon
1 litre whole milk
Juice of 1 lemon
Salt and black pepper

TIP
It really does
need to be whole
(full-fat) milk to
get the desired
curdled result.

Season the pork all over with 1½ teaspoons of salt and some black pepper. In a large flameproof casserole dish over a high heat, brown the pork on all sides in the butter and oil. Reduce the heat and add the garlic. Stir briefly – and don't allow it to burn – then add the sage leaves, fennel seeds and lemon zest.

In a separate pan, scald the milk: bring it to a simmer then turn off the heat. Pour the scalded milk and lemon juice over the pork, bring to the boil, then immediately turn the heat down to a very gentle simmer. Place a lid, slightly ajar, on the pan and cook for 1½–2 hours, turning the meat halfway through the time. Keep checking every 20–30 minutes to make sure the milk isn't burning on the bottom of the pan.

At the end of the cooking time the milk should be curdled and look like ricotta and the pork should be meltingly soft. Remove the meat from the pan and leave it to rest, covered, for 20 minutes. Check the sauce and if it has not reduced enough, transfer it to a clean pan and reduce further. Taste and season with salt if necessary. Serve the pork thickly sliced with the curdled milk sauce.

Pork chops with savoy cabbage & sloes

I came up with this recipe to highlight the pork from Mangalitsa pigs which I had filmed at a brilliant farm restaurant called Coombeshead, just outside Launceston in Cornwall. Since all of us have been subjected to nothing but very lean pork for the last 20 years, it's really quite special to come across pigs that are reared almost more for their fat than their lean, and the meat was a reminder of how good free-range pork can be. Most felicitous too that I was filming in September when there was a bumper crop of sloes – perfect to cut the fattiness of the meat.

SERVES 2

1 small savoy cabbage (about 400g), core removed and shredded
1–2 tbsp sunflower oil
2 pork chops (each about 250g)
Good handful sloes, bullaces or unripe plums

15g butter (only needed if the pork chops don't yield much fat)
1 banana shallot, finely chopped
1 large garlic clove, finely chopped or grated
100ml red wine
A few fresh thyme sprigs

100–120ml Chicken stock (page 307)
1 tbsp honey or soft brown sugar
Salt and black pepper

TIPS

Don't even think of throwing the excess fat away. Render it down for the best lard you're ever going to eat.

Pick and prepare sloes or bullaces when in season, then freeze them.

Boil the cabbage in salted water for 3 minutes, then drain. Put it in a pan with the oil, stir to coat, then season. Cover and cook over a very low heat for 20 minutes to soften.

Prepare the fruit by removing the stones with your fingers or a cherry stoner, or poach it for a few minutes in little water first. This makes it easier to remove the stones. Keep the flesh and the liquid, if poaching, for the sauce and discard the stones.

Season the pork chops on both sides. Cook them in a frying pan for 4–6 minutes on each side (depending on thickness), or until they reach an internal temperature of 71°C. Transfer the chops to a plate, cover with foil and leave to rest for about 5 minutes while you make the sauce. Leave the fat in the pan.

You want about a tablespoon of pork fat in the frying pan – just pour off any excess and keep it for another recipe. If the chops haven't yielded much fat, add the butter. Add the shallot and garlic and soften for a minute or so, then add the remaining ingredients, including the fruit and any poaching water. Bring to the boil and simmer for 3–5 minutes, then season to taste. Serve the sauce with the chops and cabbage.

Pork souvlaki with oregano

This is a recipe from northern Greece. I was quite taken with the amount of chilli in the marinade and I've now gone completely off-piste by adding pimentón to it . However, the accompaniments I include are what you will find most commonly with souvlaki, the ones that are served in pitta bread anyway. I went through a phase of trying to make my own chips to go with souvlaki, but I find chips are one of the hardest things to make at home. You have to get the right potatoes, Maris Pipers, for example, but they also have to be in the right condition. Added to that is the uncomfortableness of deep-frying in the kitchen unless you have a restaurant-quality extraction system. If I do any deep-frying I tend to do it outside, as I hate the smell of hot oil wafting through the house so much. Far better to serve with pitta or flatbread, tzatziki and a little salad.

SERVES 4

400g pork shoulder, cut into 3cm cubes

Marinade
30ml fresh lemon juice
2 tbsp olive oil
2 tsp dried oregano
1 tsp ground cumin
1 tsp cayenne pepper
1 tsp pimentón
1 small garlic clove, grated
1 tsp salt

To serve
2 tomatoes, sliced
1 little gem lettuce, chopped
1 small red onion, finely sliced
chilli flakes or 1 red chilli,
    finely sliced
Tzatziki (page 311)
Pitta or flatbread

Mix all the marinade ingredients in a bowl and add the meat. Marinate for an hour or so, then thread the cubes of meat on to skewers. Grill on a barbecue or under a hot grill for 10–12 minutes, turning until cooked through. Serve with the accompaniments suggested above.

Around Easter, souvlaki are often made with lamb. For these, I suggest leaving out the marinade and just rubbing the meat with salt, pepper, lemon juice and oregano and allow it to absorb the flavours while the barbecue heats up.

Glazed Christmas ham

Slices of hot ham with baked potatoes and salad are, I would suggest, almost as evocative of Christmas as turkey. My childhood memories are that we always had glazed ham served with spiced red cabbage on Christmas Eve, but since I became a fish cook I've adopted the continental enthusiasm for fish on that night, preferably turbot cooked in a turbot kettle and served with hollandaise sauce. Ham is now something to look forward to on Boxing Day. I have to admit to having spent four or five years of my life in the 80s and early 90s cooking about two hams a week for the deli I opened in Padstow, and never did I really work out how to stop my brown sugar and mustard glaze sliding off the ham in the hot oven and burning in the roasting tray. Now I put water in the tin so at least the mixture doesn't burn and I can remove it.

SERVES UP TO 10

1 x 2.8kg unsmoked boned
  and rolled gammon
600ml cider
1½ tsp black peppercorns
6 cloves
½ tsp chilli flakes
4 bay leaves

Glaze
3 tsp English mustard
60g soft brown sugar
12–15 cloves

Gravy
About 1 litre strained
  cooking liquor
25g unsalted butter
1 tsp cornflour (optional

TIP
Ham cooking liquor is versatile in the same way as Thai fish sauce is for boosting flavour. I use it in tomato sauces, gravy and even sometimes in a fish soup.

Some gammon can be quite salty. To test it, cut a thin slice from the end of the raw joint and add it to a pan of simmering water. Cook for about 5 minutes, then taste. If it's too salty, soak the joint in cold water overnight and then drain.

Put the gammon in a large pan or stockpot and add the cider and enough water to cover the meat. Add the peppercorns, cloves, chilli flakes and bay leaves and bring to the boil. Immediately turn down the heat so that the water is barely simmering and cook for about 1½–2 hours or until the internal temperature when tested with a probe in the centre of the meat registers 65°C. Turn off the heat and allow the meat to cool in the water. Remove the cooled meat but don't throw the liquor away.

Recipe continued overleaf

Preheat the oven to 210°C/Fan 190°C. Mix the mustard and sugar together in a small bowl. Using a sharp knife, remove any string from the meat and then take off the rind. Score the fat with a sharp knife in a diamond pattern and stud the meat with a clove at each intersection.

Set the meat on a wire rack or trivet in a roasting tin and add about 120ml of water to the tin. Then, using the back of a spoon or a brush, spread two-thirds of the glaze over the fat. Transfer to the preheated oven for 15 minutes, then brush with the remaining glaze. Top up the water if necessary and return to the oven for a further 10 minutes until browned.

Remove the tin from the oven and allow the ham to cool before carving, or serve hot with gravy. To make the gravy, reduce a litre or so of the strained cooking liquor by half, then whisk in 25g of unsalted butter. You may like to thicken the gravy slightly with a teaspoon of cornflour slaked in a little cold water.

By the way, you can use the strained cooking liquor (if not too salty) to make a tasty soup. Add soaked green or yellow split peas (see the cooking instructions on the packet) and a chopped onion and cook for about an hour or so until tender. Whizz in a blender, season to taste and add any chopped offcuts of ham.

Crisp Chinese roast pork
with steamed rice

I think the recent popularity of belly pork is down to the extreme loveliness of dishes like this. Here, a piece of belly pork is dry-marinated with Chinese spice, then slow-roasted to produce crisp and tender roast meat.

SERVES 4-6

1 x 1.5kg piece of thick belly pork, the rind scored at 1cm intervals by your butcher
1 tbsp Sichuan peppercorns
1 tsp black peppercorns
2 tbsp Maldon sea salt flakes

2 tsp Chinese 5-spice powder
2 tsp caster sugar
½ tsp fine salt
Steamed Chinese greens in oyster sauce (page 303) and Steamed rice (page 305), to serve

TIP
If all else fails in crisping up the crackling, heat the grill to high and put the pork on a low shelf to crisp up the rind.

Spike the skin of the pork with a fine skewer or a larding needle as many times as you can. Go right into the fat but not so deep that you pierce the flesh. Put the pork in a colander in the sink, then pour a kettle of boiling water (about 1.8 litres) over the skin. Leave it to drain and then dry it well.

Heat a dry, heavy-based frying pan over a high heat. Add both lots of peppercorns and shake them around for a few seconds until they darken slightly and start to smell aromatic. Grind to a fine powder in a spice grinder, tip them into a bowl and stir in the salt, spice and sugar. Place the pork flesh-side up on a tray and rub it all over with the spice mix. Cover with foil and leave it in the fridge to marinate for 8 hours or overnight.

Preheat the oven to 200°C/Fan 180°C. Turn the pork skin-side up and place it on a rack in a roasting tin containing 1–2cm of water. Sprinkle half a teaspoon of fine salt over the rind. Roast the pork for 15 minutes, then lower the oven temperature to 180°C/Fan 160°C and roast it for a further 2 hours, topping up the water in the tin now and then.

Turn the oven up to 230°C/Fan 210°C and continue to roast the pork for a further 15 minutes. Then remove it and leave it to cool a little – it's best served warm. Cut the pork into bite-sized pieces and serve with Chinese greens and rice.

Ragù Bolognese

This recipe comes from Ravenna, part of Emilia-Romagna of which Bologna is the capital, so I think it can claim to be as authentic as any other recipe from that region. What I like is its simplicity, and I do make it like this from time to time, but I suspect most Italians would add other bits and pieces from the fridge, just as I often do. Here are a few suggestions: courgettes, mushrooms, red peppers, chilli, pimentón, stock, chicken livers, ham, leeks, shallots, soy sauce, Worcester sauce, a splash of cream, chorizo or any other charcuterie, Parmesan rind.

SERVES 6-8

60ml olive oil
1 celery stick, finely chopped
2 carrots, finely chopped
1 medium onion,
  finely chopped
1 large garlic clove,
  finely chopped
300g beef mince
300g lean minced pork,
  or pork sausage meat

100g smoked bacon
  (as lean as possible),
  finely chopped
100ml red wine
500ml passata or tinned
  chopped tomatoes
2 tbsp tomato paste
1 sprig rosemary and/
  or thyme
Salt and black pepper

To serve
450-600g tagliatelle
  or spaghetti
Parmesan cheese, freshly
  grated, to taste

TIP
I really like ragù
Bolognese with
fusilli. I love the
way the spirals
trap the sauce.

In a heavy-based pan, heat the olive oil and fry the celery, carrots, onion and garlic over a medium heat for about 10 minutes. Add the beef, the pork or sausage meat and the bacon and brown them, stirring occasionally. Season with a teaspoon of salt and plenty of black pepper, then add the wine, passata, tomato paste, herbs and 60ml of water.

Continue cooking over a low heat for 1–2 hours with a lid on the pan – the longer the cooking time the softer the meat will become. Check periodically and add a little more water if the mixture is looking too dry.

Cook the pasta according to the instructions on the packet and serve with the ragù, topped with grated Parmesan and more black pepper.

Vietnamese beef noodle soup
Pho bo

Pho, and in my opinion risotto for that matter, is all about the quality of the broth. That's where the time is taken up and I tend to make a large quantity of broth and freeze what I'm not going to use immediately. Incidentally, pho is the best dish I know for those on a diet. The overall impression is freshness from the vegetables and raw meat or fish that you add at the last minute. You feel it's not fattening and is extremely good for you. It's almost cleansing.

SERVES 4

About 2 litres Asian beef broth (page 308)
300g dried 1cm-wide flat rice noodles (banh pho)
200g fillet steak
Handful each of Thai sweet basil leaves, mint leaves and coriander leaves

5 red bird's-eye chillies, thinly sliced
2 limes, cut into wedges
8 spring onions, trimmed and sliced, green and white parts separated
4 tbsp Thai fish sauce
100g bean sprouts

TIP
You can also add a couple of raw prawns per person or a few thin slices of raw salmon fillet with the steak, before ladling over the hot broth.

Bring the Asian beef broth to the boil in a pan. Drop the noodles into a separate pan of unsalted boiling water, turn off the heat and leave to soak for 10 minutes or until just tender.

Meanwhile, finely slice the steak. Put the herbs, chillies and lime wedges into separate small bowls.

Add the white part of the spring onions and the fish sauce to the broth. Drain the noodles and divide between 4 deep soup bowls. Top with the sliced beef, the green part of the spring onions and the bean sprouts. Ladle over the hot stock and serve with the garnishes, so each person can add whatever they like.

Braised beef short ribs

It's important to get the right short ribs for this. They are the elongated section of the ribs on a forequarter of beef, often called the Jacob's Ladder and comprising nine or ten rib bones. The best ones come from the middle section. This is really similar to a French daube, except that the meat is served falling off the bone. It looks great and when reheated it tastes almost better than the first time round.

SERVES 8–10

4 tbsp olive oil
9–10 beef short ribs on the bone
1 large onion, roughly chopped
2 carrots, roughly chopped
1 celery stick, roughly chopped
4 garlic cloves, bashed with
   the heel of a knife
1 bottle of red wine
400g tinned tomatoes
2 strips of thinly pared orange peel
2 bay leaves
3 thyme sprigs
1.5 litres Beef stock (page 308)
1 tsp salt
1 tsp sugar
1 tsp Rick's peppermix (page 308)

Vegetable and pancetta garnish
200g baby carrots
5 shallots, cut in half through
   the root
Unsalted butter
½ tsp sugar
½ tsp salt
250g button mushrooms
150g unsmoked pancetta,
   cut into 1cm dice
Handful flatleaf parsley, chopped

TIP
It may not look enough but one short rib per person is perfect.

Heat the oil in a large flameproof casserole dish. Add the ribs and brown them all over, then set them aside. Add the onion, carrots, celery and garlic and cook over a low-medium heat until softened. Put the ribs back in the casserole dish and add the red wine, tomatoes, orange peel, herbs and beef stock. Season with the salt, sugar and peppermix. Bring to a simmer, cover with a well-fitting lid and cook for 2–2½ hours or until the beef is tender and comes away easily from the bone.

Transfer the ribs to a plate and cover them with foil while you finish the sauce. Strain the liquid through a sieve into a bowl, pushing the vegetables down with the back of a ladle to extract as much flavour as possible. Discard the vegetables and herbs. Pour the liquid back into the casserole dish and boil hard until reduced by two-thirds to make a thickened and well-flavoured sauce.

Recipe continued overleaf

For the vegetable and pancetta garnish, put the baby carrots and shallots in a shallow pan. Add 300ml of water and a tablespoon of butter, then season with the sugar and salt. Cover with a lid and bring to the boil, then simmer until the carrots and shallots are tender. Remove the lid and reduce the liquid to a sticky glaze.

In a separate small pan, fry the mushrooms and the pancetta together in a little butter for a couple of minutes. Add them to the carrots and shallots.

Put the ribs back in the sauce and warm them through for a minute or so, then add the carrots, shallots, mushrooms and pancetta. Serve topped with some chopped parsley.

Dauphinoise potatoes (page 304) or aligot (page 305) both make good accompaniments.

Carpet bagger steak

I have a friend, Richard Glover, who is one of the main presenters on ABC radio in Sydney. He wrote a book called The Land Before Avocado, *which was really about what life and food were like in the 70s and earlier in Australia. Food not wonderful, I would suggest. However, as part of his research, he had two or three books about entertaining in the 50s and 60s, which were a delight. Saucy drawings of girls in cocktail party dresses, sipping champagne out of Marie Antoinette glasses, and recipes for dishes like crêpes suzette and steak Diane. Out of curiosity, I decided to cook the one dish that seemed synonymous with terrible showy recipes: carpet bagger steak, the origin, I've always thought, of surf and turf. It was a complete surprise to find it quite lovely. The trick is to use a thick fillet steak and slip a couple of oysters into a pocket cut into it. The steak has to be cooked rare, so the oysters are only just set, and the flavours really do work together.*

SERVES 2

4 oysters
200ml Chicken stock
(page 307)
2 x 160g fillet steaks
½ tsp Rick's peppermix
(page 308)

30g butter
½ shallot, finely chopped
100ml red wine
½ tsp sugar
½ tsp salt

TIP
It really has to be fillet steak. The meat needs to be that tender to compliment the oysters.

Shuck the oysters and add the juices to the stock. Cut a long pocket in the side of each steak, slide 2 oysters into each pocket and secure with cocktail sticks. Season with the peppermix.

Heat a ridged frying pan over a fairly high heat and add half the butter. When it's melted, add the steaks. Cook for about 2 minutes on each side – you want to keep the oysters raw and the internal temperature of the steak between 50–55°C when tested with a probe. When both sides are cooked, leave the steaks to rest on a plate covered with foil while you make the sauce.

Add the shallot to the juices in the pan and when softened, add the red wine and reduce for a minute or so. Add the chicken stock and reduce down to a syrupy sauce, then season with the sugar, salt and the remaining butter. Remove the cocktail sticks from the steaks and serve with sautéed potatoes (pages 304–5) and a lettuce and tomato salad.

Carne con chile

The classic chilli con carne made with beans and minced beef is more of a Tex-Mex recipe. In Mexico, home cooks make carne con chile for their families, using pieces of beef or pork in a rich chilli sauce with or without tomatoes, and with beans and or rice on the side. Serve this with any number of your favourite toppings, such as shredded lettuce, soured cream, crumbled Lancashire cheese, avocado, coriander, chopped onions and radishes.

SERVES 4–6

50g dried guajillo chillies, seeds shaken out
450ml boiling water
4 large ripe tomatoes, left whole
4 garlic cloves, skin on
30g lard or 3 tbsp sunflower oil
1kg braising steak, cut into 3cm chunks
1 large onion, chopped
1 tsp ground cumin
1 tsp dried oregano

4 allspice berries, bruised
1 bay leaf
1 tsp salt
2 tbsp Chipotles en adobo (page 312 or bought)

Toppings
Chopped coriander
Soured cream
Lancashire cheese crumbled
Avocado, diced
Onions, chopped
Radishes, sliced

To serve
Black beans (page 302) or rice
12–18 corn tortillas

TIP
You can now buy 100 per cent corn tortillas from most supermarkets or online from Mexican specialist suppliers, such as Mexgrocer or Cool Chile.

In a dry, heavy-based frying pan, toast the guajillo chillies for about 20 seconds, until fragrant but not burnt. Transfer them to a bowl and pour over the boiling water. Leave them to soak for 15–20 minutes.

In the same pan, dry fry the tomatoes and garlic until softened and charred. Set aside the tomatoes and garlic until cool enough to handle, then peel off and discard the garlic skins and quarter the tomatoes, skin and all.

Heat a tablespoon of lard or oil in a large flameproof casserole dish and brown the cubes of beef all over. It's best to do this in batches, adding another tablespoon of lard or oil as needed. Transfer each batch of meat to a plate.

Then add the remaining lard or oil to the pan and fry the onion for 3–4 minutes until softened. Add the cumin, oregano, allspice and bay leaf. Cook for 2 minutes, then turn off the heat.

Put the soaked chillies and about 150ml of their soaking liquid in a blender and add the garlic, tomatoes, salt and chipotles en adobo. Blend until as smooth as possible, then tip the mixture into the casserole dish with the onion and add the browned beef. Stir in about 300ml of the chilli soaking water.

Bring to the boil, then turn the heat down to a simmer, cover and cook for 1½–2 hours until the beef is tender. Check the water a couple of times and make sure that the meat doesn't dry out. Add a little more water if necessary.

While the meat is cooking, prepare the toppings. Serve with warmed tortillas, the toppings and beans or rice, as desired.

Charlie's pad kra pao

A recipe and note from my son Charlie: In Thailand, this is the ultimate comfort dish. I discovered it a couple of years ago when watching the news about the amazing rescue of the boys' football team stuck in the caves in Chiang Rai province. The boys had been dreaming about big bowls of pad kra pao and it was their first meal after their rescue. I thought: wow, that's got to be a good dish, plus it's got an egg on top! Who wouldn't like that? There are loads of different ways of making this, but here's my version. I sometimes use finger chillies instead of bird's-eye to keep the heat down.

SERVES 4

350g jasmine rice
1 tbsp Thai fish sauce
1 tbsp oyster sauce
1 tsp soy sauce
1 tsp palm sugar or
   soft brown sugar
5–6 red bird's-eye chillies,
   roughly chopped

6 garlic cloves,
   roughly chopped
Sunflower oil
450g minced pork
2 shallots, finely chopped
200g green beans,
   chopped into 2cm lengths
Generous handful Thai basil
4 eggs

Prik nam pla
3 garlic cloves, crushed
4 bird's-eye chillies,
   finely sliced
5 tbsp Thai fish sauce
6 tbsp fresh lime juice

Cook the rice according to the recipe for steamed rice on page 306. In a bowl, mix together the ingredients for the prik nam pla and set aside.

Combine the fish sauce, oyster sauce, soy sauce and sugar with a dash of water in a separate bowl. Pound the chillies and garlic to a paste with a pestle and mortar.

In a wok, fry the garlic and chilli paste in a tablespoon of oil until the garlic starts to brown. Add the pork and shallots and cook for a couple of minutes before adding the fish sauce mixture and the green beans. Cook for a couple more minutes, then remove the pan from the heat. Add the Thai basil and stir until it wilts.

Fry the eggs Thai style in plenty of oil until bubbly, with brown, crispy edges.

Serve some rice and the pork mixture on each plate, top with an egg, then spoon over the prik nam pla.

Recipes that helped me through lockdown

Somewhat unexpectedly, my wife Sas and I and our stepdaughter Olivia found ourselves in lockdown in Sydney last March and couldn't get back to the UK for five months. In those early days the lockdown was as strict in Australia as it has been here, but in time we were allowed to see one, then two other people – in our case Sas's stepmother, Janine, and her grandmother, Betty. After a while we could also invite a friend from down the road, Karen Balstrup, known by everyone as KB.

I found endless days of having not a lot to do very rewarding. We are lucky enough to have a pool at our house in Neutral Bay, so every day started with a swim, though by the time we left in August the pool temperature was down to 9 degrees. We walked every day too – it's impossible ever to be bored by the views of Sydney harbour with the bridge and opera house always somewhere there. I love a bit of DIY and gardening, so I threw myself into mending door hinges and plastering and repainting the cracks up the stairs. I planted herbs and vegetables that I thought would crop quickly before winter came – not much, just some parsley, coriander, rocket, spinach, broccoli – and I replanted a couple of tomato plants that I found growing near the compost. I didn't realise how much possums like parsley and coriander, so I had to build little wire cages round the plants to keep the creatures off. There was plenty to do, but our Thursday evening dinner was the highlight of the week.

I chose recipes from my books designed to feed five or six people with a minimum of fuss – things like fish pie, roasts, and moussaka – but the one that I ended up doing most often was pastitsio (page 199), a recipe I got from a little restaurant right in the busiest part of Corfu Town some years ago. I made up a salad on the spot to go with it – lettuce, spring onions and lots of dill.

KB would turn up early and make cocktails for us all; in the very early days we drank them two metres apart. I love a negroni but we couldn't buy any red vermouth (it was sold out), so Sas bought some Martini rosato instead and KB mixed it with Shiraz. It made the best negroni ever. She made a cosmopolitan for Sas's grandmother and margaritas for everyone else. On several occasions Olivia rustled up some tiny pink meringue shells for a sweet, which we had with whipped cream and strawberries, Eton mess style. Great memories from difficult times.

'The one that I ended up doing most often was pastitsio, a recipe I got from a little restaurant right in the busiest part of Corfu Town some years ago.'

Beef & macaroni pie with cinnamon, red wine & kefalotiri cheese
Pastitsio

I have a great affection for the Mediterranean baked dishes of meat, pasta, tomato and kefalotiri – a dry, firm, ewe's milk cheese, full of irregular holes. It ranges in colour from white through to pale yellow, depending on the grazing of the sheep, and is fresh and slightly sharp-tasting, with a distinct flavour of ewe's milk.

SERVES 8-10

500g tubular pasta,
   such as rigatoni,
   penne or tortiglioni
2 eggs, lightly beaten
50g Greek kefalotiri cheese
   or Parmesan cheese,
   finely grated
2 tbsp melted butter
10g fresh white breadcrumbs

White sauce
115g butter
115g plain flour
1.2 litres whole milk,
   plus a little extra
½ tsp freshly grated nutmeg

Meat sauce
4 tbsp olive oil
1 medium onion, finely chopped
4 garlic cloves, finely chopped
2 celery sticks, finely chopped
1kg lean beef mince
200ml red wine
400g tin chopped tomatoes
2 tbsp tomato paste
10cm cinnamon stick
¼ tsp ground cloves
1 tbsp dried oregano,
   Greek if possible
2 tbsp fresh chopped oregano
3 fresh bay leaves
Salt and black pepper

For the meat sauce, heat the oil in a pan, add the onion, garlic and celery and fry until just beginning to brown. Add the mince and fry over a high heat for 3–4 minutes, breaking up any lumps with a wooden spoon as the meat browns.

Add the red wine, tomatoes, tomato paste, cinnamon stick, ground cloves, dried and fresh oregano, bay leaves, 100ml of water, 1½ teaspoons of salt and some black pepper. Simmer for 30–40 minutes, stirring now and then, until the sauce has thickened but is still nicely moist. Remove and discard the cinnamon stick and bay leaves, then set the sauce aside.

Recipe continued overleaf

Cook the pasta in salted boiling water until al dente. Take care not to overcook, as it will cook a little more in the oven. Drain well, transfer to a large bowl and leave to cool slightly.

For the white sauce, melt the butter in a saucepan. Add the flour and cook, while stirring, over a medium heat, for 1 minute. Gradually beat in the milk, then bring to the boil, still stirring. Lower the heat and leave to simmer for 5–7 minutes, stirring occasionally. Season with the nutmeg and some salt and pepper to taste.

Preheat the oven to 180°C/Fan 160°C. Stir 250ml (about one-fifth) of the white sauce into the warm pasta together with the beaten eggs and half the grated cheese. Keep the remaining sauce warm over a low heat, stirring now and then and adding more milk if it begins to get a little thick.

Use the melted butter to grease a large, shallow ovenproof dish measuring about 23 x 33cm across and 7cm deep. Spread one-third of the pasta mixture over the base of the dish and cover with half the meat sauce. Add another third of the pasta and then the rest of the meat sauce, then cover with a final layer of pasta. Spoon over the remaining white sauce.

Mix the remaining grated cheese with the breadcrumbs and sprinkle them over the top. Bake for 30–40 minutes until bubbling hot and golden brown on top.

Sas's cottage pie

I've never written a recipe for regular cottage pie. A duck version, yes (page 153), and I wrote a shepherd's pie recipe years ago when trying to remember a dish my mother cooked with Indian spices, but never the simple British version. My wife Sas has one from her family which to all intents and purposes is bog standard apart from the courgette and the mash made from sweet potato, which makes it completely different and totally lovely.

SERVES 6

2 tsp olive oil
1kg lean beef mince
1 medium onion, finely chopped
2 carrots, sliced
1 medium courgette, finely sliced
1 celery stick, finely sliced
1 tbsp chopped fresh thyme
    leaves, plus extra to serve
250ml Beef stock (page 308)
1 tbsp Worcestershire sauce
70g tomato paste
400g tin chopped tomatoes

60g frozen peas
40g Cheddar cheese, grated
Salt and black pepper

Sweet potato mash
6 sweet potatoes (1.2kg),
    peeled and chopped coarsely
50g butter
60ml milk
Salt and freshly ground
    white pepper

TIP
Change the sweet potato mash to ordinary mash and take out the courgette and you will have the pie your mother probably made.

Preheat the oven to 180°C/Fan 160°C. Heat the olive oil in a large pan over a high heat. Working in batches, brown the beef and onion, stirring and breaking the meat up with a wooden spoon.

Add the carrots, courgette, celery, thyme, stock, sauce, tomato paste and tomatoes and season with salt and black pepper. Simmer, uncovered, for 30 minutes or until the carrots are tender. Add the peas and cook for another 10 minutes or until the peas are tender and the liquid has thickened. If the mixture starts to look dry, add a little water to moisten.

To make the mash, boil, steam or microwave the sweet potatoes until tender, then drain. Mash with the butter and, milk, then season with salt and pepper.

Spoon the beef mixture into a 2.5-litre ovenproof dish. Top with the mash and sprinkle with cheese. Bake, uncovered, for 30 minutes or until the pie is heated through and the top is golden. Serve sprinkled with extra thyme, if you like.

Reuben sandwich

*I absolutely adore any combination of salt beef and sauerkraut –
the hot salt beef sandwiches at Selfridges in London are worth
a trip into the West End. So when I saw a Reuben sandwich on
the menu at The Cheeky Dog pub next to my seafood restaurant,
Rick Stein at Bannisters, in Port Stephens, New South Wales,
I had to order it and I thought, what fantastic pub food. This
recipe is from Mitch Turner, who is head chef at my restaurant
and also looks after the pub kitchen. We both enjoy indulging
in very meaty dishes, a sort of antidote to all the fish.*

SERVES 2

4 slices rye sourdough
1 tbsp softened butter
4 slices salt beef
4 tbsp sauerkraut, drained
4 slices Emmental cheese
Bread and butter pickles,
   to serve (page 306)

Russian dressing
2 tbsp Mayonnaise (page 309 or bought)
2 tbsp crème fraiche or soured cream
½ tbsp Cholula hot sauce or Tabasco
1 tsp horseradish sauce
¼–½ tsp caraway seeds (optional)

TIP
This is quite a
messy sandwich,
so it's best eaten
with people you
know well.

In a small bowl, mix together the dressing ingredients,
adding the caraway seeds if desired.

Lightly toast the bread, butter it, then layer up the salt
beef, sauerkraut, Russian dressing and slices of Emmental.
Serve with bread and butter pickles on the side.

Roast rib of beef with Yorkshire puddings & roast potatoes

I enjoy going back to the basic instructions of any dish from time to time. The method for roasting any joint of meat is always the same. Start it in a very hot oven for half an hour or so, to brown and flavour the surface, then reduce the oven temperature to 180°C/ Fan 160°C to complete the roasting (or even 160°C/Fan 140°C if you've got time). Cooking at this lower temperature reduces the moisture loss, giving you much juicier meat. With some organisation, you can roast your beef and potatoes and bake the Yorkshires all in one oven. Start with the potatoes on a lower shelf and the beef above. Remove the potatoes after 45 minutes to an hour and keep them warm. The beef will take about an hour and a half to cook (rule of thumb: 40 minutes to the kg). Turn the oven back to very hot and finish with the Yorkshire puddings. Two ovens do make cooking a roast with all the trimmings much easier, though.

SERVES 8

2-bone rib of beef
(about 2.5kg) chined
but not trimmed
Salt and black pepper
Horseradish sauce,
to serve

Yorkshire puddings
225g plain flour
½ tsp salt
4 eggs
300ml whole milk

Roast potatoes
2kg floury potatoes,
such as Maris Pipers or
King Edwards, peeled
150g goose fat, beef
dripping or mix of both
30g polenta

Gravy
1 tbsp plain flour
300ml Chicken stock
(page 307), Beef stock
(page 308) or water

TIP
Keep all the bones
for making beef
stock (page 308).

Take the beef out of the fridge a couple of hours before roasting. Preheat the oven to 230°C/Fan 210°C.

Peel the potatoes and cut them into 5cm pieces. Put them in a pan of salted water, bring to the boil and cook for 8–10 minutes. Drain in a colander and shake a little to scuff up the surfaces. Transfer to a roasting tin big enough to take the potatoes in one layer and add the fat and/or dripping. Place in the oven for 5 minutes to melt the fat, then turn the potatoes over in the fat and sprinkle with the polenta (this gives the potatoes a lovely sandy texture). Put the tin on the bottom shelf of the oven and roast the potatoes for 45 minutes to an hour, turning them over a couple of times in the fat as they cook. Keep them warm and, if necessary, put them back in a hot oven for a few minutes to reheat before serving.

Season the beef with salt and pepper. Put it in a roasting tin, place in the oven above the potatoes and roast for 30 minutes. Then turn the oven down to 180°C/Fan 160°C and roast until the meat at the centre of the joint near the bone reaches 50°C for rare, 55°C for medium-rare or 60°C for medium – check with a temperature probe. The cooking time should be about an hour and a half in all. Remove and transfer to a tray, cover with foil and leave to rest for 30 minutes. The core temperature will rise by about 5°C. Pour off the fat from the beef roasting into a small bowl. When you've taken the beef out of the oven, increase the temperature once more to 230°C/Fan 210°C for the Yorkshire puddings

While the beef is roasting, make the Yorkshire pudding batter. Sift the flour and salt into a bowl, make a well in the centre and break in the eggs. Whisk together, then gradually add the milk to make a smooth batter with the consistency of double cream. Leave to rest for 30 minutes.

You'll need 2 x 4-cup Yorkshire pudding trays – the ones that are 10cm in diameter. Pour a teaspoon of the reserved fat into each cup and heat in the oven for a couple of minutes. Divide the batter between the 8 cups and place in the hot oven. Bake for 25–30 minutes till nicely risen and brown.

To make the gravy, place the beef roasting tin over a medium heat on the hob. Sprinkle in the flour, stir well with a wooden spoon and then add the stock or water, scraping the base of the tin to release the caramelised juices. Simmer until reduced to a well-flavoured gravy. Strain into a jug and keep warm.

Uncover the beef and pour any juices into the gravy. Run your knife between the bones and the eye of the meat in an L-shaped motion, then remove it in one piece to a board ready for carving into slices.

Serve the beef on warmed plates with the Yorkshires, roast potatoes, gravy and horseradish sauce and some type of brassica, such as cabbage, sprouts or broccoli and perhaps the glazed spring carrots on page 303.

The best chuck steak burgers

This isn't really a recipe but I am so obsessed with good hamburgers I thought it worthwhile to give you the sum total of my knowledge on making the perfect patty. Most of this comes not from me but from the butcher we use for all our restaurant meat – Philip Warren of Launceston. This is what Ian Warren, Philip's son, has to say on the matter: 'Chill the meat well before mincing as it will mince much better and the fat won't smear in the mincing blade. You want the meat to be chopped by the mincer blade, not squeezed and smeared; avoid overworking the meat and process it as little as possible. A medium mincing blade will make the meat coarse enough for texture but fine enough to hold together, as no binding agents are used.' The mixture of chuck steak and rib-cap gives the perfect proportion of the right sort of fat. Go to a good butcher for rib-cap steak; you are unlikely to find it in a supermarket.

MAKES 10 BURGERS

1.3kg chuck steak
500g rib-cap steak
Salt and Rick's peppermix (page 308)

TIP
You can freeze the raw patties, but for no more than a couple of weeks.

Using a hand-crank mincer or a mincer attachment on a food mixer, mince the cuts of steak. Combine them well and form into 10 patties. Place them on a tray lined with baking paper and chill, then bring up to room temperature before cooking.

I prefer to cook burgers on a barbecue, but obviously you can cook them under a grill or on a griddle pan if you like. Season them with plenty of salt and my peppermix or black pepper. For burgers with a good thickness of about 1.5–2cm, cook for 2 minutes on each side for rare, 3 minutes each side for medium, or 4 minutes each side for well done.

I put all the accompaniments on a large plate for everybody to help themselves: sliced onions, sliced tomatoes, torn lettuce, avocado, pickles (dill and cucumber), chilli and beetroot. I offer mayonnaise, chipotle relish, mustard and ketchup. I also ask if anybody would like cheese or bacon. I like brioche or sesame buns – I don't think buns for burgers should be anything worthy like sourdough.

Sas's beef stroganoff

One of the few dishes I was ever allowed to cook when I worked as a commis chef at The Great Western Royal Hotel in Paddington in the 60s was beef stroganoff. This was because it was an à la minute dish from the sauce section, and for me the wonder of really good Hungarian paprika and soured cream was enough to make me obsessed with this dish. It always had to be fillet steak and the trick was to serve it so the centre of each strip of steak was still rare. So when I cooked it for my wife and stepchildren, I was sort of expecting tremendous approval but what I got was, 'It's very nice but not as good as mum's'. Sas's version was cooked for her by her stepmother Janine when she was little and then by her for her children Zach and Olivia. I kept asking her to make it for me but she was unusually diffident. Finally, I persuaded her and I was perfectly truthful in saying it was delicious.

SERVES 4

30g butter
600g beef rump steak,
    thinly sliced
1 medium onion, thinly sliced
2 garlic cloves, crushed
1 tsp sweet paprika
400g button mushrooms,
    thickly sliced

2 tbsp tomato paste
2 tbsp red wine
1 tbsp lemon juice
300g single cream
1 tbsp coarsely chopped
    fresh dill
Salt and black pepper

TIP
Sas says that you could also serve this with mash or fettuccine.

Heat half the butter in a large frying pan over a high heat and lightly brown the beef in batches. Remove each batch from the pan and set aside.

Heat the remaining butter in the same pan. Add the onion and garlic and cook for about 4 minutes, stirring frequently until the onion softens. Add the paprika, mushrooms and tomato paste and cook for about 3 minutes stirring frequently.

Return the beef to the pan with the wine and lemon juice and bring to the boil. Reduce the heat and simmer, covered, for 5–7 minutes or until the beef is tender. Add the cream and dill, then cook, stirring constantly, until heated through. Don't allow the cream to boil and split. Season to taste with salt and pepper and serve with steamed rice (page 305).

Steak & kidney pudding

I enjoy the fact that the simpler you make a steak and kidney pudding, the better it tastes. You don't even need to brown the meat because the sauce will have quite enough colour, although I have taken the unorthodox step of adding a little soy sauce. Could there be, I wonder, a better accompaniment to a glass of Pomerol?

SERVES 6

700g chuck steak
225g ox kidney
2½ tbsp plain flour
1½ tsp salt
1 tsp black pepper
1 medium onion, chopped
Small handful parsley,
 chopped

A couple of thyme sprigs,
 leaves picked from the stalks
2 bay leaves
1 tbsp dark soy sauce
300ml Beef stock (page 308),
 or water
Savoy cabbage with sloes
 (page 178), to serve

Suet pastry
350g self-raising flour,
 plus extra for dusting
175g shredded suet
Large pinch of salt
225ml cold water
Butter, for greasing

Cut the steak into 2.5cm pieces. Cut the kidney in half lengthways, snip out the core with scissors, then cut into 2.5cm pieces. Put the steak and kidney in a bowl with the flour and seasoning and toss well. Mix in the onion and herbs.

For the pastry, mix the flour, suet and salt with the cold water to form a soft dough. Turn out on to a lightly floured surface and knead briefly until smooth. Roll out, using a little more flour, into a 36cm diameter circle and cut out a quarter of the circle. Set that aside for the lid and use the remainder to line the base and sides of a lightly buttered 1.75-litre pudding basin. Overlap the cut edges slightly, brushing them lightly with water and pressing them together well to seal.

Spoon the meat mixture into the basin and pour on the soy sauce and beef stock. Roll out the reserved pastry into a circle about 1cm larger than the top of the basin. Brush the edges with water, press it firmly on to the top of the pudding and crimp the edges together well to seal. Cover the basin with a floured pudding cloth and tie securely in place with string.

Place a trivet in the base of a large pan, cover with about 5cm of water and bring to the boil. Put the pudding into the pan, cover with a well-fitting lid and steam for 4 hours, topping up the water now and then. To serve, uncover the pudding and serve it straight from the basin with the cabbage.

Devilled kidneys

I originally wrote this recipe with wild mushrooms, such as chanterelles and ceps, but it is such an everyday dish that I now tend to make it with ordinary chestnut or portobello mushrooms.

SERVES 2

100g chestnut or portobello mushrooms, cleaned
3 lambs' kidneys
1 tbsp plain flour
⅛ tsp cayenne pepper

¼ tsp mustard powder
40g butter, plus extra for the toast
1 tbsp chopped parsley
4 slices sourdough bread
Salt and black pepper

Cut the mushrooms in half or into quarters or leave them whole, depending on their size. Cut the kidneys in half lengthways and snip out the cores with scissors.

Mix the flour with the cayenne pepper, mustard powder, ¼ teaspoon of salt and some black pepper in a bowl. Add the kidneys and toss well.

Heat half the butter in a large frying pan over a medium heat. Add the kidneys, shaking off any excess flour, and cook for 1½ minutes on each side. They should be lightly browned on the outside but still pink and juicy in the centre. Lift them out on to a plate and keep warm.

Add the rest of the butter to the pan and as soon as it is foaming, add the mushrooms and increase the heat to high. Season with salt and pepper and fry briskly for a couple of minutes. Put the kidneys back in the pan, add half the chopped parsley and toss together briefly.

Toast the bread and spread with butter, then spoon the kidneys and mushrooms on top of 2 of the slices. Sprinkle with the rest of the chopped parsley and serve with the remaining toast on the side.

Butterflied BBQ lamb with lemon, garlic, rosemary & thyme

I am a bit of a fan of butterflying lamb and cooking it quickly on a barbecue. This recipe comes from my series Rick Stein's Cornwall, *for which we were under pressure to cook as much food as we could outdoors because of the pandemic. We filmed in the marshy corner of a field at Nancarrow Farm, near Truro, and I remember being slightly disconcerted when told by Steve, the farmer, to beware of ticks in the marsh grass. Nevertheless, this proved to be a really lovely dish, mostly, I suspect, because the lamb from Nancarrow Farm was so very good. I think the trick with cooking with marinades on the barbecue is to avoid using too many ingredients that will burn when you cook the lamb.*

SERVES 6

1 x 2.5kg leg of lamb (see below on how to remove the bones)

Marinade
2 large garlic cloves, chopped
1 tsp dried red chilli flakes
1 tsp chopped rosemary
6 thyme sprigs, leaves picked off and stalks discarded
1 fresh bay leaf, finely chopped

Juice of 1 lemon
2 tbsp Thai fish sauce
2 tbsp pimentón
1 tsp Maldon sea salt
½ tsp coarsely ground or crushed black pepper
90ml olive oil

TIP
Salads and flatbreads are the best accompaniments.

To prepare the lamb, turn the leg over to the point where the bone runs closest to the surface. Using a sharp knife, split the meat along the bone and ease it away from the bone along both sides, leaving the bone as clean as possible. At the fatter end of the joint, there is a group of smaller bones. Continue to cut around them too, until you can lift all the bones from the meat, leaving a butterfly-shaped, bone-free joint. Trim away any excess fat and sinew. Your butcher will prepare the joint for you, if you prefer.

Mix the marinade ingredients together and rub them over the lamb. Set the lamb aside, skin-side up, for about 30 minutes.

Preheat the barbecue. When it's hot, cook the lamb for 12 minutes on each side. Leave to rest on a board, covered with foil, for 5 minutes, then carve into thick slices.

Chapter Six
VEGETARIAN

Below is what my friend Richard Glover, Australian author, journalist and radio presenter, wrote about my moussaka recipe. I like it because I'm greatly in favour of people changing my recipes to suit themselves. This is what he said:

'A few years ago, I modified one of Rick's recipes. I then served it to him and requested his opinion: "Might this be an improvement on the version you cook?" I idly inquired.

"It's superb," he lied.

Actually, Rick might not have lied. My version is pretty good, especially if you need a vegetarian take on one of the world's most comforting dishes. That was my need. A wonderful new person had joined our family, having become aware of the many virtues of our younger son. She was vegetarian, and I wanted to find a way to cook for her one of my favourite meals: the recipe Rick calls Patrick Leigh Fermor's moussaka.

The modifications I came up with are quite simple, and I think the dish retains all the lovely, nourishing, comforting qualities of the fabulous original.

In my version, the 750 grams of minced beef are replaced with lentils, cooked in a tomato and capsicum sauce. Oh, and Rick's "aubergines and courgettes are replaced by "eggplants and zucchini" since that's what they are called in Australia.'

Richard's recipe is on pages 234–35. At the time I was slightly on my best behaviour, as I realise that I do have a resistance to vegetarian cooking. It's the same as others have to fish – it's almost a psychological block, the brain telling me that this is going to be bland and lacking in excitement. As it turned out, Richard's dish wasn't boring and the lack of meat was easily compensated for by all the other rich flavours in the moussaka: tomato, garlic, lots of olive oil and pungent Greek cheese. No more are lots of other vegetarian and vegan dishes boring. The secret is making sure that they do have some sort of exaggeration in them, maybe a strong cheese, richness from butter or cream, or lots of chilli and spice in the case of dishes from the Indian subcontinent.

It's with good reason that many of the dishes in this chapter come from India or Sri Lanka when you consider that about 40 per cent of the 1.36 billion population of India are vegetarian. It's obvious that many of the dishes will be extremely good. I'm particularly fond of the potato and cauliflower curry (aloo gobi) on page 221. It seems to be one of those dishes that you find in most cuisines which are far greater than the sum of their parts – seemingly simple but carrying with them a whole bookshelf of shared experiences, comforts and memories of home. I'm thinking of dishes like Vietnamese pho, British steak and kidney pudding, boeuf en daube in France or spaghetti vongole in Italy.

I'm going to have a bit of a whinge now. What does put me off about vegetarian cooking, and even more so with vegan cooking, is the insistence that such diets will turn you physically and mentally into a better person. Also the idea that eating only plant-based food will somehow prolong your life, make your stools light and fibrous, stop your breath from smelling and keep your bones as supple as longbows. You will get up in the morning with a bounce of happy feelings and swing down the road, smiling at everyone.

This may be true, but what I really want from my food is to know it has been properly grown, sourced or reared and that it gives me and my family and friends pleasure.

As Brillat-Savarin said, 'The pleasures of the table belong to all times and all ages, to every country and every day; they go hand in hand with all our other pleasures, outlast them, and remain to console us for their loss.'

Huevos rancheros

*This is the best-known breakfast egg dish in Mexico. I seem
to have spent too many a morning in Mexico seeking out this
revitalising combination of corn tortillas, tomato, chilli and
egg, normally served with refried beans and strong black coffee.
I still like to cook this on a long Sunday morning after a
particularly lively Saturday night.*

SERVES 4

Sunflower oil,
   for shallow frying
8 large eggs
8 corn tortillas
50g Lancashire cheese,
   crumbled
Salt and black pepper

Tomato sauce
2 garlic cloves, finely chopped
1 medium onion, finely chopped
2 tbsp sunflower oil
4 serrano, jalapeño or
   medium-hot red Dutch
   chillies, roughly chopped
400g can chopped tomatoes

Refried beans (optional)
35g lard
1 medium onion, finely chopped
2 garlic cloves, finely chopped
1 green jalapeño or serrano
   chilli, finely chopped
2 x 400g cans black beans
   with some of their liquor.
½ tsp dried oregano
½ tsp salt

TIP
At last, you can
buy corn tortillas
in supermarkets.
It was a long
time coming.

For the refried beans, if including, melt the lard in a frying
pan and sweat the onion until soft and golden. Add the garlic
and chilli and continue to cook for 2–3 minutes until softened.
Use a potato masher to mash your beans in a bowl with some of
their liquor or whizz them with a blender for a smoother result.

Add the beans to the pan with the fried onions and cook over
a medium heat with the oregano and salt until the mixture
reaches your desired consistency. It's better to keep it on
the looser side as it will firm up considerably as it cools.

For the sauce, soften the garlic and onion in the oil without
browning. Add the chillies and cook for a couple of minutes,
then add the tomatoes and simmer until slightly reduced and
thickened to a pourable sauce. Season to taste and set aside.

When you are ready to serve, gently reheat the sauce and the
beans. Heat some oil in a frying pan over a medium heat. Break
in the eggs and fry to your liking, spooning a little of the hot
oil over the yolks as they cook. Slightly overlap 2 tortillas in the
centre of each warmed plate and put 2 of the eggs on top. Spoon
a generous quantity of the sauce around the eggs, scatter with
the cheese and serve with refried beans, if you've made some.

Pau bhaji

There's a rather a special blog site in Bombay called Mumbai Boss. Its strapline is 'Making Sense of the City' – a nice humorous touch. The food editor, Purve Mehra, took me to a streetside restaurant called Sardar where she felt they made the best pau bhajis in the city, probably the most famous dish there. The indulgence of eating a cracking pau bhaji is similar to that of a beautifully made hamburger: it's about the combination. It was the bhaji, a finely chopped vegetable curry cooked to a soft mash, with the buns, which seem to arrive from the bakery every half hour, and above all the slab of butter both slathered on to the bun and laid across the bhaji that made the experience so wonderful. This is a time for using ordinary bread rolls, the equivalent of Mother's Pride, but they do need to be freshly baked.

SERVES 4-6

350g potatoes, peeled
   and cut into large chunks
50g butter, plus 15g extra
1 large onion, chopped
2 tsp cumin seeds
400g ripe tomatoes, chopped
300g tin marrowfat peas, drained
3 tsp pau bhaji masala spice blend
1 tsp Kashmiri chilli powder
1 tsp ground coriander
1½ tsp salt
Handful fresh coriander

To serve
Fresh bread rolls and butter
Large handful coriander
   leaves, chopped
1–2 limes, cut into wedges
1 red onion, thinly sliced into rings

TIP
If you can't get the pau bhaji spice blend, use 2 teaspoons of Garam masala (page 308).

Boil the potatoes in a pan of salted water for 10 minutes or until tender. Drain well, then mash. Heat the 50g of butter in a large sturdy pan over a medium heat. Add the onion and cumin seeds and fry for 10 minutes until softened and golden. Stir in the mashed potato and fry for 1–2 minutes, then add the tomatoes, mix well and cook for 5 minutes, stirring often.

Add the marrowfat peas, spices and salt and cook for a further 5 minutes, stirring and mashing the mixture together. Stir through the remaining butter and a handful of coriander.

Serve with generously buttered rolls, more coriander, lime wedges and red onion rings.

Potato & cauliflower curry
Aloo gobi

This is an everyday vegetable curry which I always make a beeline for when I'm in India. I'm particularly fond of it with a fried egg on top for breakfast and it's also good with raita and chapatis. The raita should be eaten on the day of making.

3 tbsp sunflower oil
1 medium onion,
   roughly chopped
4 garlic cloves, finely chopped
1 tbsp Garam masala (page 308)
2 tsp Kashmiri chilli powder
1 tsp salt
2 medium tomatoes, chopped
500g potatoes, peeled and
   cut into 3cm chunks

1 medium cauliflower,
   cut into rough 5cm florets
Handful coriander,
   chopped, to finish

Cucumber and mint raita
175g unpeeled cucumber,
   halved lengthways
275g natural yoghurt
½ tsp caster sugar

Handful fresh mint
   leaves, chopped
1 tsp fresh lime juice
Salt and black pepper

To serve
Chapatis

For the raita, scoop out the seeds from the cucumber with a teaspoon, then grate the flesh. Toss the grated cucumber with a teaspoon of salt, tip into a sieve and leave to drain for 20–30 minutes. Mix the drained cucumber with all the remaining ingredients, adding extra salt, pepper or lime juice to taste.

Heat the oil in a heavy-based saucepan over a medium-high heat, add the onion and fry for 7 minutes until golden. Add the garlic and fry for 1–2 minutes, then stir in the garam masala, chilli powder and salt, and fry for 1 minute.

Add the tomatoes and cook for 2 minutes until slightly softened, then add the potatoes and pour in 400ml of water. Bring to a simmer, cover and cook over a medium heat for 10 minutes. Add the cauliflower and cook, covered, for 7–8 minutes, or until the cauliflower and potatoes are tender.

Scatter with fresh coriander and serve with the cucumber and mint raita and some chapatis.

Yellow dal with tomato, turmeric & fried Kashmiri chillies
Tarka dal

This is the dal I make most often, mainly because it's so incredibly easy and quick, but also because finishing it off with a tarka is so special. A tarka is a last-minute fry of spices and chilli which you pour, still sizzling, on top of the dal in the dish.

SERVES 4-6

200g yellow tur dal,
   soaked in cold water
   for 1 hour, then drained
2 medium tomatoes, chopped
1 medium onion, chopped
4 green chillies, slit lengthways
2 garlic cloves, peeled and
   left whole
Small handful fresh curry leaves
1 tsp salt
½ tsp ground turmeric

Tarka
2 tbsp sunflower oil
1 tsp black mustard seeds
2 shallots, finely chopped
4 dried Kashmiri chillies,
   each broken into 3 pieces
About 15 fresh curry leaves
Handful coriander leaves,
   roughly chopped, to garnish

Put the dal into a large saucepan and add water to cover by about 4cm. Add all the remaining dal ingredients, bring to the boil, then lower the heat to medium and simmer for 45–60 minutes. The dal should be soft but still with a little bite. Use a potato masher to break up about half of the lentils, being sure to leave plenty of texture.

For the tarka, heat the oil in a pan over a medium heat, add the mustard seeds and fry for 30 seconds until they pop. Stir in the shallots, Kashmiri chillies and curry leaves and fry for 2–3 minutes until the shallots are softened and golden.

Spoon the tarka on top of the dal, sprinkle with fresh coriander leaves and serve.

Beetroot curry
Thel dala

I ordered quite a few beetroot curries when I was in Sri Lanka because I am very fond of beetroot and this is a good example of how Sri Lankans can turn any vegetable into a memorable dish. I liked the creamy dishes with lots of coconut milk but this was a welcome change, more like a stir-fry, in which the beetroot remains slightly crunchy. It's known locally as a thel dala. I like to use coconut oil, but you might find the flavour a little too powerful. If so, use sunflower oil instead.

SERVES 4

750g raw beetroots,
    trimmed of their leaves
3 tbsp coconut or sunflower oil
1 tsp cumin seeds
1 tsp black mustard seeds
7.5cm cinnamon stick, broken
    into smaller pieces
10–12 fresh curry leaves
2 green chillies, thinly sliced
1 medium onion, finely chopped

3 garlic cloves,
    crushed or grated
1 tsp unroasted Sri Lankan
    curry powder (page 309)
1 tsp Kashmiri chilli powder
¼ tsp ground turmeric
125g chopped tomatoes,
    fresh or from a tin
1 tbsp lime juice
Salt

TIP
This is also nice made with carrots cut into batons like the beetroot.

Peel the beetroots and cut them across into 7–8mm thick slices. Then cut each slice into 7–8mm wide batons to resemble chips.

Heat the oil in a large, deep frying pan over a medium heat. Add the cumin seeds, mustard seeds, cinnamon and curry leaves and leave to sizzle for a few seconds until the mustard seeds stop popping. Add the green chillies, onion and garlic and fry for 5–6 minutes until soft and lightly browned.

Stir in the curry powder, chilli powder and turmeric, cook for a few seconds, then add the beetroot batons, tomatoes and a teaspoon of salt. Put a lid on the pan and cook over a medium-low heat for 15 minutes, stirring regularly, until the beetroot is just tender but still very slightly crunchy. Add a couple of tablespoons of water if the mixture starts sticking to the base of the pan, but ideally leave it to cook in its own juices. Uncover, stir in the lime juice and serve with rice.

Cauliflower cheese

*Cauliflower cheese is precisely the sort of British dish that most
people secretly adore, but which is often so massively overcooked
and under-cheesed that it is regarded as a typical example of
how bad our food can be. Imagine, though, if this dish was called
something like chou-fleur au Tomme de Savoie fermière and was
made with the famous mountain cheese from Savoy; it would
probably be a local speciality. A cauliflower cheese made with
good mature Cheddar and where the cauliflower is not overcooked
and plenty of the pale-green inner leaves are used is a joy.*

SERVES 4

1 large, very fresh cauliflower
(about 1kg)
40g breadcrumbs
Hot buttered wholemeal
toast, to serve

Cheese sauce
1 small onion, peeled
and halved
450ml whole milk
1 bay leaf
4 cloves
½ tsp black peppercorns
30g butter

30g plain flour
175g mature Cheddar
cheese, coarsely grated
3 tbsp double cream
1 tsp English mustard
Salt and freshly ground
white pepper

TIP
This is a great
opportunity to
use up any odds
and ends of
cheese. And you
don't have to use
only cauliflower –
add a head of
broccoli if you like.

For the cheese sauce, put the onion halves in a pan with the milk,
bay leaf, cloves and peppercorns. Bring to the boil, then remove
from the heat and set aside for 20 minutes to infuse. Strain the
milk into a jug and discard the flavouring ingredients. Melt the
butter in a pan, add the flour and cook over a medium heat for
1 minute. Remove from the heat and whisk in the milk. Return
to the heat and bring to the boil, while stirring. Leave to simmer
very gently for 10 minutes, stirring every now and then. Remove
the sauce from the heat and stir in 100g of the grated cheese,
then the cream and mustard. Season to taste.

Bring a pan of well-salted water to the boil and preheat the grill
to high. Cut the cauliflower into large florets, discarding the core
and the larger leaves. Drop the florets and young green leaves
into the water and cook for 8 minutes until tender, then drain.

Arrange the cauliflower leaves and florets in a warm, shallow
ovenproof dish and pour over the cheese sauce. Mix the rest
of the cheese with the breadcrumbs and scatter this over the
top, then slide under the grill for 3–4 minutes until golden and
bubbling. Serve with plenty of hot, buttered wholemeal toast.

Guinea pigs & friends

My first book was *English Seafood Cookery*. Though I've always been known as Rick, I called myself Richard Stein in this because it seemed a bit more serious. Back then I was cooking every day and didn't have the resource that I now have – a home economist. This marvellous person takes all my scraps of paper with scribbled recipes on them and photos taken with my phone or a little pocketbook I always have when filming, sorts them out into something resembling a formal recipe and often tests the recipes. In those days I did all the cooking for the book with my then sous-chef, Paul Sellars. Many of the recipes went on the menu straight away, but we had a process called the literary lunches where we'd invite half a dozen staff members to come to lunch and try the new dishes. Now I test most of the recipes at home, or Portia, my home economist, cooks them for her husband Julian and two children, Will and Florence, which is very valuable because they are good critics. Similarly, I try new recipes on my wife Sas and my two stepchildren Zach and Olivia, but the real fun comes when I'm testing dishes for large parties.

I completed much of the recipe testing for *Rick Stein's India* during a long summer in Australia, though at the same time my son Jack was knocking them out at a prodigious rate in our little kitchen that normally cooks for our deli. There was one occasion I remember particularly well – although as you will see later in this book, my wife's recollection is somewhat different. In my memory, we invited about 25 friends round for a curry night and I cooked 15 dishes from the *India* book. I based the whole experience around three main dishes – Mr Singh's slow-cooked lamb curry with cloves and cardamom; chicken and rose water biryani; and a Madras fish curry of snapper, tomato and tamarind, which you will find on page 96. In addition to that I prepared a myriad of side dishes: no less than three dals, tarka, black dal and the sultan's pigeon pea dal. I made a chana masala (chickpea curry), aloo gobi (page 221) and a dry curry of cabbage, carrot and coconut called a thoran, from Kerala.

I also made a fresh mango chutney, a green mint and coriander chutney and a cucumber raita as well as my favourite Indian salad, which seems to end up with everything – kachumber, made of sliced tomato and red onion with green chilli, coriander and cumin, sharpened with a little vinegar. The rice turned out to be a nightmare because I hadn't bought a big enough pot to cook it in. I found one in an Indian store in Neutral Bay, but the base was so thin it actually burnt the rice. The puddings, though, were a triumph. I made nimish – and I actually managed to buy some gold leaf for it in the same Indian shop – and a chilled mango fool served with cardamom shortbreads.

As if that wasn't already a tidy little assignment, I also decided to make my own naan bread using the griddle plate of my Aussie barbecue outdoors. These were not a success. It's hardly worth bothering to make naan unless you've got a tandoor, but the great thing about preparing so many dishes is that if one or two are a bit sub-standard it doesn't matter because there's safety in numbers. Actually, it was a very memorable evening, not least because two of our more flamboyant friends thought it was fancy dress, even though I told everyone I was 'just trying out recipes for my next book'. So we had a maharaja and maharani in our midst, turban and all. The maharaja was talking inexplicably about his latest addiction, lychee martinis. I still can't see the point, but hey ho! As ever with our parties, my wife senses when the sensible are getting ready to leave and slams on the 80s hits. Soon any slight failings in the dinner are completely forgotten.

It seems kinder to test recipes in this way. Years ago, my boys, Ed, Jack and Charlie, were also treated as guinea pigs and I can remember Jack asking their mother, Jill, who was going to be cooking one night. When told it was me he groaned, 'Oh, Dad always takes so long. It'll be forever.'

'The real fun comes when I'm testing dishes for large parties.'

Cornish briam

The thought behind this recipe was to come up with a dish that uses all the vegetables currently grown by the farmers who supply our restaurants in late August – things like carrots, courgettes, broccoli and new potatoes. Ross Geach at Trerethern Farm, also known as Padstow Kitchen Garden, grows wonderful vegetables on his land overlooking the Camel estuary. The view alone makes you feel the vegetables will taste really special, which indeed they do. I cooked this for a sequence in my Rick Stein's Cornwall *series, having remembered a lovely slow-cooked vegetable dish called briam from the island of Corfu, and it works a treat. As our local vegetables don't perhaps have the intense sweetness of Mediterranean produce, I added some chilli and feta to give it a bit more oomph.*

SERVES 6-8

150ml olive oil, plus extra
   for greasing
500g waxy new potatoes, peeled
   and cut lengthways into 5mm slices
400g carrots, peeled or scrubbed
   and sliced lengthways
2 large courgettes (about 400g)
   sliced lengthways
1 large onion, peeled and sliced
5-6 garlic cloves, peeled and sliced

300g tenderstem broccoli
4 large tomatoes (or 6 medium),
   thickly sliced
1 red or green finger chilli, sliced
Handful flatleaf parsley, chopped
A few thyme sprigs, leaves
   stripped from the woody stalks
200ml passata
100g feta cheese, crumbled
Salt and black pepper

TIP
You can use
any late summer
vegetables you
have for this dish.

Preheat the oven to 190°C/Fan 170°C. Grease a roasting tin or a shallow, lidded casserole dish with oil. Spread the potato slices in a single layer and season well with salt and pepper. Layer the carrots on top, then the courgettes, then the onion and garlic, seasoning each layer with plenty of salt and pepper.

Scatter over the broccoli and cover it with tomato slices. Add the chilli, herbs and a final sprinkling of salt and pepper. Pour over the passata and the olive oil.

Cover the roasting tin tightly with foil or put a tight-fitting lid on the dish and place in the oven for about 1¼ hours. Sprinkle over the crumbled feta and return the tin to the oven, uncovered, for a further 15–20 minutes.

Allow it to cool slightly before serving as a side dish or as a main with crusty bread or rice.

Debra's achiote chickpeas

Our friend Debra Oswald has two recipes in this book. I tried to cut them down to one to be fair to everyone else, but I don't want to drop either of them. The reason for keeping this one is that I'm obsessed with the flavour of achiote, which you can buy from Mexican suppliers or on the internet. This recipe can be vegan if you leave the feta out.

SERVES 4
as a main meal
or 8 as a side

50g achiote paste
125ml olive oil
4 garlic cloves, crushed
1 large onion, chopped
4 tomatoes, diced
2 x 400g tins chickpeas,
    drained and rinsed
¼ tsp cayenne pepper
1 tsp salt

1 tsp black pepper
1 tbsp fresh oregano leaves
    or ½ tsp dried oregano
¼–½ tsp chilli flakes or
    chipotle flakes
200g feta, crumbled
2 large handfuls baby spinach
12 corn tortillas, if serving
    as a main meal

TIP
This recipe works
well prepared
ahead of time.
Just stop before
adding the feta
and spinach and
add them when
you reheat.

Blend the achiote paste with a few tablespoons of boiling water to soften it.

Pour the oil into a large pan and cook the garlic and onion until soft and translucent. Add the achiote and the tomatoes and stir for 5–10 minutes or so until softened.

Add the chickpeas, cayenne, salt, pepper, oregano and chilli or chipotle flakes. Stir to mix and cook for 5–10 minutes. Then add the feta and stir it through until it starts to melt. Finally fold through the spinach until it starts to wilt.

Serve as a side dish or as a filling for warmed tacos.

Richard Glover's vegetable moussaka

As you will see from the introduction to the chapter, this is Richard's vegetarian version of my moussaka. I suppose I am a bit of a recent convert to vegetarian cooking. This recipe and my stepson Zach's vegan chilli dish on page 242 are examples of my growing realisation that dishes written specifically for meat-free eating can be very good indeed. The reality is I don't like the cruel way in which we 'grow' animals for food any more than vegans do.

SERVES 6-8

1 aubergine, sliced lengthways
3 courgettes, sliced lengthways
Olive oil
2 large potatoes, sliced lengthways
100g red lentils, or 200g cooked puy lentils

2 small onions, chopped
1 red pepper, chopped
2 garlic cloves, chopped
50g tomato paste
3 beefsteak or 4 large tomatoes, chopped
1 cinnamon stick
Salt and black pepper

Béchamel sauce
100ml butter
100g plain flour
750ml whole milk
3 eggs
1 tsp grated nutmeg
150g Graviera cheese (or Gruyère if Graviera is unavailable), freshly grated

TIP
This dish is also very good the following day, served just warmed through, not piping hot.

Begin by salting the aubergine and courgette slices and leaving them for about 30 minutes. Rinse them and dry on kitchen paper. Fry them in plenty of oil over a medium heat until lightly browned and starting to soften, then drain on kitchen paper and set aside. Fry the potatoes in the same way. If using red lentils, cook according to the packet instructions.

In a separate pan, heat about 70ml of olive oil and fry the onions, red pepper and garlic for 5 minutes until softened. Stir in the tomato paste and cook for about 5 minutes, until the vegetables are soft and coated in the tomato paste. Add the chopped tomatoes and cinnamon stick, then season with salt and plenty of black pepper. Simmer for another 5 minutes. Throw in the cooked lentils and simmer for 5 minutes, then remove the cinnamon stick.

In a deep ovenproof dish, measuring about 24 x 35cm, arrange the potatoes in a single layer and top with a third of the lentil sauce. Add the slices of aubergine, cover with another third of the sauce, then the courgettes and finish with lentil sauce.

Preheat the oven to 220°C/Fan 200°C. Now make the béchamel sauce. Melt the butter in a pan over a gentle heat, stir in the flour and cook for 2 minutes, so the flour loses its raw taste. Slowly incorporate the milk and continue stirring until the sauce thickens. Remove the pan from the heat and whisk in the eggs, nutmeg and 100g of the grated cheese.

Spread the béchamel over the layered lentils and vegetables and top with the remaining 50g of grated cheese. Bake for 30 minutes, then take the dish out of the oven and leave to cool slightly. Serve warm.

Egg roast en route to Thekkady

This intro is from my book India *and I've kept it in as I rather like it: I find that a good recipe can often be found at the lunch place a driver selects for Western sensibilities – such as air conditioning. It never ceases to amaze me how good the cooking in these restaurants can be, though the places themselves are completely devoid of atmosphere, with the curtains drawn against the glare of a hot day, lots of tiled surfaces, maybe a picture on the wall of Ganesha the elephant god, lord of success and destroyer of evils, riding on a mouse. I was intrigued to see 'egg roast' on the menu of the Green Mango multi-cuisine restaurant in the hotel ABM Grande in Theni, between Madurai and Thekkady. Nobody quite knows why it's called an egg roast because the eggs are actually boiled, peeled, then simmered in a pan with an intense red masala flavoured with Kashmiri chillies, tomato passata and coconut oil. I love an egg curry and this is possibly my favourite.*

SERVES 4-6

6 eggs
2 tbsp coconut oil
Small handful fresh
    curry leaves
1 tsp fennel seeds
2 medium onions (250g), sliced
2 dried Kashmiri chillies,
    torn into pieces
4 garlic cloves, finely crushed

4cm root ginger,
    finely chopped
1 tsp ground coriander
1 tsp ground cumin
1 tsp Kashmiri chilli powder
1 tsp ground black pepper
1/2 tsp ground turmeric
400g passata
1 tsp salt

To serve
Handful fresh coriander
    leaves, chopped
Chapatis

TIP
The Kashmiri chillies and the powder are as much about their deep colour as their heat. If you can't get them, use 3 parts sweet paprika to 1 part cayenne pepper.

Bring a pan of water to the boil, add the eggs and cook them for 10 minutes. Drain and run under cold water before peeling.

Heat the coconut oil in a heavy-based pan over a medium heat. Add the curry leaves and fennel seeds and fry for 30 seconds, then add the onions and fry for 10 minutes until softened and golden brown. Add the dried chillies, garlic and ginger and fry for 2–3 minutes, then stir in the ground spices and fry for 30 seconds. Stir in the passata and salt, then simmer for 5–10 minutes until the sauce is rich and reduced.

Add the whole peeled eggs, put a lid on the pan and simmer for a further 4–5 minutes to heat the eggs through. Sprinkle with the chopped coriander and serve with chapatis.

Store cupboard

These days when journalists are few and far between, the most popular way of communication with newspapers and magazines is the Q and A. Frankly they drive me bonkers because the questions are always the same: what would your last supper be? What gadget couldn't you live without? What's your favourite cuisine from all the countries you've visited? Living or dead, who would you invite to your dream dinner party? And the big one – name the top ten ingredients you couldn't do without in your store cupboard.

My store cupboard is actually quite large but extends to a number of hastily put up Formica shelves in the garage. This is because I've had to buy in so many bottles, tins and jars for each of the various cuisines I have written about all over the world, coupled with the extreme generosity of companies trying to get their products into our deli or for me to be seen spooning them out in my next TV series.

The problem for me is sell-by dates. I've still got masalas and Kashmiri chillies from my India trip (2013), chillies from Mexico (2016), sauces and vinegars from Southeast Asia (2008), pul biber from the Venice to Istanbul journey (2014), which I'm still using, although officially out of date. Yesterday, I found a jar of capers from Salina – an island off the coast of Sicily – from 2004. I've long given up throwing stuff out by looking at the date on the label. I have to smell it and taste it and if it seems all right, I continue to use it. Deep down I know perfectly well that if I had a fresh pot it would be at least twice as good, but I do hate waste. At the moment, during another lockdown, I'm throwing away lots but, my gosh, there is still plenty left!

In a perfect world there are a number of things I always need in my cupboard, which incidentally is 1.2m wide, 2m high and 50cm deep. It's got five shelves and two deep drawers at the bottom. The bottom shelves contain two baskets for vegetables and the double doors have five narrow shelves attached to them for spice jars. The interior is wood but its exterior is painted a tasteful colour called Stiffkey Blue. There is plenty of space – it's possibly a little too deep because things tend to languish at the back and go out of date. There is some order. Bottled sauces and chutneys at the top, a shelf of oils, vinegars and condiments, then a shelf for flours, pasta and rice, and the bottom shelf for biscuits, cereals, sugar, chocolate nuts, desiccated coconut and anything to do with desserts.

Rather regrettably, the two big drawers at the bottom are filled with plastic containers. Nobody knows where else to keep them. Should you store them with the lid on or off? Or should you buy them all the same size so that they stack? But this cupboard is a joy to me. Referring back to that irritating question, here is the definitive list of what I really need and what you'll see recurring in ingredients lists.

Bottled sauces – soy sauce, Thai fish sauce, Japanese mayonnaise (Kewpie), HP sauce, tomato ketchup, sriracha, Worcestershire sauce, Tabasco and chipotle ketchup, which I like with my eggs and as a barbecue sauce.

Oils - three olive oils. I don't bother with brands. I just use ordinary supermarket extra virgin for salad dressing, a regular olive oil for cooking, and a single-estate olive oil for sprinkling on food or dipping bread into. I generally use sunflower oil for frying and I like to have a toasted sesame oil, some walnut or hazelnut oil and a cold-pressed rapeseed oil.

Vinegars – I'm trying to deal with a surfeit of balsamics, the best of which come from Modena and are, I think, almost not vinegars at all. You could certainly sprinkle them on your strawberries. But generally I like red wine, white wine, sherry, cider, distilled malt vinegar for pickles and Chinese black rice vinegar (chinkiang) for Chinese stir-fries and red braised pork. I've also got a couple of vintage French vinegars – a Banyuls, which makes a great dressing, and a bottle of Château Cheval Blanc made into vinegar that was given to me as a 70th birthday present. Needless to say, there's always a bottle of malt vinegar for fish and chips. There is now someone producing an artisan malt vinegar whose address is The Old Nuclear Bunker, Coverack, Cornwall. I also have a rice wine vinegar for Southeast Asian dishes. Oh, and I've got a double magnum of my own vinegar, which I started with a mother about 15 years ago and empty the remains of any unfinished bottles of wine into. I keep the flies out with a bit of muslin and a loose-fitting cork.

Jars and tins – chopped tomatoes, various tins of beans and pulses – usually chickpeas, butter beans and black beans; tomato paste, capers, olives, gherkins, mustard (English and French), chipotles en adobo, horseradish sauce, mint sauce and mint jelly, redcurrant jelly and Branston pickle; plus a selection of my own home-made preserves – usually plum chutney, green tomato chutney and bread and butter pickles.

I'm currently having a lovefest with a couple of jars of shrimp balachan, which is so good for adding to curries, particularly Goan fish curries, and there are always jars of the spice pastes that we make for the restaurants, such as nasi goreng and the Balinese spice mix, basa gede.

As far as jams and other, shall we say, spreadables are concerned, Portia, who helps me with writing the books, keeps me supplied annually with her quince jelly, and my friend Maud from Treyarnon, near Padstow, does the same with crab apples. My favourite jams are raspberry and the marmalade we make at our own production kitchen. Being of divided loyalties, there are always jars of both Marmite and Vegemite – I used to hate the latter but now I rather like it – and perhaps for me only, there is Bovril.

The rest – the other shelves contain various pastas, flours, including plenty of strong flour for sourdough, rice and panko breadcrumbs for deep-fried breaded fish. I guiltily always have a little bottle of gravy browning called Parisian Browning Essence that I bought in Australia. I don't usually hold with food dyes but it doesn't half make sausage and mashed potato with onion gravy look better.

The bottom shelf, as I said, is for biscuits, chocolate and so on – which I buy for baking but end up eating anyway – and for cereals. I am particularly fond, from my childhood, of grape nuts with full-cream milk and brown sugar, and here's a little idea: poached dark cherries with Greek yoghurt sprinkled with grape nuts and a spoonful of honey.

Rabo Estofado (Cont)

Add olive oil about 130ml
to hot frying pan browns
Oxtail brings it then
removes the pieas

Now fries veg then
a saucepan? Add
when the cooking is Add
all the veg dish fries
Add ... veg brandy ... lit
100 ml brandy
100 ml red wine
500 ml beef stock (see Espagnole)
1 ... white pork

1 rabo
2 onion
2 zenahorias (zer carrots)
1 puerro
2 dientes de ajos (cloves)
Puerro de campo

Add red wine
Half litre wine
1 copa de cognac

cooks for 1-2 hours

Finally
Takes out the meat
whizzes up veggies in
game # to form puree

The proper recipe

1½ kg oxtail
2 medium onion
2 carrots
1 leek
3/4 clover garlic or 2 large
100 ml EV olive oil
salt - 1 tsp
1 tablespoon parsley
100 ml brandy
500 ml red wine
1 litre good beef stock
(1 cup)
garnish
2 pieces luke

E8g

Zach's vegan chilli

I wanted a proper vegan dish in my book, but I'm not capable of coming up with something at my age, so I asked my stepson, Zach. He's not actually vegan but would prefer to be I think, except that he can't resist turbot and hollandaise sauce. He does keep the fridge stuffed full of soya milk, tofu and such things as vegan crème fraiche, though. I like this dish. It's colourful and there is plenty of depth of flavour. I particularly like the creaminess of the crème fraiche made with cashew nuts.

SERVES 4

4 sweet potatoes, skins scrubbed
2 tbsp sunflower oil, plus extra
    for the sweet potatoes
100g broccoli florets
1 red onion, finely sliced
1 large garlic clove, finely
    chopped or grated
1½–2 tsp cayenne pepper
1 tsp ground cinnamon
1 tsp ground cumin
1 red pepper, chopped

600g tinned chopped
    tomatoes
170g tinned chickpeas,
    drained and rinsed
100g fresh, frozen or tinned
    sweetcorn kernels
170g tinned black beans,
    drained and rinsed
170g tinned kidney beans,
    drained and rinsed
Salt and black pepper

Vegan 'crème fraiche'
65g cashews soaked in
    120ml water for 30
    minutes, then drained
Juice of ½ lemon

To serve
75g edamame beans
1 avocado, peeled,
    stoned and sliced
Lime wedges

TIP
You can use any leftover beans in a soup or salad or, if you prefer, just use one type of bean. This is also delicious with plenty of fresh coriander leaves on top.

Preheat the oven to 200°C/Fan 180°C. Rub the sweet potatoes all over with a little oil and season, then bake for about 45 minutes, depending on size. Steam the broccoli until tender.

To make the vegan crème fraiche, put the soaked and drained cashew nuts in a blender with the lemon juice. Season with salt and blitz to form a cream.

Heat the oil in a large pan and add the onion, garlic and spices. Cook over a medium heat for a few minutes until softened, then add the red pepper and tomatoes and cook for a couple of minutes. Add the chickpeas, sweetcorn, black beans and kidney beans, season with salt and cook for 10–15 minutes. If the mixture starts to look too dry, add a little water. Then add the steamed broccoli and mix to warm it through.

Trim the ends off the sweet potatoes and cut them in half but don't cut right through the other side. Place a potato on each plate and spoon over the chilli. Top with some edamame beans and crème fraiche, then serve with avocado and lime wedges.

Chapter Seven
DESSERTS & DRINKS

My wife Sas has a secret passion for desserts which, because she is someone who is very strict about what she eats for weight reasons, is very hard to perceive. I have only circumstantial evidence, the first of which is that she regards puddings as the very heart of home cooking: tarte tatin, apple Charlotte, rhubarb crumble, tiramisu, even Christmas pudding are to her the ties that bind families together. When, however, we go out to a restaurant she never orders a sweet and I always say, 'Are you sure you don't want one?' to which she replies, 'Absolutely not.'

There then follows what our friend Barry Humphries calls the darting fork. He divides the world into those who admit to their passion and those who try to disguise it and the result is that whatever I order, but particularly if it's sticky toffee pudding, a fork will dart over to my plate. If I complain righteously because I asked her and she said no, she'll say, 'Sharing is caring and you're not a sharer.' So then there follows lots of spluttering and irritation from me, when even desserts she says she can't abide, like panna cotta, seem to disappear on the darting fork.

The reality is that Sas has a no-nonsense approach to food, which means that she doesn't like to eat anything she sees as a waste of calories. The prime candidates are first courses, so when I'm planning a dinner she will show faint praise for first courses. But I actually think she's right in that desserts are what really do count in family meals.

Interestingly, the most popular dish in my last television series, which was about Cornwall, was apple Charlotte (page 254). I cooked this, fittingly enough, in an apple orchard. I felt rather embarrassed at the time, as it was my mother's recipe and there's nothing much to it other than apple purée, sugar, lemon zest and lots of buttered bread, but everyone loved it. I suspect this had a lot to do with the company I was keeping at the time – a lovely man named John Harris, head gardener at Tresillian House, near Newquay, where we were staying. John designed and built the orchard in the grounds of the house in the early 90s and now it is splendidly mature, with 84 different varieties of apples. The orchard is planted in a diamond shape that allows maximum light to the trees, but which you can only appreciate from above. Thanks to drones, that's not a problem these days.

John's knowledge of apple orchards was like gold for a television programme, and his enthusiasm for the varieties he grows is so charming: apples such as Cornish Gilliflower, Cornish Aromatic, Crimson Queen and Lord of the Isles. When I asked John about a variety known as the pear apple because of its shape, he told me that it was grown to make 'soft cider for ladies' because 'rough cider was for the men'.

The other reason I think for the great success of the apple Charlotte is that it is so much a part of many people's memories of childhood.

Rhubarb crumble

Rhubarb crumble – the light-brown crust splitting and darkening round the edge of the dish with the rhubarb bubbling up from below, the smell of butter and baked flour with the sour tang of the rhubarb – is a pudding which is about as close to the heart of British cooking as you can get. Yet why is it so often disappointing? Usually it's the crumble that's wrong. It might be too lean, making it rather dry and everlasting to eat, or it's undercooked so that it has the pasty flavour of uncooked flour. The rhubarb is usually less of a problem, though getting the balance of sugar right is critical; it should be tart but not so much as to pucker the mouth. This last point is dependent on the variety of rhubarb chosen. I enjoy the early forced rhubarb, with its pale pink and delicate skin, which appears in long rectangular boxes in January and February. This is surprisingly sweet, not having received much of the teeth-biting oxalic acid present in greener rhubarb stalks and in poisonous quantities in the leaves. So who's the hero here? Well, my mother; it's her recipe and she never got it wrong.

SERVES 6-8

225g plain flour
175g chilled butter, cut into cubes
275g caster sugar
900g rhubarb, trimmed and wiped clean
Clotted cream, to serve

TIP
You could add orange zest or a tablespoon of chopped stem ginger to the rhubarb for a change.

Preheat the oven to 190°C/Fan 170°C. For the topping, put the flour and butter into a food processor and pulse together until the mixture looks like coarse breadcrumbs. Alternatively, put the flour and cubed butter in a bowl and rub them together with your fingertips. You want the mixture to be clumpy rather than fine and dusty. Stir in 100g of the sugar.

Cut the rhubarb into 2.5cm pieces, put them in a bowl and add the rest of the sugar. Mix well and set aside for 15–20 minutes, stirring now and then, until slightly moistened.

Spread the fruit over the base of a shallow ovenproof dish and sprinkle over the topping. Bake for 45–50 minutes until the rhubarb is tender and the top is golden brown. Serve with some clotted cream.

Egg-free meringues

Who would have dreamed that the liquid from canned chickpeas had very similar properties to egg white? I must add here that it's really important to use chickpeas in unsalted water, otherwise your meringues will taste rather savoury. When Portia, my home economist, first suggested egg-free meringues I was typically unenthusiastic but after tasting them, I realised I could substitute my sense of trickery for my strong waste-not-want-not feelings. And Portia says that the joy on the faces of a couple of friends, parents of recent vegan-convert children, at discovering perfectly lovely egg-free meringues was a wonder. Having a stepson who would prefer to be vegan, I am in no way as dismissive of a meat- and dairy-free life as I used to be.

SERVES 8-10

100ml of aquafaba (liquid drained
    from a 400g tin chickpeas
    in UNSALTED water)
½ tsp cream of tartar
110g caster sugar
Seeds scraped from a vanilla pod

To serve
Coconut cream
Fruit

TIP
These meringues can be made to serve as petits fours. Just put teaspoons of the mixture on lined baking sheets and cook as described but for only about 2 hours. Sandwich together with whipped coconut cream or vegan lemon curd.

Preheat the oven to 110°C/Fan 90°C.

Whisk the aquafaba with the cream of tartar for 12–15 minutes in a stand mixer or with electric beaters until it's white, voluminous and holding its shape. You should be able to turn the whisk upside down without the mixture dropping. Add the sugar and vanilla seeds in a couple of batches and whisk again briefly to incorporate.

Spoon on to baking sheets lined with parchment, either using serving spoons to make individual servings or shaping a disc to make a pavlova. Bake for 2½–3 hours until the tops and bottoms are crisp and firm. Turn off the oven and leave to cool in the oven or transfer to a wire rack to cool in a dry place. Store in an airtight tin for up to 2 days.

Serve with whipped coconut cream, mango, papaya and passion fruit or strawberries and raspberries.

Gooseberry fool

Where are the gooseberry bushes of yesteryear? Everyone with a decent-sized garden used to have gooseberries, but nowadays they are quite hard to get hold of. Remembering those in our garden in the Cotswolds – we referred to them as goosegogs – I think they were either very sour or overripe and splitting. As far as I can work out, the French only serve them with mackerel. We try harder – while gooseberry jam isn't much to write home about, a gooseberry fool is a great thing.

SERVES 4

200g gooseberries, topped and tailed (frozen are fine, as are tinned and drained at a push)
40g caster sugar

150ml double cream
150ml Greek-style yoghurt
1–2 tbsp sifted icing sugar, to taste
Ginger biscuits, to serve

TIP
Tart fruit, such as blackcurrants, redcurrants or rhubarb, make great fools. Just adjust the amount of sugar to taste.

Put the gooseberries in a saucepan with the sugar and 3 tablespoons of water. Place over a low heat and stir until the sugar has dissolved. Then turn up the heat and cook for 3–5 minutes until the gooseberries are soft and falling apart. Keep stirring and crushing the fruit with the back of a wooden spoon until you have a pulpy sauce. Take the pan off the heat, tip the fruit into a bowl, leave to cool and then refrigerate until cold.

In a separate bowl, whisk the cream until thickened and forming soft creamy peaks. Stir in the yoghurt, then fold in the gooseberry pulp and add the icing sugar. Spoon into glasses or small bowls and serve with crisp ginger biscuits.

Apple Charlotte

I've mentioned the television series that I recently filmed in Cornwall often in this book, mainly because most of the recipes in the programmes are for dishes I cook at home a lot. The runaway success of the series was this apple Charlotte, which I cooked in an orchard at Tresillian House, near Newquay. It's a very special recipe – my mother's and one of her favourites.

SERVES 4

125g butter
350g Bramley apples
350g Cox's apples
2 tbsp sugar

A little grated lemon zest, to taste
6-8 slices white bread, about 5mm thick, crusts removed

Custard, clotted cream or ice cream, to serve

TIP
I love the clean taste of apple and lemon in this, as cooked by my mum, but you could add a good pinch of ground cloves or some ground cinnamon if you like.

Grease a pudding basin, about 15cm in diameter and 10cm deep, with plenty of the butter. Peel, core and finely slice the apples. Rinse in cold water and put them in a saucepan with the sugar, lemon zest and 30g of the butter. Cook to a pulp over a low heat and then beat to a purée with a wooden spoon. Allow to cool. Preheat the oven to 200°C/Fan 180°C.

Melt the remaining butter. Dip each slice of bread into the butter and then line a pudding basin with about three-quarters of the slices. Pack them in tightly and don't leave any gaps. Spoon in the cooled apple purée and cover with the remaining buttered pieces of bread and gently push down.

Tightly cover the pudding with foil and bake for about 30 minutes. Remove the foil and bake for a further 8–10 minutes until the top is golden brown. Leave the pudding to rest for 5 minutes before turning out on to a serving plate. Serve with custard, clotted cream or ice cream.

Foraging – a walk with a purpose

I'm writing this during what is now the third lockdown of the Coronavirus pandemic. It's a lovely sunny day in Padstow in January and actually quite mild – about 11 degrees. Yesterday was even milder, 14. As I walked to my normal place on the Camel Estuary for my swim, I was reflecting on the reality that the weather in the summer in Cornwall is normally wetter, cloudier and often colder than London, but in the winter the climate is much warmer and probably accounts for why so many different crops can be grown here.

The swim itself was a bit grim – browny-grey water, lots of seaweed and pigeons flying all around the little bay. There were two lads fishing where I normally change, and they seemed rather surprised to see anyone swimming at this time of year. Sometimes I find it hard to explain why I do, but my great PA Vivienne Taylor gave me a special towelling robe for my birthday a couple of weeks ago and it's changed my winter swimming life.

Part of the fun of walking to the little cove is that at every time of the year there are things to pick up: field mushrooms and crab apples in September, shaggy inkcap mushrooms in October and November; limpets, of course, and in spring and early summer there's parsley, sorrel and wild garlic. In summer, I go to Harlyn Bay and Mother Ivey's a lot and often come back with some seaweed, a bit of rock samphire and a capful of mussels from the beach for my breakfast. I'll steam the mussels with a drop of cider, some butter, a few chopped shallots and a lick of cream. I don't eat the seaweed and the samphire, but they add to the flavour.

I do really like walking and walk almost every day, but I feel a bit guilty in that a good walk only becomes a great one if I find something to gather. For this reason, autumnal walks are the most attractive to me. I'm inordinately fond of blackberries, but I can never quite work out why the wild ones taste so much nicer than cultivated. Maybe it's the same reason that vines that have to exist in thin, rocky soils produce such interesting grapes. Maybe it's simply that gathering blackberries is a labour of love and it takes effort. For a start, there's the prickles, then there's always going to be nettles nearby and flies and the irritation that the best crop is always slightly out of reach. Your struggle to get them will always result in prickles and stings because you'll drop your guard and then you'll probably step in a cow pat as well. I still think the whole adventure of gathering wild fruit or anything else edible is bound to be better for you all round than eating the equivalent from the supermarket.

While I'm on the subject of blackberries, wild plums in the shape of sloes and bullaces bring back fond memories of the days when I was a young father taking my boys out on weekend walks. All three of them couldn't believe you could eat anything so sour. Both sloes and bullaces are great for sloe gin and there's actually a very nice recipe on page 178 for using them in a sauce with pork chops. The sourness is fantastic for cutting through the fattiness of meat from breeds of pig like Gloucester Old Spot, Cornish Black or Mangalitsa.

The main reason for going on foraging trips with my boys when they were little was to find wild mushrooms. Unfortunately, Cornwall isn't the best county for mushrooming, for one thing because it's not got a lot of forests. Also, I suspect the frequent salt-laden westerly winds don't bring out the best in many a mushroom, so the walks were always full of hope and anticipation but sadly not often rewarded. We were always looking at mushrooms that could have been edible but equally could have been death caps, which we never dared to pick. We had much more success with gathering samphire in the summer because that grows a lot in the Camel Estuary and we also became quite expert in identifying wild salad leaves.

I seem to remember rewarding the boys financially for the samphire, as well as for little buckets of winkles, both of which I actually needed for the platters of fruits de mer we were starting to serve in the restaurant in those days. I also paid them for the shore crabs, which they would catch in an onion net baited with a little mackerel off the quayside in Padstow. I used to like to think that the life-cycle of the green shore crab involved finding food in a little net bag, being dragged to the surface and put in a little bucket of water, then being returned to the harbour waters by parents who didn't want to have to take the crabs home to die and become really smelly. With my boys, the crabs were not so lucky because they do make the most excellent seafood stock, which I used as part of a sauce for grilled lobster in the restaurant.

It's interesting to look back now and realise that a lot of the things I suggested gathering to keep the boys having fun have now become really trendy, like samphire and elderflowers. Elderflowers, though, bring a sense of regret to me because the elder tree flowers in late May-early June and sadly 'summer's lease hath too short a date'. I think I only managed to gather enough elderflowers to make cordial on a couple of occasions when my boys were little. I was always meaning to go after the spring bank holiday weekend when we'd been very busy in the restaurant with no time to venture out, but sadly all that was ever left were a few single flowers.

'I do really like walking and walk almost every day, but I feel a bit guilty in that a good walk only becomes a great one if I find something to gather.'

Apple tarte tatin

This recipe comes from my book French Odyssey *and I note
that the introduction to the recipe is as apt now as it was then:
The points to note in making tarte tatin are first, the apples –
you need a nice firm apple that won't fall apart, so I go for Cox's
– and second, the making of the caramel. It needs to be done over a
medium heat, taking your time to allow the butter, sugar and apple
juices to reach a nice toffee colour before topping the dish with the
puff pastry and baking it. One of the best puddings in the world.*

SERVES 6

250g puff pastry (preferably all butter)
75g softened butter
175g caster sugar
750g firm dessert apples, such as Cox's
Vanilla ice cream or crème fraiche, to serve

TIPS

You can also
make this with
pears, nectarines,
peaches, plums or
apricots, and we
do rather a nice
pineapple version
in the Seafood
Restaurant.

Savoury versions
with vegetables
like tomatoes or
aubergines are
good too, but
slow-cook them
first and leave
out the sugar.

Roll out the pastry on a lightly floured surface and cut out a
26cm disc, slightly larger than the top of a tarte tatin dish or
a reliably non-stick cast-iron frying pan. Transfer it to a baking
sheet and chill for at least 20 minutes. Spread the butter over
the base of the tarte tatin dish or frying pan, then sprinkle
over the sugar in a thick, even layer.

Peel, core and halve the apples, if large, trimming them
very slightly if necessary to fit but keeping their nicely
rounded shape. Tightly pack them on top of the sugar. Place
the tatin dish or frying pan over a medium heat and cook for
20–25 minutes, gently shaking the pan now and then, until
the butter and sugar have amalgamated with the apple juices
to produce a rich toffee-coloured sauce. Just don't let it burn.

Preheat the oven to 190°C/Fan 170°C. Place the pastry on top
of the apples and tuck the edges down inside the pan. Prick
the pastry 5 or 6 times with the tip of a small, sharp knife,
transfer to the oven and bake for 25 minutes until the pastry
is puffed up, crisp and golden.

Remove the tart from the oven and leave it to rest for 5 minutes.
Then run a knife round the edge of the tart and invert it on
to a round, flat serving plate. Serve warm, cut into wedges,
with vanilla ice cream or crème fraiche.

Christmas cake

*I wouldn't say there was anything unique about my recipe.
Most are much of a muchness, but what I love about Christmas
cake is feeding it with fortified wines or spirits. Personally,
I prefer using fortified wine because brandy or whisky are too
strong, although last Christmas I used vintage port and my wife
claimed you could get tipsy just from the smell of the cake. I'm a
great fan of proper marzipan and some royal icing too. In the early
days of the restaurant I once spent a winter on a cake-decorating
course. I was the only man and all the women were unbelievably
skilled. Why they were on the course, I don't know. I still cringe
at the memory that for some reason I chose to make a square
Christmas cake, even though we all had cake turntables.
As a beginner, if you ever think of making a square cake, don't.*

**MAKES A 20CM
ROUND CAKE**

175g sultanas	225g butter, softened,	*Marzipan*	*Royal icing*
275g currants	plus extra for greasing	250g ground almonds	3 egg whites
175g raisins	Sunflower oil	125g icing sugar, plus	675g icing sugar, sifted
50g glacé cherries, halved	225g dark muscovado sugar	extra for dusting	1½ tsp glycerine
50g mixed peel	4 eggs, beaten	125g caster sugar	1-2 tsp lemon juice
Grated zest of 1 orange	225g plain flour	1 tsp almond extract	1 drop of blue food
Grated zest of 1 lemon,	60g chopped mixed nuts	1 egg white	colouring (if very
75ml brandy or sherry,	or ground almonds	2-3 tbsp apricot jam,	bright white icing
or orange juice if	1 tsp mixed spice	warmed and sieved	is desired)
you prefer	¼ tsp freshly grated nutmeg		

The day before you make your cake, mix the dried fruit,
cherries and peel with the citrus zest. Stir in the brandy,
sherry or orange juice, cover and leave to soak overnight.

You will need a 20cm round cake tin. To line it, cut 2 discs
of baking parchment to fit the base. Then cut a length of
parchment about 10cm longer than the circumference of the
tin and about 5cm taller than the tin depth. Along the long
edge, fold over a strip about 2cm wide and then snip along
the folded edge about every 2cm. Butter the tin very well
and lay a disc of parchment in the base. Then line the sides
of the tin with the long strip of parchment, fitting the snipped
edge into the base and pressing it into the edges of the tin.
Add the second disc to the base, covering the snipped edges,
then brush with a little oil. The tin is now ready to use.

Preheat the oven to 140°C/Fan 120°C. Using a food mixer or an electric beater, mix together the butter and sugar until well combined and fluffy. Add the beaten eggs, a little at a time. If the mixture starts to look as though it's curdling, add a tablespoon of the measured flour, then continue to add the eggs. Stir in the remaining flour, chopped nuts, spices and the soaked dried fruit.

Spoon the mixture into the prepared tin and flatten the surface. Cover the top with a double layer of baking parchment and cut a hole 4cm in diameter in the middle to allow steam to escape. Bake the cake on the lowest shelf in the oven for 4 hours and 15 minutes. Test with a skewer pushed into the middle of the cake and if it comes out clean, remove the cake and place it on a wire rack. If not, put the cake back in the oven and cook for up to another 30 minutes, checking after 15, until a skewer comes out clean. Leave the cake to cool on a wire rack until completely cold.

If you're making the cake weeks in advance, store it in an airtight tin. To feed it, skewer holes in the surface and add a few teaspoons of brandy, sherry, port or rum. Do this several times a week for a few weeks.

Alternatively, you can marzipan the cake as soon as it's fully cold. At least a week before you want to ice your cake, make the marzipan by combining the ingredients, except the jam, in a food processor and pulsing until combined. Turn it out on to a board dusted with icing sugar and knead briefly to form a dough, then wrap it well in cling film or store in a plastic box in the fridge until ready to use.

Measure up the side of the cake across the top and down the other side to get a diameter for your disc. Roll out the marzipan on a board dusted with icing sugar until large enough to cover the top and sides of the cake. Brush the cake all over with the warmed apricot jam. Drape the marzipan over a rolling pin and line up the centre of the marzipan with the centre of the cake. Place the marzipan over the cake, smooth it over and trim off any excess. Cover with a clean tea towel and leave it to dry out for a day or so in a cool dry place.

Recipe continued overleaf

Royal icing

This makes just one layer of icing. If you want to do 2 layers and get a very smooth finish, make 2 half-quantity batches of the icing and allow the first coat to dry completely for about 24 hours before top coating.

Beat the 3 egg whites together in a bowl or a stand mixer. Add enough of the sifted icing sugar, a little at a time, until you have a thick paste (you may not need all of the icing sugar). Whisk for 10 minutes or so until the icing is whipped and shiny. Add the glycerine to prevent the icing from becoming rock hard, and then a teaspoon of the lemon juice and the blue colouring, if using. The icing should be glossy and stiff and should stand up in stiff peaks. Add a little more lemon juice if it is too stiff to work with.

Pile about 80 per cent of the icing on top of the cake and smooth over the top and sides. Working with a palette knife, smooth the icing over the top until it is level, then around the sides to make it as even as possible. If you prefer, do a rough snow scene, using a palette knife or fork to create texture. Spoon the remaining 20 per cent of the icing into an airtight container until the next day.

The next day, check the icing consistency. If it has stiffened, add a few drops of lemon juice until you get a pipeable consistency. Spoon the icing into a piping bag fitted with a decorative nozzle and pipe around the base where the cake meets the board and around the top rim of the cake. Add a ribbon and any other festive decorations, as desired.

Chocolate fondants
with coffee ice cream

Unusually, I have adapted a recipe we use at the restaurant which was for 21 chocolate fondants and 15 litres of ice cream. Normally the restaurant recipes are scaled-up versions of those that appear in my books, but it was our patissier Stuart Pate who came up with this years ago. I still think it's the best and it's lovely served with some coffee ice cream.

SERVES 4

100g unsalted butter, plus extra, melted, for greasing the basins
15g cocoa powder, plus extra for dusting the basins
100g dark chocolate (70% cocoa solids), chopped
2 eggs, plus 2 extra yolks
50g caster sugar

Coffee ice cream
Makes 1.25–1.5 litres
600ml whole milk
300ml double cream
2 eggs, plus 1 extra yolk
225g caster sugar
15ml Camp coffee

TIP
Make the fondants to the chilling stage before your guests arrive. When you're ready, take the ice cream from the freezer to soften at the same time as you place the fondants in the preheated oven.

You will need 4 individual 7cm-diameter metal pudding basins. Brush the inside of each one with melted butter and dust with cocoa powder.

Put the butter and chocolate in a bowl and set it over a pan of simmering water. Leave until the butter and chocolate have melted, then stir. Sift the cocoa powder into the chocolate and butter mix and set aside.

In a separate bowl, whisk the whole eggs, egg yolks and caster sugar to ribbon stage – until the mixture is thick and pale and the whisk leaves a ribbon trail in the mixture when lifted out.

Add the melted chocolate mixture to the eggs and fold together. Divide the mixture between the individual pudding basins and chill until required.

Preheat the oven to 180°C/Fan 160°C. Bake the fondants for 10–12 minutes until they have risen and the tops are firm to the touch. Remove from the oven and cool for 2 minutes before running a knife around the top of each basin to release them. Turn out on to each serving plate and serve immediately with the coffee ice cream.

Recipe continued overleaf

Coffee ice cream

In a large saucepan, bring the milk and cream just to the boil, then take off the heat. In a bowl, mix the whole eggs, egg yolk and sugar together and add the milk and cream. Return the pan to a low heat and stir until the mixture has thickened. Do not allow it to get too hot or the eggs will scramble.

Leave to cool completely, then add the coffee and churn in an ice cream maker.

If you don't have an ice cream maker, pour the mixture into a plastic box with a lid and freeze for a couple of hours. Remove from the freezer and blitz in a food processor, then put it back in the freezer. Repeat this process another couple of times and then leave to freeze for the final time for 6–8 hours. Take the ice cream out of the freezer 10–15 minutes before serving.

Olivia's Baileys truffles

My stepdaughter Olivia was taught this recipe at Westminster Kingsway College, but changed it to give the truffles a taste of Baileys. She says it reminds her of late-night snacks, sitting by the fire on Christmas night with maybe a glass of spiced rum.

MAKES
ABOUT 28

100g dark chocolate, chopped into small pieces
100g milk chocolate, chopped into small pieces
10g butter (at room temperature)
150ml double cream
60ml Baileys Irish Cream
30g cocoa powder

TIP
You could use finely chopped nuts as a coating, or dip the truffles into melted white or dark chocolate, then chill them until set. Use a different liqueur, if preferred.

Put the chopped chocolate and butter in a bowl. Pour the double cream into a small pan and bring to a boil, then immediately pour it over the chocolate and butter. Stir until the chocolate has melted and the mixture is smooth, then stir in the Baileys. Refrigerate for 4 hours until firm.

Scoop up a few generous teaspoonfuls of the mixture and drop them into a bowl with the cocoa powder. Roll the balls of coated chocolate between your palms and set aside. Continue with the remaining mixture, then return them to the cocoa powder for a final dusting.

Put the truffles in the fridge and chill for at least a couple of hours. Store in the fridge between pieces of baking parchment until ready to eat.

Spiced pears poached
with blackberries & red wine

This recipe is from Sas's stepmother, Janine. During the months of lockdown we spent in Sydney in 2020, she must have made it five times, as it was popular with us all. One reason I love it so much is the inclusion of blackberries in the poaching liquor which has the effect of making the pears a really dark red. Plus I like the way the sauce is thickened by reducing the cooking liquid.

SERVES 8

1 orange
1 lemon
750ml red wine
200g root ginger
1 cinnamon stick
4 whole cloves
1 fresh bay leaf
5 fennel seeds

1 rosemary sprig
500g caster sugar
300g fresh or frozen
   blackberries
8 pears, peeled, leaving
   the top stem intact
Custard or ice cream,
   to serve

TIP
This is a great choice for a dinner party, as it can happily be earlier in the day, or even the day before, ready to serve to guests.

Using a vegetable peeler, pare the zest from half the orange and half the lemon, then squeeze the juice from each fruit.

Put the orange and lemon zest in a large pan with the wine, ginger, spices, bay leaf, fennel seeds, rosemary, sugar and blackberries and bring to the boil. Reduce the heat to low and simmer for 10 minutes. Strain the liquid into a clean pan and return the cinnamon stick to the strained mixture. Add the pears and the citrus juices and simmer over a very low heat for about 45 minutes or until the pears are tender, turning once.

Carefully lift the pears from the liquid and set them aside. Simmer the liquid until reduced by two-thirds and then drain. Pour the sauce over the pears and serve warm or at room temperature with custard or ice cream.

Maud's chocolate fridge cake

Maud Old is a friend of ours with a farm at Treyarnon Bay and, like many Cornish farmers' wives, is enormously generous with her lovely lunches, dinners and hospitality in general. Sadly, her husband Geoffrey died some years ago and a testimony to the long and happy years they spent together is how much she misses him. Nevertheless, she is filled with the realisation that life goes on and for her that means cooking for friends and family all the time. When she first gave me this cake it reminded me of my own childhood in the 60s, when fridge cakes were all the rage.

MAKES ABOUT
16 SQUARES

250g butter, plus extra for greasing
4 tbsp golden syrup
250g plain chocolate, broken into pieces
300g rich tea or shortbread-type
    biscuits, chopped into 1cm pieces
85g raisins or sultanas
100g glacé cherries, halved
100g chopped mixed nuts

Icing
100g dark chocolate
50ml double cream
50g icing sugar, sifted
Grated dark chocolate (optional)

TIP
You can add whatever you like to this cake – for example, dried apricots or cranberries, hazelnuts or walnuts, mixed peel and so on.

Grease a 20–22cm square tin. Melt the butter and golden syrup in a pan. Put the chocolate in a bowl and place over a pan of barely simmering water until melted. Add the chocolate to the butter and syrup, then add the chopped biscuits, dried fruit and nuts. Stir well, turn into the greased tin and refrigerate overnight.

The cake is delicious with icing too. Melt the dark chocolate and stir in the cream and icing sugar. Cover the cold fridge cake with the icing, add grated chocolate, if desired, then put it back in the fridge for an hour or so to set.

Millionaire's shortbread

My wife has realised that she has been eating millionaire's shortbread all her life, but in Australia it was always known as caramel slice or caramel square. It's through her that I discovered a love of it. A square plus an Aussie flat white coffee is my perfect choice while sitting outside a café somewhere in Sydney. Millionaire's shortbread sounds much posher.

MAKES 16–24
(depending on bar size)

Base
250g plain flour
70g caster sugar
175g salted butter
   (at room temperature)

Caramel
1 x 397g tin full-fat
   condensed milk
100g light soft brown sugar
100g butter
½ tsp flaked sea salt
   (if you want a salted
   caramel version)

Topping
200g dark chocolate
1 tsp vegetable or coconut oil

TIP
Adding oil to the chocolate makes it easier to cut and less likely to shatter. Fine to use milk or white chocolate or a marbled mixture if you prefer.

Preheat the oven to 180°C/Fan 160°C. Line a baking tin measuring about 22 x 25cm with baking parchment.

Put the flour, sugar and butter in a bowl or food processor and combine until the mixture resembles breadcrumbs. Bring it together to form a rough dough, then press firmly into the tin using the back of a spoon. Prick the base with a fork. Bake for about 20 minutes until lightly golden and firm, then remove from the oven and set aside to cool completely in the tin.

While the base is cooling, make the caramel. Put all the ingredients into a non-stick pan and place over a medium heat until the butter has melted, the sugar has dissolved and the mixture comes together. Turn up the heat and bring to the boil. Lower the heat and cook for a further 5–10 minutes until the mixture thickens. Stir constantly to prevent the mixture from catching on the bottom of the pan. Pour over the cooled base and sprinkle over the sea salt, if using. Cool completely.

For the topping, put the chocolate in a bowl set over a pan of barely simmering water. When the chocolate has melted, stir in the oil. When the caramel has completely cooled, pour over the melted chocolate and leave to set. Cut into 16, 20 or 24 pieces and store in an airtight tin.

Passion fruit soufflés

Having spent some time making soufflés in my own restaurant when I did a spell of being the pastry cook, I can reassure anyone that making them is not difficult. What is difficult, though, is getting the timing right. I once took part in a banquet for about 1,000 people run by an exceptionally organised chef named Peter Cromberg. He hired about 30 fan ovens for the soufflés so that they could all be cooked at once, but still the skill came from making sure the waiters got them all out to the table in time. Once they are at the table nobody minds if inevitably they deflate. What I love about this passion fruit soufflé is that I've mischievously included the seeds, which bring a very satisfying crunch, almost in counterpoint to the ethereal nature of the dish.

SERVES 4

Sauce	For the ramekins	Soufflés
1 ripe mango, peeled and stoned	10g butter, melted, for greasing	25g butter
2 passion fruits, pulp and seeds	1 tbsp caster sugar, for dusting	20g cornflour
A little fresh lime juice, to taste		55g caster sugar
1–2 tsp caster or icing sugar, to taste		140ml milk
		3 or 4 passion fruits, pulp and seeds
		4 medium eggs, separated
		Icing sugar, for dusting

TIP
Any leftover mango and passion fruit sauce is delicious poured over ice cream.

For the sauce, blitz the mango flesh to a smooth pulp in a liquidiser. Pour it into a jug, add the passion fruit pulp with the seeds, then stir in the lime juice. Sweeten with sugar to taste. Cover and refrigerate until ready to use.

You need 4 x 150ml ramekins. Brush the insides of the ramekins with melted butter and dust with caster sugar. Preheat the oven to 220°C/Fan 200°C and place a heavy baking tray in the oven to heat up.

To make the soufflés, melt the 25g of butter in a pan and add the cornflour and about half the caster sugar. Stir over the heat for a couple of minutes until you have thick paste. Take the pan off the heat and add the milk gradually, whisking after each addition until smooth. Then put the pan back over a medium heat and cook for 2 minutes until the mixture comes to the boil and you have thick custard. Remove from the heat and whisk in the passion fruit, seeds and all, and the egg yolks, then set aside.

Whisk the egg whites in a clean bowl. Once they are at soft peak stage, add the remaining sugar in 3 batches, whisking after each addition, until you have a glossy meringue mixture.

Add a large spoonful of the meringue to the passion fruit custard and stir well to 'loosen' the mixture. Then, using a large metal spoon, fold in the rest. Divide the mixture between the 4 prepared ramekins and run a butter knife or teaspoon handle around the edge of each ramekin to a depth of about 1cm to encourage the soufflés to rise.

Place the ramekins on the hot baking tray and cook for 10 minutes until the soufflés are well risen and golden on top. Put the sauce on the table and get your sieve charged with icing sugar for sifting. Have 4 dessert plates and the mango sauce ready.

Remove the soufflés from the oven very swiftly, dust them with icing sugar and put them on the plates. Take them to the table immediately, as they sink fast once out of the oven. Each person can make a hole in the centre of their soufflé and pour in some of the sauce.

If you want to get ahead with these, refrigerate the custard mixture once you have added the passion fruit and egg yolks. Just cover the surface with a piece of greaseproof paper to prevent a skin from forming. Remove it from the fridge half an hour before you want to cook. You may need to rewhisk the mixture briefly to loosen it, then whisk the egg whites and incorporate and cook as above.

Hummingbird cake

One of the joys of baking cakes in Australia is the availability of tropical fruit with much more regularity than in the UK, but Aussies share the same cake-making skills, so the result is a delight like this hummingbird cake. It's similar to a carrot cake but stuffed full of bananas and pineapple. I'm particularly fond of this cake because Sas's family produced one for my 60th birthday in Mollymook. I had become inured to celebratory cakes, as they always seemed to be just sponge with a dull filling of jam or buttercream, so this was a bit of a mind-blower.

SERVES 6-8

200ml sunflower oil,
 plus extra for greasing
275g plain flour
240g caster sugar
1 tsp ground cinnamon
1 tsp bicarbonate of soda
100g chopped walnuts
3 medium eggs, beaten
200g (2 or 3) ripe bananas, mashed
150g canned crushed pineapple,
 juice reserved

Icing
175g cream cheese
4 tbsp unsalted butter
 (at room temperature)
1 tsp vanilla extract
430g icing sugar, sifted
Handful of walnuts halves,
 to decorate (optional)

TIP
If you want to coat the sides with the icing, just up the quantities by about 30 per cent.

Preheat the oven to 180°C/Fan 160°C. Grease 3 cake tins of about 20cm in diameter with oil and line the bases with discs of baking parchment.

Sift the flour into a large bowl and add the oil, caster sugar, cinnamon, bicarbonate of soda, walnuts, beaten eggs, bananas, and the pineapple with about 4 tablespoons of the juice. Stir well and divide the mixture equally between the 3 cake tins. Bake for about 25 minutes until risen and a skewer comes out clean when inserted into the centre of the cakes. Cool on wire racks and turn out and peel off the parchment.

While the cakes are cooking, make the icing. In a food mixer, beat together the cream cheese, butter and vanilla, then add the sugar a third at a time, making sure each batch is incorporated before adding the next. Chill until ready to use.

Layer up the cake layers with the icing and spread the rest generously on top. Decorate with walnut halves if desired.

Panna cotta with salted pistachio cream

This is an ideal recipe for a dinner party. It can all be made in advance, it looks smart and the pistachio brittle is irresistible. You'll hear people say, 'Oh my God, this is amazing,' to which I reply that it came from Bologna. The pistachio brittle makes more than you need, so keep the rest to sprinkle on ice creams or cakes.

SERVES 8

Panna cotta
4 x 2g gelatine leaves
700ml double cream
200ml whole milk
1 vanilla pod
225g caster sugar

Salted pistachio cream
130g shelled pistachios
30g butter, plus extra for greasing
¼ tsp flaked sea salt
80g caster sugar
300ml double cream

TIP
Rinse and air dry the vanilla pod (after scraping out the seeds), then add it to a jar of caster sugar. Within a week or so you will have vanilla-scented sugar, delicious for sprinkling on cakes and desserts.

Soak the gelatine in a bowl of cold water for 5 minutes. Pour the cream and milk into a pan, add the vanilla pod and sugar and warm over a medium-low heat until the sugar has dissolved. Bring up to a simmer, then take off the heat. Take out the pod, split and scrape the seeds into the milk mixture.

Drain the gelatine, squeeze out any excess water and stir into the mixture until dissolved. Divide between 8 small glasses or cups. Cool, then chill for at least 4 hours or overnight.

Toast 100g of the pistachios in a dry pan over a medium heat for 1 to 2 minutes. Roughly chop the nuts. Butter a shallow metal baking tray and scatter the nuts and sea salt over it.

Put the 30g of butter and the sugar into a heavy-based pan and add 3 tablespoons of water. Heat gently to dissolve the sugar. Increase the heat and boil for about 5 minutes or until the mixture turns deep golden brown. Working fast, pour the caramel over the nuts, then set aside to cool and harden. When hard, break up with a rolling pin and blitz in a processor into a very coarse 'powder'. Fold about 80g of the pistachio powder into the cream, and keep the rest for serving.

Roughly chop the remaining, untoasted nuts. When you're ready to eat, unmould the panna cottas and serve with the pistachio cream. Sprinkle with the chopped nuts.

Tiramisu

This is a family recipe from Sas's cousins, Jane and Tim. It's so special because, unlike many a tiramisu, it doesn't collapse. The custard is cooked in a bain-marie before folding in the cream and mascarpone, so holds its shape but is still as light as a feather.

SERVES 8-10

6 egg yolks
200g caster sugar
300g mascarpone
   (at room temperature)
300ml whipping cream

175ml espresso coffee, cooled
125ml Baileys Irish Cream
About 30 savoiardi biscuits
Cocoa powder, for dusting

TIP
It's quite an Aussie thing to use Baileys in this, but you can use the more traditional Marsala instead.

Put the egg yolks and sugar in a bowl and place over a pan of just-simmering water. Whisk for about 8 minutes, then remove from the heat and continue to whisk until thick and pale yellow in colour. Allow to cool slightly before mixing in the mascarpone.

Whip the cream with an electric beater until thickened and holding its shape. Gently fold the cream into the egg mixture and set aside.

You'll need a serving dish measuring about 20 x 28 x 10cm. Mix the cold espresso with the Baileys in a shallow bowl. Dip the biscuits into the coffee mix, but don't soak them or they will fall apart. Place half the dipped biscuits in the base of your serving dish and top with half the mascarpone custard. Add another layer of dipped biscuits and the remaining mascarpone custard, then dust the top liberally with cocoa powder. Refrigerate for a minimum of 4 hours, preferably overnight, before serving.

Vodka lemon drizzle pancakes with blackberry compote

There is, I have to confess, no need to put the vodka in the blackberry compote that accompanies these, but it does add to the sense of occasion. The reality is that the director Matt Bennett asked me to come up with a recipe using vodka after a filmed visit to a potato farm and vodka distillery, Colewith Farm near St Austell, for my Cornish TV series. It was actually a celebration of autumn blackberries too.

SERVES 4-6

Pancakes
125g plain flour
Pinch salt
1 egg, beaten
300ml milk
1 tbsp sunflower oil,
   plus extra for cooking

Blackberry compote
250g fresh (or frozen)
   blackberries
1 tbsp fresh lemon juice
1-2 tbsp caster sugar
   (depending on
   sweetness of berries)

Vodka lemon drizzle
4 tbsp caster sugar
4 tbsp freshly squeezed
   lemon juice
2-3 tbsp vodka

To serve
Clotted cream or
   vanilla ice cream

First make the batter. Sift the flour and salt into a bowl and make a well in the centre. Add the egg together with a little the mixture is the consistency of thick cream, add the tablespoon of oil and beat in the remaining milk. Set the batter aside for a few minutes while you make the compote.

Put the blackberries, lemon juice and sugar in a pan. Heat gently until the berries start to soften and release some of their juice and the sugar dissolves. Stir gently until you have a syrupy mixture but the berries are still holding their shape. Take the pan off the heat and set aside.

Heat a 20–23cm non-stick frying pan and swirl in a little oil, then pour out any excess. The pan should be just coated. Pour in enough batter to coat the bottom of the pan evenly and place over a medium heat. After about a minute or so, loosen the edges and flip the pancake over to cook the other side. Repeat to cook the rest, placing each one on a warm plate and covering with a clean tea towel to keep warm.

Mix together the sugar, lemon juice and vodka. To serve, drizzle each pancake with the vodka mixture, roll it up and spoon over some compote. Serve with cream or ice cream.

Preserving

I read in the paper this morning that our government is intending to pressurise manufacturers to provide many more spares, dating back far longer, enabling us all to keep our washing machines, vacuum cleaners, coffee makers and electric whisks, not to mention printers, mobile phones and computers for longer. All the bits of my latest laptop appear to be glued in place, so there's no chance of getting it repaired. Officially, this is all down to reducing landfill, but I think it's been engendered by everyone being in lockdown.

It goes without saying that the negatives of lockdown have been terrible, most notably the effect on our children's education and the claustrophobia of living in confined spaces, but there have been some positives. A delight shared by me and many of my friends is the realisation, or should I say reinforcement, of the fact that, in the kitchen, preserving things we might otherwise throw away changes their taste, in many cases most interestingly, but also satisfies a basic need – full security. There is nothing that feels more secure for many cooks than having a store cupboard full of jams, chutneys and pickles. I suppose the whole of cooking is an affirmation of life, and preserving things that might otherwise go to waste is life affirming.

The reality of preserving is that generally we are all too busy. It's not quite the mentality of life is too short for boning oxtails, but actually making jams, pickling cabbage, making cordials and, even though it's not exactly preserving, baking sourdough bread, requires a knowledge built up over time that many of us simply don't have. Lockdown has shown that such things are the way to a feeling of happiness brought about by concentrating on small details. I believe this is called mindfulness, in other words 'being in the moment'. Apart from cooking, my other source of mindfulness is DIY. What sends me to sleep of a night is wondering which screw to use that will perfectly match in a hinge but which also has the strength to support the door.

Preserving is a series of very simple processes, which only become easy after many years of mistakes. It's the mistakes that infuriate when you repeatedly make them but then there's the complete euphoria when you finally get it right.

Take jam, for example, and maybe a particularly tricky one to make – marmalade (page 289). In theory, all it is is Seville oranges, sugar and water, but the process by which these three ingredients become jam depends on a number of possibilities, all based on many people's experiences. It's not like boiling an egg! It depends on what you want from your marmalade. What I want is clarity, a very soft set, peel that I can see as being hand cut, bitterness and a lovely deep-orange colour.

Or take bread and butter pickles (page 306). What I like in bread and butter pickles is the crunchiness of the cucumbers, the light yellow colour from the turmeric and the balance of vinegar, sugar and salt which emphasises the sweetness. That and the scent of coriander and fennel seeds and the presence of yellow mustard seeds. For my money, most chutneys are better for having more salt and sugar than you would put in if you were being sensible.

What I love about preserving is the ritual of doing it: choosing the right day, trying to remind yourself that you can't do this while juggling ten other things – it's not a multi-tasking job. You need to take pleasure in the process and your equipment. Get a good preserving pan with a measuring scale up the side and proper jars; everything looks better in good-quality preserving jars. Don't be tempted by the cheaper imitations with thin clamping wires. When you've got your preserves cooling on the windowsill, backlit by the sun, you don't want to be regretting the cheapness of your jars.

Another thing about preserving or indeed making sourdough bread or, I suspect, cheese or wine, is that no recipe will quite give you the finished product. It's a blend of the recipe and your experience and no batch will be quite the same as another. The magic is in using your skills to manage these variables and that's the beauty of home-made preserves over supermarket alternatives.

Light plum tart

This is my most often cooked dessert, realistically because it's so easy to make and I'm always pushed for time when cooking for more than four. I also like this because it's clear that I haven't gone to a lot of trouble to make it, and by the time we get to this stage of a meal I'm normally so deep in conversation with whoever I am sitting next to that it seems almost a slightly irritating diversion to have to stop and accept approval for something more tricksy. I use whatever fresh fruit is available but plum is a favourite.

SERVES 8

500g puff pastry
    (preferably all butter)
Flour, for dusting
10–12 ripe plums, halved
    and stoned
4 tsp sugar
3 tbsp redcurrant jelly
Crème fraiche, to serve

TIP
This would also work with ripe apricots, peaches or nectarines or with figs, apples or pears.

Preheat the oven to 220°C/Fan 200°C. Roll out the pastry on a lightly floured surface into a rough circle. Cut it into a disc about 28–30cm in diameter, using a large dinner plate as a guide. Transfer to a baking tray.

Cut each plum across into 4 or 5 slices and arrange them slightly overlapping on the pastry. Sprinkle over the sugar and bake for about 20 minutes, until the pastry is puffed up, crisp and golden and the sugar has lightly caramelised.

Meanwhile, put the redcurrant jelly into a pan with 2 teaspoons of water. Warm over a gentle heat until melted. Leave aside to cool slightly but do not let it set.

Remove the tart from the oven and brush with the redcurrant glaze. Cut into 8 wedges and serve with crème fraiche.

Mincemeat

If you don't have the precise amounts of fruit listed, it's fine to play around with the ratios. Keep a mix of dried fruits and the same overall weight but, for example, if you only have sultanas and no raisins, just use more sultanas.

MAKES ABOUT
4 X 400G
JAM JARS

350g (1 very large or 2 smaller) cooking apples, peeled and grated
150g raisins
250g currants
200g sultanas
75g soft dried figs, chopped to the size of sultanas, or dried cranberries, if preferred
225g beef or vegetable suet

250g soft dark brown sugar
75g chopped mixed peel
Grated zest and juice of 1 large orange,
Grated zest of 1 lemon
2 tsp ground ginger
1 tsp ground cinnamon
½ tsp freshly grated nutmeg
¼ tsp ground cloves
45ml Cointreau, Grand Marnier or brandy

TIP
To sterilise jars, wash them well, then put them in a 160°C/Fan 140°C oven for about 15 minutes. Soak the lids in a bowl of boiling water for a few minutes.

Preheat the oven to 140°C/Fan 120°C. Put all the ingredients, except the alcohol, into a large flameproof casserole dish with a lid and mix well.

Put the casserole dish over a low heat to warm the mixture through until the suet begins to melt. Then put the lid on and transfer to the oven for about an hour. Allow to cool before adding the alcohol.

Spoon the mincemeat into sterilised jars and seal.
It keeps well for at least a year.

Mince pies

I am conscious that I've brought many of my mother's recipes into this book. She was a very good cook and, as I am fond of saying, I'm always trying to cook the food my mother cooked for me as a child because those were the best things I have ever eaten. Her mince pies are a case in point. The extreme 'sandiness' of the pastry is what makes them so special. Her recipe calls for more fat to flour than your average shortcrust and can be a little too rich in some cases but not in mince pies.

MAKES 12

1 jar of mincemeat
(see opposite)
Icing sugar, for dusting
Milk, for brushing

Shortcrust pastry
225g plain flour, plus extra for dusting
1/2 tsp salt
65g lard or vegetable shortening,
   cold and cubed
65g butter, cold and cubed
1 1/2–2 tbsp ice-cold water

TIP
This pastry is delicious but very short and crumbly which makes it a bit delicate to handle. Keep it cool and handle as little as possible. You can re-roll the trimmings but the less you do, the better the pastry.

To make the pastry, combine the flour, salt, lard (or shortening) and butter in a food processor and pulse until the mixture looks like breadcrumbs. Transfer to a bowl and stir in just enough of the ice-cold water to get the pastry to come together in a dough.

Turn the pastry out on to a lightly floured board and form it into a thick disc. Cover with cling film or baking parchment and leave to rest in a cool place or the fridge for about 30 minutes. If you put the pastry in the fridge, allow 15 minutes or so for it to come back up to room temperature before rolling it out.

Roll the pastry out on a floured board to a 2–3mm thickness. Using a pastry cutter, cut 12 discs large enough to fill 12 cups of a shallow bun tin. Then use a smaller cutter to cut another 12 discs to form the lids. Preheat the oven to 180°C/Fan 160°C.

Add a tablespoon or so of mincemeat to each pastry-lined cup. Brush the edges of the pastry with a little cold water and put the lids on top, pressing the edges to seal. Make a couple of slits in each lid to allow steam to escape and brush the pies with milk, then bake for about 25 minutes until golden and crisp. Serve warm, dusted with icing sugar. If you want to make the pies ahead of time, warm them through in the oven before serving.

Saffron buns for afternoon tea

A recipe from my Cornish TV series, these make your house smell lovely and as I said at the time, is there anything better, apart perhaps from enjoying a slice of Christmas cake, than sitting by an open fire with a mug of tea and a hot buttered saffron bun.

MAKES 10

325ml whole milk
Big pinch saffron strands
90g clotted cream
50g butter (at room temperature)
550g strong white bread flour,
    sifted, plus extra for dusting

1¼ tsp fine sea salt
50g caster sugar, plus 50g for glaze
1 x 7g sachet fast-acting dried yeast
70g raisins
30g chopped mixed peel
Butter or clotted cream, to serve

TIP
If you do have any buns left, slice and butter them to make a delicious bread and butter pudding.

In a saucepan, heat the milk almost to boiling point, then remove from the heat. Lightly crumble the saffron strands between your fingers into the milk and stir. Stir in the clotted cream and butter and continue to stir until fully melted. Set aside to infuse for 15–20 minutes or until the mixture is about blood temperature and golden yellow in colour.

Combine the sifted flour, the salt, sugar and yeast in the bowl of a food mixer fitted with a dough hook. Add the warm milk mixture and combine. Knead at a slow speed for about 5 minutes, then add the raisins and mixed peel and continue to knead for a further 5 minutes until the dough feels springy and elastic. It should bounce back when pressed. Cover the bowl with cling film or a clean tea towel and leave to rise in a warm place for about 45–60 minutes or until the dough has doubled in size.

Alternatively, combine all the ingredients – except the raisins and peel – in a bowl and add the warm milk mixture and knead by hand briefly until you have a smooth dough. Add the dried fruit and knead for a further 6–8 minutes until smooth and elastic and proceed with the rising process.

Preheat the oven to 200°C/Fan 180°C. When the dough has risen, turn it out on to a lightly floured board and knock it back (knock the air out of the dough) and knead for a couple of minutes, until smooth and elastic.

Recipe continued overleaf

Divide the dough into 10 pieces and roll each piece into a smooth ball. Place them on a baking sheet, leaving some space between them as they will rise again. Cover the buns with a tea towel or cling film and leave them to rise in a warm place for about 30 minutes.

Transfer to the oven and bake for 20–25 minutes until risen and golden. While the buns are in the oven, dissolve 50g of caster sugar in a pan with a couple of tablespoons of water and boil for about a minute to create a glossy syrup.

Remove the buns from the oven and place on a wire rack, then brush the tops with the syrup and leave to cool slightly. Serve warm with butter or clotted cream, or allow to cool and serve halved, toasted and spread with butter.

Seville orange marmalade

You will be best off with a very large wide pan, and you'll need jam jars, muslin and string. The muslin bag of pulp and pips is really important, as the pips are full of pectin and are what gives the marmalade its setting properties. I've never been tempted to use jam sugar (which contains pectin), even when making marmalade for sale in our deli. The result is a much softer set, which can cause some complaints, but better to live a bit dangerously I say.

MAKES 10
X 450G JARS

1.5kg Seville oranges
Juice of 3 lemons
2.5–3kg granulated sugar

Cut the oranges in half, squeeze the halves and reserve the juice in a measuring jug. Set any pips aside. Then cut the orange halves into quarters and scoop out the pulp and any remaining pips. Put the pips and pulp in a bowl lined with a muslin. Cut the peel into strips as thick or thin as you like. Put a few saucers in the freezer for testing setting later.

Put the peel and orange and lemon juice in a pan. Tie the muslin containing the pips and pulp with string to form a bag and add it to the pan. Measure the juice, make it up to 3 litres with water and add it to the pan. Bring to the boil, then turn down to a simmer and cook for 1–1½ hours or so until the peel is tender and the volume has reduced by about half.

Lift out the muslin bag into a bowl. Press it hard with a wooden spoon to extract as much of the pectin-rich juice as possible. When cool enough to handle, squeeze again and add the juice to the pan. Measure the contents of the pan (pulp and liquid) and for every litre, add about 800g of sugar.

Put the pan back over a medium heat and stir until the sugar is fully dissolved. Increase the heat and boil rapidly for 15 minutes, then start testing. Drop a teaspoon of marmalade on to a cold saucer and put it in the fridge for about a minute. If it wrinkles when pushed with your finger, it is ready. If not, continue to boil, testing every 5 minutes – it can take half an hour. When ready, leave to cool for 20 minutes, then stir. Ladle into sterilised jars (see page 284) and leave to cool before labelling. Keeps well for at least a couple of years.

Elderflower cordial

I mentioned in my piece on foraging (page 256) how when I was really busy cooking in the Seafood Restaurant in Padstow I always meant to gather elderflowers and make cordial but never had enough time. Now I can.

MAKES ABOUT
2 X 750ML
BOTTLES

1.25kg granulated sugar
2 unwaxed lemons
25 elderflower heads,
   leaves removed
50g citric acid

In a large saucepan, heat the sugar and 1 litre of water, stirring until the sugar has dissolved, then bring to the boil.

Pare the zest from the lemons with a vegetable peeler, then slice the naked lemons. Shake out any insects from the elderflower heads but do not wash the flowers.

Take the pan off the heat and stir in the elderflower heads, lemon zest, lemon slices and citric acid. Cover the pan with a lid or a clean tea towel and leave to infuse for about 24 hours until fragrant.

Strain the liquid through a piece of muslin and, using a funnel, transfer to sterilised bottles. Store in the fridge and serve diluted with still or sparkling water or use in cocktails.

Mulled wine

What makes my recipe so special is the black cardamom.
It gives a wonderful smoky flavour to the wine, just right
for sipping outdoors on a cold evening in some Cotswolds
village, with the smell of woodsmoke on the breeze.

**SERVES
ABOUT 6**

1 bottle (750ml) cheap red wine
60ml vodka or gin
50ml vincotto (optional, page 312)
½ orange, cut into slices
100g sugar
6 cloves
7cm cinnamon stick
1 black cardamom pod, crushed

TIP
You really only
need cheap wine.
I've tried it using
more expensive
stuff and it makes
no difference to
the taste.

Put all the ingredients in a large saucepan, add 200ml
of water and slowly heat to dissolve the sugar. Bring to
just below a simmer, but do not let it boil at any time.
Keep the wine hot over a low heat for about 30 minutes
to allow the flavours to infuse. Ladle into glasses to serve.

The perfect negroni

I'm very boring because I'm not really interested in cocktails. I always order a negroni and Sas always has margaritas. Debate rages over the icing of a negroni. Some say one single large cube; others go for normal cubes. I favour the latter because there is always one last mouthful trapped in the cubes.

SERVES 1

30ml gin
30ml Campari
30ml sweet vermouth
   (preferably Antica Formula)
Ice cubes
Pared zest of an orange

Combine the gin, Campari and vermouth. Pour over plenty of ice and garnish with a curl of orange zest.

SERVES 1

Sas's margarita

45ml 100% agave blanco tequila
25ml Cointreau
20ml freshly squeezed lime juice

For the glass
Lime wedge
Fine salt

Prepare the glass by running the lime wedge around the rim and then dipping it into a saucer of fine salt. Set aside.

Shake the tequila, Cointreau and lime juice very hard over a full shaker of cubed ice until the shaker is frosted. Double strain into the prepared cocktail glass, without ice, and serve.

I asked Sas, my wife, to write down a few thoughts about having people round to eat and drink at home. I didn't do much of this before I met her, but I have to say she's made up for that big time! The thing about her – and her children say the same – is you never know who she's going to invite and often it's people I wouldn't dare ask, because I'd be certain they wouldn't really want to come, but then they seem perfectly happy. The other thing, which completely unhinges me, is what I thought was going to be eight guests turns out to be 16, which she swears she told me about.

I love nothing more than to throw a party

I can't remember a time when I didn't do this in some way, shape or form. My best friend Trace and I moved into our first flat when we were 17. We were unloading the last of our furniture, when friends started arriving with bottles of cheap vodka and Passion Pop. Trace looked at me and said, 'Don't tell me you've invited people over for a party?' Oops. I spent the next day, extremely hungover, convincing Mrs Leach, our landlady who lived in the flat above, not to evict us.

In the early 90s, I was very into proper dinner parties. *Australian Women's Weekly* cookbooks were my bible and I would invite three other couples and serve a classic three-course dinner on my prized Wedgwood china – a wedding present. I thought I was very grown up, folding napkins into the shape of swans and serving cheap sparkling white wine.

These days, Ricky and I generally end up having 14 people to dinner. My thinking is that if you are going to be shopping, prepping, cooking, organising decorations and making playlists you might as well maximise the fun with lots of family and friends, so here are my ideas.

Choose a theme
Deciding on a theme for an occasion helps you to coordinate everything, from the dress code, table setting and food menu to the music. It gets you excited about the event, as there's nothing nicer than looking forward to family and friends coming over for food, fun and frivolity.

Being Australian, I love outdoor parties (weather permitting). Things centre around the barbecue and a grass area in the garden is great for an impromptu dance floor. I set up a large round cheese board with a selection of cured meats, bread, crackers, some dips, dried apricots, grapes and nuts so guests have something to nibble on when they arrive. They can help themselves to a drink and have a chat while the main part of the meal is cooked on the barbecue. Favourites are butterflied lamb or chicken or pork souvlakis, served with big bowls of salad. Dessert has to be pavlova.

A Mexican-themed evening is also popular. I decorate the table and surrounding areas with cacti and succulents – fresh and fake – along with coloured pom-poms, paper skulls and traditional tissue-paper decorations known as papel picado. My daughter Olivia is a big fan of piñatas filled with lollies and smash cakes, which make a great talking point. Last but not least, get the mariachi music playing.

I set up a serving table with bowls and platters of food so everyone can help themselves. Mexican beers are mandatory and I have jugs of margaritas, my favourite cocktail. Lots of restaurants, wine stores and online companies now deliver wonderful ready-mixed cocktails to your door, if you don't want the hassle of making your own.

Spanish tapas parties are another great idea for an informal dinner. Have some large boards laden with Spanish ham, cheeses, padron peppers, olives, mini croquetas and sliced Spanish tortillas. Serve Spanish wines and jugs of sangria. Play Spanish guitar music in the background and then, after dinner, put on the salsa and get everyone dancing.

When Ricky was writing *Rick Stein's India*, we used to invite family and friends to taste dishes. One night, I think we had about 40 people over. They dressed up in brightly coloured outfits – one couple wore traditional saris – and we ate sitting on large cushions on the floor. I lit loads of candles and we ended up dancing to wonderful Bollywood music. For an Indian-themed feast, begin with a selection of starters, such as samosas, chicken tikka, and bhajis, as well poppadoms and a selection of chutneys. For the main course, serve big bowls of curry and rice.

Set a date, prepare a guest list and send invitations
It's not a good plan to invite people who are all strangers to one another. As much as it might be tempting to introduce all your favourite friends to each other, it can make things awkward if you are the only common factor. I also like to invite a mixture of singles and couples. Keep a record of guests invited and food and drinks served. Note any incidents that have occurred. I've had guests end up in hospital from too much good cheer.

I like to send out invites three weeks in advance. If it's a birthday or special occasion, I send invitations by post, otherwise I email. I do like a last-minute phone round for Friday night nibbles at home or a Sunday roast or barbecue.

Decorations
Everything on the table should have a purpose, so select with care. Collect things from around your home for decorations, like seashells you have collected from beach days. Add some flowers and other beautiful items, such as lemons. Coloured glasses and crockery look great on a plain white tablecloth

Have one thing in huge volume. For example, oysters or prawns piled high with chunks of lemons and dipping sauces make a lovely centrepiece and can be served as the starter.

Candles set the mood and it's lovely to go into a home with a nice scent, so scatter them around – always with an eye to fire safety!

Make sure the bathroom looks pretty and welcoming. Add a big candle, a beautiful scented flower like a gardenia, plenty of hand towels and some smart coffee table books.

Fairy lights, festoon lights, fire pits and lamb's wool covers on wooden benches add a romantic feel to the garden.

Music
Let's face it, a lunch, dinner or drinks party isn't fun without music. Use a music-streaming service for making eclectic playlists, or iTunes if you want to make pre-dinner, mid-dinner and post-dinner lists, using music you already own.

The trick here is moderation. Too fast or too loud and you risk distracting guests from chatting and enjoying the food. Too quiet or too slow when mixed with a few bottles of bubbles and your guests will want to be in their PJs on the couch at home. Go for the mid-range – it's background music.

Try to match the feel of the night. Think about the evening as an adventure with a start, a middle and an end. Upbeat is great to start with, when guests are on their feet and arriving, conversation is louder, people are catching up. Drop the volume and tempo as your guests sit down for the meal. Towards the end of the night, it depends on whether you want your guests to stay and party or call a cab and leave. I never want guests to go home, so I continually blare 'Don't You Want Me Baby' by The Human League, 'Don't Stop Me Now' by Queen, 'Don't Stop Believin' by Journey or Ricky's favourite, 'We Built This City' by Jefferson Starship.

The day before
Make sure you have more alcohol than you think you need. There's nothing worse than running out of drinks when everyone is really getting stuck into the party.

Stock up on headache tablets, band aids and safety pins and most important – toilet paper. It's awful for a guest to have to text their partner from the bathroom asking for toilet paper.

Check the stereo system works and the playlists are sorted. The amount of fights I've had with Ricky over the speaker not working or him having decided it's a great opportunity to listen to some obscure 19th-century cathedral music, just as our friends want to dance to disco and sing into spoons.

Check the seating plan is correct and the names are spelt correctly on the place cards.

Make sure the glasses are polished and cutlery is sparkling. No one wants to sip delicious Riesling from a glass with lipstick marks around the rim.

Before your guests arrive
Empty the dishwasher. My husband is very keen on giving the kitchen a spring clean an hour before guests arrive. He stuffs the dishwasher with odd things, so later, when you want to load the mountains of dishes, you have to spend ages emptying and trying to find where rarely used containers live.

Empty the rubbish bin and make sure there are plenty of bags and boxes for empty bottles to make clearing up easier.

Have at least one vase ready in case a generous guest brings a bunch of flowers.

Make sure there is plenty of room in the centre of the table to put dishes for sharing.

Set up a drink and snack station for guests as they arrive with champagne, wine, water and something to nibble on.

Put jugs of water on the table. People will thank you in the morning, when their head doesn't feel like it's going to combust from a lack of hydration.

Delegate a helpful family member or friend to help serve food and clear plates and glasses if you can. You want to be able to chat, giggle and dance with your guests. You certainly don't want to spend the entire night with your marigolds on and cursing your husband's name under your breath, as he yells from the table, 'Would you mind getting me another bottle of red while you are up?'

Get dressed up for the evening. It's a fair assumption that your guests will have made an effort with their outfits and it's nice to reciprocate the gesture.

Light candles and put on your first playlist to set the mood for the evening. It's so nice for guests to arrive to a sweet-smelling scent and music wafting through the house.

Have a glass of bubbles or wine or take a moment for yourself. As much I love having people round, it can be stressful. It's amazing how often a family fight can occur just before the guests are about to arrive.

And afterwards
Do start the clean up before bed. Even if you have had a few drinks. You'll be so happy to wake up to a clean kitchen instead of a bomb site.

SIDE DISHES & BASICS

TOMATO, SHALLOT & BASIL SALAD
Serves 4–6

3 beef tomatoes
1 shallot, thinly sliced
6–8 basil leaves,
    finely shredded
Dressing
4 tbsp extra virgin olive oil
1 tbsp sherry vinegar
¼ tsp caster sugar
Salt and black pepper

For the dressing, whisk together the oil and vinegar with the sugar, half a teaspoon of salt and some black pepper.

Thinly slice the tomatoes and lay them in a single layer over the base of a large serving plate. Sprinkle with the sliced shallot, the dressing and shredded basil leaves.

Finish with a little more coarsely ground black pepper and serve immediately.

LETTUCE & SPRING ONION SALAD WITH DILL & OREGANO
Great with pastitsio, souvlaki or vegetable moussaka.
Serves 4

1 cos or romaine lettuce
4 spring onions, sliced
Small handful dill, chopped
Dressing
60ml extra virgin olive oil
    (preferably Greek)
10ml red wine vinegar
10ml lemon juice
1 small garlic clove, mashed
1 tsp Dijon mustard
½ tsp salt
1 tsp Greek dried oregano
½ tsp of honey

Cut the lettuce into 2cm slices and mix with the spring onions and dill. Whisk the dressing ingredients together and toss with the salad.

LETTUCE, TOMATO, AVOCADO & BASIL SALAD
Serves 4

2 tomatoes, cut into thin wedges
1 cos or romaine lettuce,
    leaves torn
1 avocado, sliced
6 basil leaves, torn
Salt
Dressing
3 tbsp sunflower oil
1 tbsp mild olive oil
1 tbsp red wine vinegar
½ tsp salt
¼ tsp sugar

Prepare this salad just before serving. Sprinkle the tomato wedges with salt 2 or 3 minutes before assembling. Put everything in a salad bowl, whisk the dressing ingredients together and toss with the salad.

CRISP CABBAGE, WALNUT & APPLE SALAD
Serves 4

¼ salad cabbage,
    thinly shredded
15g walnuts, chopped
15g raisins or sultanas
1 celery stick, thinly sliced
1 crisp apple, cored and diced
1 small handful parsley,
    roughly chopped
A generous handful
    of rocket leaves
1 tbsp mayonnaise
Dressing
3 tbsp sunflower oil
1 tbsp mild olive oil
1 tbsp red wine vinegar
½ tsp salt
¼ tsp sugar

In a large bowl mix all the salad ingredients. Whisk the dressing ingredients together, add to the salad and stir well to coat the salad with the dressing.

GREEN BEAN & FRESH COCONUT SALAD
Serves 4

250g fine green beans,
    cut into pieces
6 tbsp vegetable oil
25g shallots, sliced
3 garlic cloves, sliced
1 medium-hot red chilli, chopped
150g fresh coconut, finely grated
100g bean sprouts
2 Kaffir lime leaves, shredded
2 red bird's-eye chillies,
    thinly sliced
Salt
Dressing
½ tsp shrimp paste
4 tsp lime juice
1 tbsp vegetable oil
2 tsp soft brown sugar
½ tsp salt

Cook the green beans for 3 minutes in boiling, salted water, then drain and refresh under cold water. Dry the beans well and put them in a bowl.

Heat the oil in a small pan, add the shallots and fry until crisp and golden. Lift out on to kitchen paper to drain, then set aside. Add the garlic to the pan and do the same, then add the chopped red chilli and fry for just a few seconds.

Add the fried shallots, garlic and chilli to the beans in the bowl, along with the coconut, bean sprouts, lime leaves and sliced chillies.

For the dressing, mix the shrimp paste with the lime juice in a small bowl, then whisk in the oil, sugar and salt. Add to the salad and toss everything together well, then serve. Great with the Indonesian seafood curry on page 104.

RADICCHIO & ANCHOVY SALAD
Serves 4 –8

2 garlic cloves
4 anchovy fillets
1 tbsp lemon juice
4 tbsp olive oil
½–1 radicchio

Blend the garlic, anchovy fillets, lemon juice and oil in a food processor.

Shred the radicchio and dress it with the anchovy mixture.

GREEN BEANS IN TOMATO SAUCE
Taze fasulye
Don't be afraid to let the beans stew for a long time. The flavour improves as they lose their fresh greenness and turn khaki. You can use runner beans or pulses like butter beans too.
Serves 6

8 tbsp olive oil
1 small onion, chopped
2 garlic cloves, crushed or grated
5 medium tomatoes, chopped
1 tbsp tomato paste
450g green beans, trimmed
Salt and black pepper

Heat 6 tablespoons of the oil in a pan over a medium heat, add the onion and cook until soft. Add the garlic, tomatoes and tomato paste, season and cook for 2 minutes.

Add the green beans with just enough water to cover them. Put a lid on the pan and bring to the boil, then turn down to a simmer and stew the beans for about 45 minutes.

Take the lid off the pan and cook for a further 15–20 minutes to allow the juices to thicken. Stir in the remaining oil, then serve.

PETITS POIS À LA FRANÇAISE
Serves 4

4 little gem lettuce hearts
12 spring onions or 225g very
    small button onions or shallots
50g butter
700g fresh or frozen petits pois
½ tsp sugar
Salt and white pepper

Remove the outer leaves from the lettuce hearts if necessary, then trim the bases and slice each one across quite finely. Trim the spring onions and cut into 2.5cm pieces or peel the button onions or shallots.

Melt half the butter in a shallow, flameproof casserole dish. Add the onions and cook for 2–3 minutes until tender but not browned. Add the petits pois, lettuce, sugar and 100ml of water and season with salt and white pepper. Simmer rapidly for 3–4 minutes until the peas have started to soften and about three-quarters of the liquid has evaporated.

Dot the rest of the butter around the pan. Shake the pan over the heat until the butter has melted and amalgamated with the cooking juices to make a sauce.

CAVOLO NERO WITH FENNEL SEEDS & GARLIC
Serves 4

450g cavolo nero,
    the younger the better
3 tbsp olive oil
1 garlic clove, sliced
Pinch fennel seeds
Salt and black pepper

Cavolo nero can get quite woody as it gets older, so if the leaves are large, strip them away from the stems with a sharp knife and discard the stems. Otherwise, just bunch the leaves together and cut

them across into 3. Bring a pan of salted water to the boil, add the leaves and cook them for 4 minutes or until slightly undercooked, turning them over regularly. Drain and refresh in cold water, then drain again.

Put the olive oil and sliced garlic into a large pan and place over a medium-high heat. As soon as the garlic starts to sizzle, add a good pinch of lightly crushed fennel seeds and cook gently without colouring for 1 minute. Add the cavolo nero leaves and stir-fry for 1–1½ minutes until heated through. Season well to taste and serve.

BLACK BEANS WITH GARLIC, ONION & BAY LEAF
Frijoles
Most black beans don't need pre-soaking but check the packet just in case.
Serves 4

300g black turtle beans
    or pinto beans
1 onion, peeled and halved
4 garlic cloves, bashed with
    the heel of a knife
1 bay leaf
1 tsp salt

Rinse the beans very well and pick out any stones. Tip them into a large saucepan and cover with about 2 litres of water, then add the onion, garlic, bay leaf and salt. Bring to the boil. Skim off any scum that rises to the top and continue to boil, uncovered, for 10 minutes.

Turn the heat down and simmer the beans gently for up to an hour or until they are tender but not disintegrating. Drain and reserve about 150ml of the cooking liquid to use if you're going to make refried beans (page 218).

STEAMED CHINESE GREENS IN OYSTER SAUCE
Serves 4–6

8-12 small pak choi
2 tsp sunflower oil
1 tsp sesame oil
4 tbsp oyster sauce
1 tbsp dark soy sauce

Cut the pak choi lengthways into quarters and put them on an opened-out petal steamer. Lower them into a shallow pan containing about 1cm of simmering water, cover and steam for 3–4 minutes or until tender.

Meanwhile, mix together the sunflower oil, sesame oil, oyster sauce and dark soy sauce in a small pan and leave to warm through over a low heat.

Transfer the pak choi to a warmed serving plate, spoon over the sauce and serve.

GLAZED SPRING CARROTS WITH TARRAGON & CHIVES
Serves 4

450g small spring carrots
½ tsp honey
½ tsp salt
15g butter
½ tsp chopped tarragon leaves
½ tsp chopped chives

Scrub the carrots and trim down their tops. Put them in a wide, shallow pan and add 600ml of water to barely cover, then add the honey, salt and butter. Cover with a tight-fitting lid and simmer until just tender.

Uncover the pan, increase the heat and boil rapidly to reduce the liquid, shaking the pan now and then, until just before the carrots start to catch on the base of the pan. They should just be allowed to colour very slightly here and there. Add the chopped tarragon and chives, toss well and serve.

COURGETTES WITH CHIVES
Serves 4

350g courgettes (very small and freshly picked, if possible)
25g butter
1 tbsp chopped chives
Salt and black pepper

Slice the courgettes across into thin discs. Melt the butter in a large sauté pan, add the courgettes and fry them gently over a low heat until they are just tender. Sprinkle them with the chopped chives and a little salt and black pepper about 1 minute after they have started cooking.

STIR-FRIED BRUSSELS SPROUTS WITH SHALLOTS & CHESTNUTS
Serves 6–8

100g diced pancetta (optional)
2 tbsp sunflower oil
3 banana shallots, peeled and finely sliced
600g Brussels sprouts, trimmed and halved, then finely shredded
180g vacuum-packed whole chestnuts, quartered
Salt and black pepper

Heat a large frying pan or wok and fry the pancetta, if using, over a high heat for 3 or 4 minutes until crispy. Add the oil to the pan and fry the shallots until softened, then add the sprouts and chestnuts. Season with salt and black pepper (you may not need much salt if using pancetta). Cook over a medium heat for 3–5 minutes until just tender. Serve immediately.

Tip
If you have any leftovers, add some cream or crème fraiche, a splash of chicken stock and some grated Parmesan and warm through to make a delicious pasta sauce. Or, mix with some leftover chicken or turkey and some cream and chicken stock to make a pie filling.

STEAMED SPINACH
Serves 4–6

900g spinach, well washed and dried in a salad spinner
25g butter
A few rasps nutmeg
Salt and black pepper

Put the spinach in a saucepan, add about 50ml of water, then cover and place over a high heat. Stir a little as the leaves wilt down by about four-fifths. Tip into a colander and lightly press out the excess water with the back of a wooden spoon.

Melt the butter in the pan, add the spinach and season with nutmeg, salt and pepper. Toss briefly over a high heat and serve immediately.

CELERIAC & POTATO MASH
Serves 4

450g floury potatoes, such as King Edwards or Maris Pipers, peeled
450g celeriac, peeled
50g butter
50ml milk
1 garlic clove, crushed or grated
Salt and black pepper

Cut the potatoes and celeriac into 5–6cm chunks, put them in a saucepan and cover with water. Bring to the boil, then turn the heat down and simmer for 15–20 minutes. Drain in a colander and return to the pan. Mash with a potato masher or using an electric hand whisk, then add the butter, milk and garlic. Season with salt and black pepper.

PURÉE OF SWEDE, CARROT & POTATO WITH ROCKET
Serves 4

225g peeled swede,
    cut into chunks
225g peeled carrots,
    cut into chunks
225g peeled potatoes,
    cut into chunks
25g butter
Good handful roughly
    chopped rocket
Salt and black pepper

Cook the swede, carrot and potato in well-salted, boiling water for 20 minutes or until tender. Drain well.

Transfer them to a food processor with the butter and blend briefly into a smooth purée. Tip back into the pan and leave to cook over a gentle heat, stirring now and then, until the mixture has thickened.

Add the rocket, season with salt and pepper and serve.

LOBSTER MASH
Serves 4

900g floury potatoes, such as
    Maris Pipers or King Edwards,
    peeled and cut into chunks
60ml Shellfish reduction
    (page 307)
25g butter (room temperature)
60g cooked lobster meat,
    langoustines or prawns,
    chopped, or crab meat
Salt and black pepper

Put the potatoes in a pan of salted water. Bring to the boil and cook for about 20 minutes until tender. Drain well.

Pass the potatoes through a potato ricer or beat them in the pan with an electric hand whisk until smooth and fluffy. Add the butter and shellfish reduction and mix well, then stir in the cooked chopped lobster, prawns or crab. Season with salt and pepper and serve with any grilled or fried fish.

POMMES ANNA
Serves 6

1.25kg floury potatoes,
    such as Maris Pipers or
    King Edwards, peeled
50g butter
Salt and black pepper

Preheat the oven to 220°C/Fan 200°C. Slice the potatoes very thinly by hand, on a mandolin or in a food processor.

Heat an ovenproof frying pan over a medium heat. Add half the butter and let it melt, then neatly overlap the first layer of potatoes in the base. It's worth taking care over this, as it is what you will see when the potatoes are turned out. Layer in the rest of the potatoes, seasoning each layer with salt and pepper, and dot the remaining butter over the top.

Transfer the pan to the oven and bake for 1 hour. To serve, invert on to a warm serving plate and cut into wedges.

QUICK DAUPHINOISE POTATOES
Serves 6

900g floury potatoes,
    such as Maris Pipers or
    King Edwards, peeled
300ml double cream
300ml whole milk
1 garlic clove, crushed
Freshly grated nutmeg
15g butter, for greasing
Salt and black pepper

Preheat the oven to 200°C/Fan 180°C. Slice the potatoes very thinly by hand, on a mandolin or in a food processor.

Put the cream, milk and garlic into a large non-stick saucepan and season with plenty of salt and pepper. Add the sliced potatoes and simmer for 10 minutes until

they are just tender when pierced with the top of a small, sharp knife. Stir them now and then, but be very careful not to break up the slices. Season with freshly grated nutmeg and salt and pepper to taste.

Lightly butter a 1.5-litre shallow ovenproof dish. Spoon in the potatoes and liquid, overlapping the slices in the top layer neatly if you wish. Bake for about 20–25 minutes or until golden and bubbling. Allow to stand for 5–10 minutes before cutting and serving.

SAUTÉED POTATOES
Serves 4

750g floury potatoes,
    such as Maris Pipers or
    King Edwards, peeled
25-30g polenta, semolina
    or breadcrumbs
40g butter
3 tbsp oil
Salt and black pepper

Cut the potatoes into 3cm pieces. Put them into a pan of well-salted water, bring to the boil and simmer for about 7 minutes until tender. Drain well, then shake the colander to rough up the edges. Sprinkle with the polenta, semolina or breadcrumbs.

Heat the butter and oil in a large frying pan. It's important not to overcrowd the pan, so if you don't have a really large pan, use 2 smaller ones. Add the potatoes and fry them over a medium heat for about 10 minutes, turning them over as they brown, until they are crisp, golden brown and sandy. The outside of the potatoes should break off a little as you sauté them to give them a nice crumbly, crunchy crust. Season with salt and pepper and serve immediately.

If there's a lot of oil or fat towards the end of the cooking time, use some kitchen paper to absorb it to obtain a sandy texture.

POMMES COQ D'OR
Serves 4

900ml Chicken stock (page 307)
2 garlic cloves
750g floury potatoes,
    such as Maris Pipers or
    King Edwards, peeled
50g butter
Salt and black pepper

Preheat the oven to 180°C/ Fan 160°C. Pour the stock into a pan and boil until reduced to 175ml. Leave to cool slightly.

Mash the garlic cloves with a little salt with the blade of a knife to make a smooth paste, then stir into the stock. Season with a teaspoon of salt and plenty of black pepper.

Thinly slice the potatoes on a mandolin or using a food processor.

Use about half the butter to liberally grease the inside of a large cast-iron gratin dish. Starting on the outside and working inwards, layer the sliced potatoes in the dish, overlapping the slices slightly as you go. The potatoes should only be a maximum of three layers thick.

Add the chicken stock, which should come just below the top layer of potatoes, and dot the top with the remaining butter. Cook in the oven for 1 hour. Good with grilled fish.

ALIGOT
This is a version of a great potato dish from the Auvergne. It's usually cooked with one of the local Tome cheeses, notably Tome de Laguiole, which is made from skimmed milk so is reasonably

low in fat. It's hard to get though, so I often use Emmental.
Serves 4

1kg floury potatoes,
    such as Maris Pipers or
    King Edwards, peeled
    and cut into chunks
60g butter, cut into cubes
3 garlic cloves, finely chopped
    or grated
250g Emmental cheese, grated
100–150ml whole milk
Salt

Put the potatoes in a pan of salted water, bring to the boil and simmer for 15–20 minutes until tender. Drain, then mash roughly.

Add the butter, garlic, cheese and a teaspoon of salt to the pan of hot mash. Using an electric hand whisk, whisk in enough milk to get a light fluffy consistency. I usually add about 125ml.

Eat this on its own, maybe with a salad, or serve as a thoroughly OTT addition to a pork chop or steak.

PILAU RICE
Serves 4

2 tbsp sunflower oil
3 cloves
3 green cardamom pods,
    cracked
5cm piece cinnamon stick
1 bay leaf
350g basmati rice
600ml boiling water
Salt

Heat the oil in a saucepan. Add the cloves, cardamom pods, cinnamon stick and bay leaf and cook gently over a low heat for 2–3 minutes until the spices start to smell aromatic.

Stir in the basmati rice and fry gently for 1 minute. Add the boiling water and half a teaspoon of salt and quickly bring to the boil. Stir once, cover with a tight-fitting lid

and cook over a low heat for 10 minutes.

Remove the pan from the heat and leave undisturbed for 5 minutes. Uncover, fluff up the grains with a fork, then serve.

STEAMED RICE
Serves 4

350g basmati, jasmine
    or long-grain rice

Put the rice in a pan with 600ml of water. Quickly bring to the boil, stir once, then cover with a tight-fitting lid and reduce the heat to low.

Simmer basmati rice for 10 minutes and jasmine or long-grain rice for 12–15 minutes. Turn off the heat and leave to steam, covered, for a further 5 minutes. Uncover, fluff up the grains of rice with a fork, and serve.

BUTTERY RICE PILAF
Serves 4

15g butter
2 shallots, finely chopped
1 bay leaf
350g long-grain rice
600ml Chicken stock
    (page 307)
1 tsp salt

Melt the butter in a pan. Add the shallots and cook gently until soft but not browned. Stir in the bay leaf and rice and fry gently for 1 minute.

Add the chicken stock and salt and quickly bring to the boil. Stir once, cover with a tight-fitting lid and simmer for 10 minutes. Turn off the heat and leave to steam, covered, for a further 5 minutes.

Uncover, remove the bay leaf and fluff up the grains with a fork before serving.

BRAISED SAUERKRAUT
Serves 6

40g butter or goose fat
1 medium onion, sliced
1 carrot, thinly sliced
6 juniper berries, crushed
2 bay leaves
3 cloves
3 garlic cloves, finely chopped
500g jar of sauerkraut
600ml Chicken stock (page 307)
120ml dry white wine

Melt the butter or goose fat in a pan. Add the onion, carrot, juniper berries, bay leaves, cloves and garlic and cook gently for 3–4 minutes until soft but not coloured.

Add the sauerkraut, stock and white wine. Cover and simmer very gently for 1 hour.

BREAD & BUTTER PICKLES
Makes about 2 x 350g jars

400g baby cucumbers
1 medium onion, peeled, halved and sliced
25g fine salt
200g light brown soft sugar
200ml apple cider vinegar
¼ tsp turmeric
1 tsp coriander seeds
1 tsp yellow mustard seeds
½ tsp fennel seeds

Cut the cucumbers into slices 3–4mm thick on the diagonal. Place them with the onion slices in a bowl and sprinkle over the salt. Cover and refrigerate for 2–3 hours. Tip them into a colander over the sink and rinse with cold water. Give everything a good shake and drain again.

Put the sugar, vinegar and spices in a pan and stir over a medium heat until the sugar has dissolved. Bring to the boil and cook for 5 minutes, then turn off the heat. Add the drained cucumber and onion and leave the mixture to cool. Pour into 2 sterilised jars and store in a cool, dark place for up to a year.

GREEN TOMATO CHUTNEY
Makes about 3 jars

4 tbsp sunflower oil
600g onions, chopped
4 garlic cloves, chopped
5cm cinnamon stick
2 tsp yellow mustard seeds
1 tsp chilli flakes
2 bay leaves
½ tsp ground cloves
1kg green tomatoes, roughly chopped
500g cooking apples, peeled, cored and chopped
500ml apple cider vinegar
400g sultanas
300g soft light brown sugar
4 tsp salt

Heat the oil in a preserving pan or large, wide pan, add the onions and cook for about 10 minutes until softened. Add the garlic, cinnamon stick, mustard seeds, chilli flakes, bay leaves and ground cloves and cook for another 5 minutes.

Add the tomatoes, apples and half the vinegar and simmer for about 15 minutes or until the tomatoes and apples have softened. Then add the sultanas, sugar, salt and remaining vinegar and stir until the sugar has dissolved. Turn up the heat until the chutney is gently bubbling.

Cook for about 1¼–1¾ hours or until thickened – a wooden spoon pulled along the bottom of the pan should leave a path that slowly fills from the sides. Start checking after 1¼ hours, as the time will vary depending on the water content of the fruit and the size of your pan. Stir regularly to avoid the chutney catching on the bottom.

Remove the cinnamon stick and bay leaves, then ladle into sterilised jars. Store in a cool, dark place. This keeps for at least a year.

VEGETABLE STOCK
Makes about 2 litres

2 large onions
2 large carrots
1 celery head
1 fennel bulb
1 garlic bulb
3 bay leaves
1 tsp salt

Wash and roughly slice the vegetables – you don't need to peel the garlic. Put everything in a large pan with 3 litres of water and bring to the boil Simmer for an hour, then strain it through a fine sieve. If not using immediately, allow to cool, then refrigerate or freeze for later use.

FISH STOCK
Makes about 1 litre

1kg fish bones and heads (lemon sole, brill and plaice all good but any fish is fine, except oily ones like mackerel, sardines, herrings, salmon and tuna)
1 onion, chopped
1 leek, washed and sliced
1 fennel bulb, sliced
100g celery, sliced
1 thyme sprig
30ml sunflower oil
100ml white wine

Cut up the fish bones into 5–6cm pieces and put them into a large pan. Add the vegetables, thyme and oil. Put a lid on the pan, place over a medium heat and cook everything gently for 5 minutes, not allowing it to colour. Add the white wine and 2.25 litres of water and bring just to the boil, then turn the heat down and simmer very gently for 20 minutes. Strain through a sieve. Use as required.

If not using immediately, leave to cool, then chill and refrigerate or freeze. You may like to reduce the volume by simmering the strained stock.

SHELLFISH STOCK

Makes about 1 litre of stock
or 150ml shellfish reduction

15g unsalted butter
50g carrot, chopped
50g onion, chopped
50g celery, chopped
350g shell-on prawns
    (or shrimp or small crabs)
75ml white wine
A couple of tarragon sprigs
200ml tinned tomatoes
1.2 litres Fish stock (page 306)
Pinch cayenne pepper

Melt the butter in a large
pan. Add the carrot, onion
and celery and fry gently for
3–4 minutes until they start
to soften. Add the prawns
and fry for another 2 minutes,
then add all the remaining
ingredients. Lower the heat
and simmer for 40 minutes.

Strain the stock, pressing
out as much liquid as possible
with the back of a ladle. This
can now be used as a shellfish
stock or reduced further for
a stronger-tasting reduction.

For the reduction, bring the
stock back to the boil and boil
rapidly until you are left with
about 150ml of liquid.

CHICKEN STOCK

Makes 1.5 litres

Bones from 1.5kg uncooked
    chicken or 500g chicken
    wings or a leftover carcass
    and bones from a roast chicken
1 large carrot, roughly chopped
2 celery sticks, roughly sliced
2 leeks, washed and sliced
2 fresh or dried bay leaves
2 thyme sprigs

Put all the ingredients into
a large pan with 2.5 litres of
water and bring to the boil.
Skim off any scum that rises
to the surface. Leave to simmer
gently for about 2 hours –
don't let it boil as an emulsion
will form and make the stock

cloudy. Strain through a fine,
sieve and use as required.
If not using immediately,
leave to cool, then chill
and refrigerate or freeze. Or
simmer the strained stock to
reduce further before storing.

ROAST CHICKEN STOCK

Makes about 1.75 litres

Bones from a 1.5kg chicken
    or 500g chicken wings
1 tbsp vegetable oil
1 large carrot, roughly chopped
2 celery sticks, roughly chopped
2 leeks, washed and roughly
    chopped
2 bay leaves
2 thyme sprigs

Preheat the oven to 210°C/
Fan 190°C. Roast the chicken
bones or wings for 30–45
minutes, until they've taken
on a good rich brown colour.
Heat the oil in a large pan
and fry the vegetables over a
medium heat until browned,
but not burnt. Add the
browned chicken bones or
wings and add 2.5 litres of cold
water to cover, then the herbs.
Bring to the boil and skim off
all of the fat that rises to the
surface. Turn down the heat
to a gentle simmer and cook
for about 2 hours.

Strain the stock through a
fine sieve into a clean pan and
continue to cook to concentrate
the flavour, if necessary. It is
now ready to use, chill or
freeze as required.

DUCK BROTH

Makes 2 litres

1 large roasted duck carcass
1 bunch spring onions, sliced
25g root ginger, peeled
    and sliced
6 black peppercorns
2 star anise
3 cloves
10cm cinnamon stick

Put all the ingredients into a
large pan, cover with 3 litres
of water and bring to the boil.
Skim off any scum as it rises to
the surface. Leave to simmer
gently for 3 hours, skimming
regularly to remove any fat,
until the stock has reduced by a
third to 2 litres. Strain the stock
through a fine sieve into a clean
pan. If you have time, chill the
stock overnight in the fridge
and then skim the congealed fat
off the surface. If not, then skim
off as much as you can, then
use immediately or refrigerate
or freeze for later use.

VEAL STOCK

Makes about 2.4 litres

2kg veal bones, roughly chopped
    (ask your butcher to do this)
1 tbsp oil
1 onion, halved
2 carrots, roughly chopped
2 celery sticks, roughly chopped
Bunch parsley stalks, crushed
2 bay leaves
1 thyme sprig
½ tsp black peppercorns

Preheat the oven to 220°C/
Fan 200°C and roast the bones
for an hour until browned.

Heat the oil in a large pan and
brown the onion, carrots and
celery over a medium heat for
about 5–10 minutes. Add the
browned bones to the pot,
together with the herbs and
peppercorns, and completely
cover with cold water. Bring to
the boil, skimming off any scum
that rises to the surface. Turn the
heat down to a gentle simmer
and cook for 4–6 hours, topping
up the water as it evaporates and
skimming off the fat that rises
to the surface from time to time.

When ready, strain through
a fine sieve into a clean pan.
Cool until ready to use. It can
now be reduced down by rapid
boiling to make a stronger
stock or to freeze.

BEEF STOCK
Makes about 2.4 litres

2 celery sticks, roughly chopped
2 carrots, roughly chopped
2 onions, roughly chopped
900g beef shin
2 bay leaves
2 thyme sprigs
1 tbsp salt

For a pale brown stock, put all the ingredients, except the bay leaves, thyme and salt, into a large pan with 5 litres of water and bring to the boil. Skim off any scum that rises to the surface. Simmer for 2½ hours, adding the herbs and salt for the last 15 minutes. Strain through a fine sieve into a clean pan. The stock is now ready to use, chill or freeze for later use, or you can continue to cook to reduce the liquid for a richer stock.

For a richer-tasting brown beef stock, start by heating 2 tablespoons of vegetable oil in the pan. Add the vegetables and beef and fry for 10–15 minutes until nicely browned. Then add the water and cook as above, adding the herbs and salt 15 minutes before the end of cooking.

ASIAN BEEF BROTH
Make 2.75 litres

40g root ginger,
  cut into 6 pieces
350g shallots, sliced
4 star anise
2 x 7.5cm cinnamon sticks
½ tsp fennel seeds
900g beef shin
1kg beef marrow bones
2 celery sticks, roughly sliced
2 carrots, roughly sliced
2 onions, roughly sliced
8 cloves
1 tsp black peppercorns
1 tbsp salt

Put the ginger and shallots on a chopping board and bash them lightly with a rolling pin. Heat a large, dry frying pan over a high heat, add the star anise, cinnamon sticks and fennel seeds and shake them around for a few seconds until they darken slightly and start to smell aromatic, then tip them on to a plate. Add the ginger and shallots to the frying pan and cook for 10 minutes until nicely toasted. Add these to the roasted spices.

Put the beef shin, beef bones, celery, carrots, onions, cloves, peppercorns, and the roasted spices, ginger and shallots into a large pan and add 5 litres of water. Bring to the boil, skimming off the scum as it rises to the surface. Lower the heat, add the salt and leave to simmer very gently for 3–5 hours – the longer, the better.

Strain the broth into a clean pan. If you can, leave it to chill overnight, which will allow you to lift off and discard the fat from the surface before using. Freeze for later use.

RICK'S PEPPERMIX
1 chipotle chilli (seeds removed)
1 pasilla chilli (seeds removed)
2 tbsp black peppercorns
2 tbsp white peppercorns
2 tsp Sichuan peppercorns
1 tbsp salt

Blitz all the ingredients in a spice grinder and store in a jam jar until required.

INDONESIAN SPICE PASTE
Basa gede

1½ tsp black peppercorns
½ nutmeg
25g candle nuts, macadamias,
  cashews or roasted peanuts
1 tsp sesame seeds
60g shallots, roughly chopped
25g root ginger, peeled and
  roughly chopped
40g galangal (or extra ginger),
  peeled and roughly chopped
15g fresh turmeric, chopped,
  or 1 tsp turmeric powder
3 fat lemongrass stalks,
  core chopped
4 garlic cloves
2 medium-hot red chillies,
  roughly chopped
3 red bird's-eye chillies,
  roughly chopped
1 tsp shrimp paste
1 tbsp soft brown sugar
1 tsp salt
3 tbsp sunflower oil
Juice of ½ lime

Put the peppercorns, nutmeg, nuts and sesame seeds into a spice grinder and grind to a fine powder. Tip into a mini food processor, add all the other ingredients and blend everything into a very smooth paste. This keeps for a couple of weeks in the fridge.

GARAM MASALA
This is my own garam masala recipe, which is essentially a balanced combination of the most popular spices. Even more important than the mix is having them freshly roasted and ground. I can't stress too strongly how much better it is to make your own garam masala than to buy it. It's important to make this regularly. I would suggest renewing it every 3 months.
Makes 50g

1 tbsp black peppercorns
2 tbsp cumin seeds
2 tbsp coriander seeds
2 tsp cardamom seeds
  (from 30-40 green pods)
4 tsp whole cloves
7cm cinnamon stick
1 whole nutmeg

Toast all the spices apart from the nutmeg in a dry frying pan over a medium heat for a couple of minutes until toasted and aromatic. Cool. Grate the nutmeg and add it to a spice grinder along with whole spices – you might want to break up the cinnamon stick – and grind everything coarsely. Store in a sealed container out of sunlight; it will keep at its most aromatic for 3 months.

UNROASTED & ROASTED SRI LANKAN CURRY POWDER

1 tbsp uncooked long-grain or basmati rice
50g coriander seeds
25g cumin seeds
25g fennel seeds
7.5cm cinnamon stick
1½ tsp fenugreek seeds
½ tsp cloves
½ tsp cardamom seeds (from about 10 green pods)
½ tsp black mustard seeds
1 tsp black peppercorns
3 dried red kashmiri chillies
1 tsp turmeric (for unroasted curry powder only)

For the unroasted or 'raw' curry powder, heat a dry frying pan over a medium heat. Add the rice and shake it around until it is lightly golden. Tip it into a small bowl and leave to cool. Then mix with the spices, dried chillies and turmeric powder and grind everything (in batches if necessary) coarsely.

For the roasted or 'black' curry powder, heat a dry frying pan over a medium heat. Add the rice and shake it around for about 3 minutes until medium-brown in colour, taking care not to let it get too brown or to burn. Tip the rice into a bowl and leave to cool while you do the same to the spices, and then to the dried chillies. Mix the rice, spices (no turmeric) and chillies together and grind (in batches if necessary) to a powder. Store in a screw-top jar. Use within 3 months.

QUICK HOLLANDAISE SAUCE
Serves 4

2 egg yolks
Juice of ½ lemon
225g Clarified butter (see page 312), warmed
Good pinch of cayenne pepper
¾ tsp salt

Put the egg yolks, lemon juice and 2 tablespoons of water into a blender or food processor. Turn on the machine, then slowly pour in the warm butter through the hole in the lid until the sauce is thick. Season with the cayenne and salt.

OLIVE OIL MAYONNAISE
Makes 300ml

1 whole egg or 2 egg yolks
2 tsp white wine vinegar
½ tsp salt
300ml olive oil

The simplest way is to put a whole egg, the vinegar and salt in a food processor. Turn on the machine and very slowly trickle the oil through the hole in the lid until you have a thick emulsion.

To make the mayonnaise by hand, make sure all the ingredients are at room temperature and use 2 egg yolks, rather than a whole egg. Put the egg yolks, vinegar and salt into a mixing bowl and rest the bowl on a damp cloth to stop it moving around. Lightly whisk the yolks to break them up and, using a wire whisk, beat the oil in, a few drops at a time, until it is all incorporated. Once you have added the same volume of oil as the original mixture of egg yolks and vinegar, you can add the oil a little more quickly.

This keeps in the fridge for at least a fortnight.

MUSTARD MAYONNAISE
Makes 300ml

1 egg
1 tbsp English mustard (made up, not powder)
1 tsp salt
1 tsp white wine vinegar
300ml sunflower oil

Blend the egg, mustard, salt and vinegar in a food processor. With the motor running, gradually add the oil in a slow trickle until it is all incorporated. Store in the fridge.

AÏOLI
Makes about 175ml

4 garlic cloves, peeled
½ tsp salt
1 medium egg yolk
175ml olive or sunflower oil

Crush the garlic under the blade of a large knife, add the salt and work with the side of the blade to make a smooth, salty paste. Scrape the garlic into a bowl. Add the egg yolk and whisk together with an electric beater, adding the olive oil in a thin steady stream to create a mayonnaise-like mixture.

FISH VELOUTÉ
Makes 600ml

600ml Fish stock (page 306)
60g butter
45g plain flour

Bring the stock to the boil. Melt the butter in another pan, add the flour and cook for 2 minutes, stirring constantly; don't let it brown. Remove from the heat and gradually whisk in the stock, a little at a time, until it is all incorporated and you have a smooth sauce. Put the pan back over the heat. Turn the heat right down and allow the sauce to simmer for 40 minutes, stirring occasionally to prevent it from catching. Pass the sauce through a sieve. If not using immediately, cover with baking parchment to prevent a skin from forming and chill until needed.

SAUCE VIN BLANC
Serves 6

600ml Fish velouté (page 309)
50ml white wine
70ml double cream
1 egg yolk
50g cold butter, cubed
Salt and black pepper

Put the velouté, wine and cream into a pan and reduce over a medium heat till the sauce is thick enough to coat the back of a spoon.

Put the egg yolk and a teaspoon of water in a bowl over a pan of simmering water. Whisk until a light and fluffy sabayon is formed and you can clearly see the marks of the whisk. Take off the heat and stir in the reduced velouté. Finish the sauce by whisking in the cubes of butter.

SAUCE ESPAGNOLE
Serves 6–8

50ml sunflower oil
100g carrots, peeled
    and roughly chopped
100g onions, peeled
    and roughly chopped
60g plain flour
25g tomato paste
1 litre beef stock
    (page 308), heated

Heat the oil in a large pan. Add the carrots and onions and cook over a medium heat until softened and lightly browned. Add the flour and continue to cook, stirring frequently, until

the flour is browned to a good biscuit-brown colour, then stir in the tomato paste. Gradually add the boiling stock and bring to the boil. Skim off the impurities and simmer for 4–6 hours skimming as necessary. Strain.

DEMI-GLACE
A demi-glace is a refined espagnole, made by simmering 1 litre of brown beef stock with 1 litre of espagnole (see above) and reducing the liquid by half – from 2 litres to 1 litre. Skim off any impurities and pass through a fine sieve, then reboil and correct the seasoning with salt.

ONION GRAVY
Use the demi-glace sauce here to make the best onion gravy for sausage and mash.
Serves about 6

60g butter
2 large onions, finely sliced
Pinch caster sugar
400ml demi-glace

Melt the butter in a pan and add the onions and sugar. Cook over a low heat for about 30 minutes until the onions are meltingly soft and have turned a golden brown. Add the demi-glace and bring to the boil, then immediately turn down to a simmer and cook for a couple of minutes. Great with sausages and mashed potatoes.

SOY, BUTTER & CORIANDER SAUCE
Serves 4

600ml Chicken stock (page 307)
2 tbsp dark soy sauce
75g unsalted butter
1 tomato, skinned,
    deseeded and diced
1 heaped tsp chopped coriander

Put the chicken stock and soy sauce into a pan and boil rapidly until reduced by half. Add the butter to the sauce and whisk it in. Remove from the heat and stir in the tomato and coriander. Perfect with white fish or chicken.

ROUILLE
Makes about 300ml

25g slice day-old white
    bread, crusts removed
A little fish stock or water
3 fat garlic cloves, peeled
1 egg yolk
250ml olive oil
Salt
Harissa
1 roasted red pepper
1 tsp tomato paste
1 tsp ground coriander
Pinch saffron strands
2 medium-hot red chillies, stalks
    removed, roughly chopped
¼ tsp cayenne pepper
½ tsp salt

First make the harissa. Put the roasted red pepper, tomato paste, ground coriander, saffron, chillies, cayenne pepper and ¼ teaspoon of salt into a food processor and blend until smooth. Transfer to a bowl and set aside.

For the rouille, soak the slice of bread in the fish stock or water and leave to soften. Squeeze out the excess liquid and put the bread into the food processor with 2 tablespoons of the harissa, the garlic, egg yolk and ¼ teaspoon of salt. Blend until smooth. With the machine still running, gradually add the oil until you have a smooth, thick mayonnaise-like mixture. This can be stored in the fridge for at least a fortnight.

If you don't want to make the harissa paste, use bought harissa, adding as much as you need – about 2 tablespoons depending on the brand.

ROASTED TOMATO SAUCE
Makes about 400g

About 1.25kg ripe tomatoes
5 or 6 garlic cloves in their skins
4 tbsp olive oil
Pinch of sugar
Basil, thyme or oregano
    leaves, torn (optional)
Salt and black pepper

Heat the oven to 180°C/
Fan 160°C. Halve or quarter
the tomatoes, depending on
size, or leave them whole if
using cherry tomatoes. Place
the tomatoes and garlic in a
single layer on a baking tray,
drizzle over the oil and season
with salt and pepper. Roast
for 30–40 minutes until
the tomatoes and garlic are
softened. At this point, if the
skins are soft, they can be left
on, or if you prefer a smoother
sauce or the skins are tough,
slip them off.

Slip the garlic cloves from
their skins and put the soft
flesh in a blender with the
tomatoes. Pulse until you have
the desired texture. Taste for
seasoning and add sugar and
more pepper and sugar as
required. Add the herbs, if
using. The sauce is now ready
to use, refrigerate or freeze.

TZATZIKI
Serves 6

1 large cucumber
2 garlic cloves
500g Greek sheep's yoghurt
75g spring onions, trimmed
    and finely chopped
2 tbsp chopped fresh dill or mint
2 tbsp extra virgin olive oil
1 tsp white wine vinegar
Dill or mint sprigs or slices of
    cucumber, to garnish (optional)
Salt and black pepper

Peel strips of skin off the
cucumber – you want some
skin but not all of it. Then
coarsely grate the cucumber,

pile it into the centre of a clean
tea towel and squeeze out
most of the excess liquid.

Put the garlic cloves on a
chopping board, sprinkle with
a large pinch of salt and crush
into a smooth paste with the
flat blade of a large knife.

Tip the yoghurt into a
bowl and stir in the cucumber,
garlic, spring onions, dill or
mint, olive oil, vinegar and
salt and pepper to taste. Serve
garnished with extra dill or
mint sprigs or a few peeled
cucumber slices, if you like.

PICO DE GALLO SALSA
Serves 4–6

2 large ripe tomatoes, deseeded
    and cut into 5mm dice
1/2 onion, chopped
Handful coriander, chopped
1 green serrano or jalapeño
    chilli, finely chopped
1/4 tsp salt
Juice of 1/2–1 lime

Mix all the ingredients
in a bowl. Start with the
juice of half a lime and add
more to taste, if desired.
Serve immediately.

GUACAMOLE
Serves 4

1 jalapeño or serrano green
    chilli, deseeded and
    finely chopped
1/2 small white onion,
    finely chopped
1/4 tsp salt
1 large ripe avocado or
    2 small, stoned and peeled
Juice of 1/2–1 lime
Small handful coriander,
    chopped

Using a pestle and mortar,
pound the chopped chilli
with the onion and salt.
When they're broken down
to a lumpy paste, add the
avocado and break up the

flesh roughly with a fork.
Stir in the lime juice to taste
and the chopped coriander,
then serve immediately.

You can also make this in a
food processor, but don;t over
process, as guacamole is much
better when a little lumpy.

CHIPOTLE CREMA
Serve 2–4

2 Chipotles en adobo
    (page 312 or bought),
    finely chopped or mashed
    with a pestle and mortar
2 tbsp soured cream
2 tbsp mayonnaise
Squeeze of lime juice
Pinch of salt

Mix all the ingredients
together and set aside.

CHIPOTLES EN ADOBO
Makes a 370g jar

8 chipotle chillies
150ml boiling water
3 large ripe tomatoes,
    roughly chopped
1 medium onion,
    roughly chopped
4 large garlic cloves,
    peeled and sliced
60ml cider vinegar
3/4 tsp salt
2 tsp brown sugar

Wash the chillies, remove
the hard stems but leave the
seeds in place. Put the chillies
in a bowl with the 150ml of
boiling water and cover with
cling film. Leave the chillies
to soak for about 20 minutes.

Remove 3 of the soaked
chillies, leaving the rest in the
water, and put them in a food
processor or blender. Add the
tomatoes, onion, garlic,
vinegar, salt, the soaking
liquid and the sugar, then
process to make a smooth
paste. Tip this paste into a
pan and add the remaining

whole soaked chillies. Bring to the boil, then reduce the heat and simmer the chipotles for about 1 hour. Check them every 20–30 minutes and add a little more boiling water if needed.

Leave to cool slightly, then pour into a sterilised glass jar. Cool completely and store in the fridge for up to a month.

CLARIFIED BUTTER

Place some butter in a small pan and leave it over a very low heat until it has melted. Then skim off any scum from the surface and pour off the clear golden liquid into a bowl. Discard the milky white solids that will have settled on the bottom of the pan.

DRIED BREADCRUMBS

Put some crustless white bread in a food processor and blitz into crumbs. Spread the crumbs on a large baking tray and bake at 140°C/Fan 120°C for 20 minutes. Stir the crumbs and return to the oven for a further 15–20 minutes until crisp and dry but not browned. Leave them to cool and store in an airtight container. They keep very well.

BEURRE MANIÉ

Blend equal quantities of butter and plain flour together into a smooth paste. Cover and keep in the fridge until needed. It will keep as long as butter. Whisk into hot sauces to thicken as required.

VINCOTTO

500ml red wine (or 400ml or so of red wine and up to 100ml white wine)
60g sugar

Pour the wine into a pan and add the sugar. Bring to the boil and simmer until thick and syrupy. Cool, then store in a bottle. Great for adding colour and body to stews.

RICH SHORTCRUST PASTRY
Makes enough for 12 mince pies

225g plain flour, plus extra for dusting
1/2 tsp salt
55g chilled butter, cubed
55g chilled lard, cubed
1 1/2–2 tbsp cold water

Sift the flour and salt into a food processor or a mixing bowl. Add the chilled butter and lard and process or work together with your fingers until the mixture looks like fine breadcrumbs. Stir in the water with a round-bladed knife until it comes together into a ball. Turn out on to a lightly floured work surface and knead briefly until smooth. Roll out and use as required.

For a slighter leaner and more malleable pastry, reduce the butter and lard to 45g each.

DUCK CONFIT
Makes 4

50g salt
1 tbsp thyme leaves
Leaves from a large rosemary sprig
2 bay leaves, finely shredded
2 garlic cloves, roughly chopped
4 large duck legs
900g duck or goose fat

Put the salt, thyme, rosemary, bay leaves and garlic into a spice grinder and grind together until the mixture looks like wet sand. Sprinkle half the mixture over the base of a shallow dish, put the duck legs on top and then cover with the rest. Cover and leave in the fridge for 6 hours, turning them over halfway through. Don't leave the duck any longer or it will become too salty.

Preheat the oven to 140°C/ Fan 120°C. Rinse the duck legs, pat them dry with kitchen paper and put them in an oven dish. Melt the duck or goose fat and pour it over the duck legs, making sure that they are completely submerged. Cover and cook in the oven for 1½ hours.

Remove and leave the duck to cool in the fat, then chill until needed. To use, lift the duck out of the fat and wipe off as much as you can with kitchen paper.

COOK'S NOTES

Generally, I don't specify the weight of garlic cloves, tomatoes, carrots or onions because the reality of cooking is that you just take a clove or two of garlic or a whole onion. However, in case it's helpful, I thought it would be sensible to suggest the weights (unpeeled) I have in mind.

1 garlic clove: 5g
1 small onion: 100g
1 medium onion: 175g
1 large onion: 225g
Small handful fresh herbs: about 15g
Large handful fresh herbs: about 30g

All teaspoon and tablespoon measurements are level unless otherwise stated and are based on measuring spoons:

1 teaspoon: 5ml
1 tablespoon: 15ml

Readers in Australia will need to make minor adjustments, as their tablespoon measure is 20ml.

Oven temperatures
We have given settings for regular and fan ovens throughout the book. Should you need gas settings, they are as follows:

°C	°C FAN	GAS
120	100	½
140	120	1
150	130	2
160	140	3
180	160	4
190	170	5
200	180	6
220	200	7
230	210	8
240	220	9

Eggs and chicken
Use medium free-range eggs in the recipes, unless otherwise specified. And use free-range chicken if possible.

Temperature probe
I use a temperature probe to determine the correct internal temperature of meat, poultry and fish. This is a cheap gadget and you get far more accurate results than by relying on cooking times alone. Always bring meat and poultry up to room temperature before cooking.

Bear in mind that meat and fish continue to cook after being removed from the heat; their temperature rises by about 6°C. Meat and poultry benefit from resting after being cooked and before serving.

Cooking steak
The temperatures below are just before taking the meat off the heat. The meat must be at room temperature before you start cooking. Here are suggested timings for 2cm-thick steak.

Blue: 1 minute on each side (47–49°C)
Rare: 1½ minutes on each side (50°C)
Medium rare: 2 minutes on each side (55°C)
Medium: 2¼ minutes on each side (60°C)
Medium well done: 2½–3 minutes on each side (65°C)
Well done: 4 minutes on each side (71°C)

A note about finding equivalent fish and shellfish outside the UK
Most of the species I've written recipes for have easy alternatives. Lobsters. prawns, crabs and bivalves, such as mussels, clams, oysters and scallops, are pretty much the same everywhere, as are flat fish. Round fish for cooking whole are easy to find – I'm thinking particularly of small snapper, sea bass and bream. Sardines and mackerel occur everywhere, as do tuna and salmon. Cod and other members of the cod family, like hake, haddock, ling and pollack, are not so easy to suggest equivalents for. In Australia or New Zealand I would choose large meaty fish with thick fillets, like blue-eye trevalla, large snapper and hapuka. The other fish I'm very fond of but which does cause problems is monkfish, as there is no real equivalent. I tend to recommend John Dory as a substitute – it's not the same shape but it does have fillets of firm flesh like monkfish. Blue-eye trevalla would be another option.

ACKNOWLEDGEMENTS

Thanks to the following at Ebury Books: Joel Rickett, Managing Director; Albert DePetrillo, Publishing Director; Lizzy Gray, Publishing Director, a very enthusiastic Joanna Stenlake, Editor, and my publicist Claire Scott.

Once again, big thanks to Portia Spooner for pulling everything together and testing so many of the recipes on Jules, her husband, and their children, Will and Flo. Thanks to Alex and Emma Smith for the fabulous ideas behind the book design, particularly the collage on the endpapers, and again thanks to James Murphy for the photographs, which so often catch a special moment. Have a look at the picture of John Harris in the apple orchard on page 244 to see what I mean. Thanks to Aya Nishimura for the sheer scrumptiousness of the food in the photos, and to Penny Markham for the kitchen-dresser-look of all the crockery pans, casseroles and glasses. I missed my usual trips to the photography studio because of Covid restrictions, but the one I did make was very special, so thank you to James Murphy's assistant, Lucia Lowther, for organising a great lunch and fabulous coffees, and to Flora Lowther who arranged all the location photography so well.

Great to have been working with project editor Jinny Johnson again; she is so quick and decisive. A big thank you to my PA Viv Taylor for keeping us all in touch from Padstow, and the biggest thank you to my wife, Sas, who has always been completely supportive and has contributed so much to this book, both to the written pieces and the recipes, and above all for having an editor's scrutiny of what's good and what isn't.

And absolutely lastly, thanks to all those of my family and friends who feature in the book: Richard Glover and Debra Oswald, married in all but name; Maud Old; Janine Van Heynsbergen, Sas's stepmother; Sas's sister, Georgina Senes; her cousins, Jane and Tim Martin; Sas's cousin Sacha's partner, Rose Ka; my stepchildren, Zach and Olivia Burns; and my sons Ed, Jack and Charlie. In the photo in the pub on pages 2–3 are, clockwise from the left, Dave Brown, Penny McGregor, Chris Arnold, Hugo Wooley, me, Sas, John Bradford and Johnnie Walter. In the photo of an early dinner in the garden at Chiswick on pages 294–295 are, clockwise from the left: Sas, Barry Humphries, Olivia Burns, Zach Burns, Lizzie Humphries, me, Oscar Hibbert, Brian O'Doherty and Kathy Lette.

I would also like to thank Karen & Andrew Smith for the sloes for the recipe photo on page 178, and a big thank you to the following suppliers.

Giel Spierings – Cornish Gouda Company (pages 12–13)
Tim Marshall – Porthilly Oysters (pages 78–79)
Gary Dutton – Gary Dutton Butchers (pages 122–123)
Sam Bishop – Trevear Farm (pages 122–123)
Philip & Ian Warren – Philip Warren Butchers (pages 164–165)
Ross Geach – Padstow Kitchen Garden (pages 214–215)
John Harris – Tresillian House (pages 244–245)

1

BBC Books, an imprint of Ebury Publishing
20 Vauxhall Bridge Road, London SW1V 2SA

BBC Books is part of the Penguin Random House group of companies whose addresses can be found at global.penguinrandomhouse.com

Penguin
Random House
UK

Text copyright © Rick Stein 2021
Photography copyright © James Murphy 2021
Design copyright © Woodland Books 2021

Rick Stein has asserted his right to be identified as the author of this Work in accordance with the Copyright, Designs and Patents Act 1988

First published by BBC Books in 2021
www.eburypublishing.co.uk

A CIP catalogue record for this book is available from the British Library

ISBN 9781785947087

Printed and bound by Firmengruppe APPL, aprinta druck, Wemding, Germany

Penguin Random House is committed to a sustainable future for our business, our readers and our planet. This book is made from Forest Stewardship Council® certified paper

MIX
Paper from
responsible sources
FSC® C018179

Publishing Director: Lizzy Gray
Editor: Joanna Stenlake
Home economist: Portia Spooner
Design and art direction: Smith & Gilmour
Photographer: James Murphy
Project editor: Jinny Johnson
Food stylist: Aya Nishimura
Prop stylist: Penny Markham
Proofreader: Elise See Tai
Indexer: Hilary Bird